iPod,
Therefore I Am

iPod,
Therefore I Am

DYLAN JONES

Weidenfeld & Nicolson

LONDON

First published in Great Britain in 2005
by Weidenfeld & Nicolson, a division of
the Orion Publishing Group Ltd
Orion House
5 Upper Saint Martin's Lane
London
WC2H 9EA

'Being Boring'
Words and Music by Neil Tennant and
Chris Lowe.
© 1990 Cage Music Ltd. Sony/ATV
Music Publishing (UK) Ltd

10 9 8 7 6 5 4 3 2 1

A CIP catalogue record for this book is
available from the British Library

ISBN-13 9 780297 848752
ISBN-10 0 297 84875 5

Typeset, printed and bound in Great Britain by
Butler and Tanner Ltd, Frome and London

www.orionbooks.co.uk

For Michael Jones

Contents

Appendices

Acknowledgements

I'd like to thank my employers at Condé Nast, Nicholas Coleridge and Jonathan Newhouse, for all their help and encouragement, my brilliant agent Ed Victor (who got the idea immediately), Alan Samson (who bought it), Daniel Walter (who originally suggested it), Mel Agace, Richard Campbell-Breeden, Tony Parsons, Oliver Peyton, Adrian Deevoy, Stuart Morgan, Robin Derrick, Bill Prince, Julian Alexander, Andrew Hale, Debra Bourne, Camilla McPhie, Andy Morris, Daniel Jones, Danielle (for the typing), Edie and Georgia (for continually asking) 'Is Daddy iPodding again?') and my wife Sarah, the iPod widow, who essentially told me to get on with it.

Some of the material here has appeared, in a radically different form, in *GQ*.

'The iPod is the most interesting artistic creation in pop since the electric guitar' – Bono

Introduction
I am a Jukebox

'My name is Dylan Jones and I am addicted to music . . .'

> 'There are other things in life besides music,' said Hoagy
> Carmichael, the composer of "Stardust" and "Georgia On My
> Mind".
>   'I forget what they are, but they're around.'

My transparent Macally mouse glows red as my index finger
clicks left. I'm opening iTunes on the vertical panel bar, slipping
into my library, a library that currently contains 4399 songs
(enough for 12.2 days of continuous music, taking up 29.96 GBs).

I open a jewel case and slip the CD into the disc port in my
PowerBook G4. Seconds later, an icon appears on my desktop,
half an inch in diameter, a fairly accurate approximation of a
disc: Audio CD, it says (although it really looks like an old-
fashioned vinyl disc in miniature); I'm at home and have not
dialled up – broadband is some weeks away as BT struggles to
reach detente between my modem and their phone lines.

The track listing springs up on my screen, fifteen songs, all
Beatles covers, one of two free CDs given away with *Mojo*
magazine. This is *Beatlemania/Volume 1*, and I'm about to
upload The Cyrkle's rather inspired, slightly odd (and seemingly
randomly but deliberately out-of-tune) version of 'I'm Happy
Just To Dance With You', the Lennon and McCartney song
originally from *A Hard Day's Night* (I think it's inspired and
odd because it changes key when you least expect it to, under-
scoring my theory that all really exceptional songs change key
when you least expect them to).

I highlight the song with the bright blue horizontal 4 mm-deep band, drag it across into the library and then gaze through the window at the top of iTunes as it uploads. It still feels magical, and watching the input bar fill up, I'm reminded of all those *Mission Impossible*-type films where a computer whiz tries to defuse a briefcase bomb before his laptop starts flashing 'ABORTED'. Fifteen seconds later – 'I'm Happy' is two seconds shy of two minutes – the song is nestling at the bottom of my library, waiting for me to punch in its details. And after I do – typing the album and song title first, so the song doesn't move before I've finished – it bounces up into its rightful alphabetical place, track number 4400, ready and waiting, and now very much part of my life. I go and look for it – why, I don't know, as it's always going to be there, unless I get tired of it and delete it – and of course it's there, nestling quietly, quite properly, between 'Move On Up' by Curtis Mayfield and 'You're The One For Me' by D Train.

And so I double-click on it and play.

And then I go wandering, scrolling up and down the library, looking for songs the way I once flicked through albums in record shops, back when I was twelve, flicking through for no other reason than to convince myself they are still there. And as I scroll I find something I thought I'd deleted – fantastic! – a Groove Armada song I no longer like. More room for something else, more gigabytes for the CDs I'm going to buy tomorrow, for the Rufus Wainwright song I'm going to download from iTunes ('Rebel Prince' from *Poses*). I press the right-hand side of my mouse and scroll down to 'Clear', and after my PowerBook asks me twice if I really, *seriously* want to delete the song not only from my playlist but also from my library, it is gone, banished to that ungodly place where unwanted MP3 files presumably go to die. And having deleted it I move on, move up, scroll down, wander around and wallow in a lifetime's love and affection.

Every record I've ever owned and kept is on this machine,

from Alice Cooper's 'Elected' right up to Shapeshifter's happy house classic 'Lola's Theme'. One is a record I bought after seeing it performed on *Top of the Pops*, the other after I heard it in an Ibizan nightclub. My whole life is here, 40 GB of memory, thirty years of memories. Every song I've ever cared about is in here somewhere, waiting in its chosen spot hugging the wall until it's chosen to dance.

I feel as though I'm in a pinball or a computerised one-arm bandit, bouncing arbitrarily between 1950s doo-wop and 1990s alt-country, from the Delfonics to the Thorns via Creedence Clearwater Revival and The Pogues. I am a jukebox, and it feels good.

I open the cupboard in my den and take out my PowerPod, the white lead that I use to connect the iPod with the G4. The connection is made, and the iPod begins uploading the new additions to the library, a further 154 songs. A few minutes later the exercise is completed, and my Pod is full – prone but proud. The iPod lies on the desk in front of me. Looks a little like a speaker box. It is white, oblong, ergonomic, with perfectly rounded corners and a pale blue two-inch LCD window that lights up super brightly for exactly two seconds when I touch one of the iPod's buttons (I have told it to do this and it does what it's told). It's made from this most remarkable plastic, a double-crystal polymer Antarctica that looks like the most modern material ever invented.

As the light recedes and then jumps back into life, it's winking at me, letting me know it's available and ready. It's willing and able, too, hinting that its vast library is there for the taking; all I need to do is press the menu button and spin the wheel. All my 3G Pod needs to spring into action is for me to press a button, then hit the raised rim in the centre of the scroll wheel, spin, browse, then scroll down the songs to, let me see, how about, 'A Man Needs A Maid' by Neil Young, from *Harvest*, during that period when he wanted to be James Taylor, and I was trying to persuade my mum to buy me my first pair of flared jeans. My iPod tells me this is the first song I'm playing from a possible 4400 (I knew that!), and, right now as I'm typing, that it's 1 minute 22 seconds into the song with, oh damn it, 1.41, no, 1.33 left. How clever is that? This is a facility I never really thought about, a facility I never realised I wanted, or needed, but now of course can't live without. At least I don't think I can. But I feel that way about the iPod generally. The feelings I have towards my iPod (my intuitive little iPod), towards my G4, towards the Pod's iconic white headphones, towards everything associated with it are almost unnatural.

The iPod has consumed my life like few things before it. It sits in my office, daring me to play with it, like some sort of sex toy. As well as being the greatest invention since, oh, that round thing that cars tend to have four of, or those thin slivers of bread that come in packets, the iPod is also obviously a thing of beauty. And I think I'm beginning to really fall in love. Seriously ...

1 Steve Jobs Changes His World

What you didn't know about the Apple CEO

Sometimes, critical mass happens when we least expect it. Early in 2004 Steve Jobs noticed something as he was walking through New York City. 'I was on Madison,' said the Apple CEO, 'and it was, like, on every block, there was someone with white headphones, and I thought, "Oh, my god, it's starting to happen."' Bizarrely, Jonathan Ive, the company's sought-after style guru, and the man behind the design of the iPod, had a similar experience in London: 'On the streets and coming out of the Tube, you'd see people fiddling with it.' By the summer of 2004 Apple had sold over three million iPods to over three million people for whom the little plastic and chrome computer with the capacious disc drive had become a way of life. They had sold them to Will Smith, Gwyneth Paltrow, Bill Clinton, Jamie Cullum, Sheryl Crow, Kevin Bacon, Public Enemy's Chuck D, Alanis Morissette, David Bowie, Ice T, Robbie Williams and every other compressed, digitised celebrity worth his salt. The couturier Karl Lagerfeld bought himself sixty of the damn things, coded on their backs by laser etching so he could tell them apart (he even commissioned a pink copper rectangular purse to hold twelve at any one time). *Vanity Fair* editor Graydon Carter was given his by downhome rocker Steve Earl (who had already filled it with five thousand of his favourite songs).

In April 2002 Apple's iPod had 51 per cent of the digital music player market, the remaining 49 per cent being split with the Rio, RCA Lycra, iRiver and Digital Way (digital music players you never, ever wanted to be seen with). By 2008 there will be eighteen million digital players in the world, and over ten million of those will be iPods.

People are no longer listening to their Walkmans – why would they, when they can carry their entire record collection around with them? Why limit yourself to 60, 90 minutes of music when you could have 40,000 minutes on tap, at the turn of a wheel? I mean, *why*? Seemingly overnight the iPod had galvanised a generation. In a Yahoo survey, a fifth of British backpackers said they wouldn't leave home without one. Although, unlike previous musical revolutions, this was embraced by a much wider demographic, a demographic that had a) access to a computer, b) the means to buy a digital music player, c) taste in music – any taste. The fans of the iPod were not just eighteen years old; they were twenty-five, thirty, forty-five, *sixty*. Owners consumed everything from Maroon 5 to Beethoven, from Nirvana to *Dark Side Of The Moon*. They listened to their little white machines on the bus, on the Tube, on the train, in the bath. Everywhere.

Almost overnight, the iPod became a private club with a membership of millions. And not only did people begin buying iPods, they started buying iPod accessories – often third-party accessories – with a frenzy not seen since the dotcom boom at the end of the last century: external speakers (Altec Lansing in particular), microphones, leather carriers, plastic 'skins', iTrip transmitters which amplified your iPod through your car stereo, even special adaptors to fit your BMW or Smart car, enabling you to play your iPod on the journey to work (or, if the inclination took you, to Shanghai ...). It was the first piece of kit that really appealed to the fickle consumer as well as to the computer nerd. And everyone found a different use for it – sure, you could store your entire collection of Bob Dylan albums on it (should any such thing be attractive to anyone), but its vast storage space made it a useful vault for all manner of digital files: the makers of the *Lord of The Rings* films eve used iPod to transport dailies from the film set to the studio.

When Steve Jobs returned to the company he co-founded in 1997, there were no plans for a digital music player, far from it. But having failed to notice the impending explosion in digital music, he set about creating a piece of 'jukebox' software soon to be known as iTunes.

The story of Apple is a convoluted one, but a story nonetheless that makes for easy reading. Having dropped out of university in Oregon in the early 1970s, this long-haired, sandal-wearing, vegetarian teenager, who lived entirely on fruit, teamed up with school friend Steve Wozniak and, in true American dream fashion, invented the world's first bonafide personal computer in Jobs' stepfather's garage. The computer, he'd tell anyone who'd listen, was going to be the bicycle of the mind. When the two met, doing summer work at Hewlett-Packard, Wozniak was only eighteen and Jobs, just thirteen. Jobs was never an underachiever (how could he be? After all, he was born and raised in Palo Alto in California, soon to become Silicon Valley) – he was a believer.

To finance the company – Apple was named after his favourite fruit – Jobs sold his Volkswagen camper van and Wozniak his treasured programmable computer to raise $1300. Weeks later, Jobs secured his first order of 50 Apple I computers. Semi-cased in timber and initially costing $666.66,[1] the original 1975 Apple is today enshrined in the Smithsonian Institute, where it looks so much older than it actually is (once compared to

---

[1] While working at HP, Stephen Wozniak started a 'business' called, without a hint of irony, Dial-a-Joke. Each morning he'd record a joke into his home answering machine which people were then encouraged to call. At its peak, over two thousand people called per day, making it one of the numbers most dialled in the Bay Area. But of course Wozniak made no money from it, since no one at the time knew how to charge for such calls. Wozniak's Dial-a-Joke phone number was 255-6666. Repeating numbers appealed to Wozniak immensely, and when Jobs suggested a retail price of $650 for the Apple I, Wozniak countered with $666, then eventually $666.66.

a component from a 1930s telephone exchange, it made a Mackintosh chair look positively hi-tech). Unreliable and bulky, it was not a great success, and so they started again, coming up with Apple II, not the world's first personal computer, but soon the most popular (plastic case, built-in keyboard, coloured graphics, the lot). It defined low-end computers for decades to come, and it was said that twenty-third century archaeologists excavating some ancient PC World stockroom would see no significant functional difference between an Apple II from 1978 and an IBM PS/2 from 1992.

Many schools found that buying a few Apples was a cheap way to add computing to their curriculum. Apple II's breakthrough was an application called VisiCale, the first proper spreadsheet. released in 1979, when Jobs was twenty-four. Between 1978 and 1983, Apple sales grew by 150 per cent a year, but those sales were based on the home and education markets. Jobs realised that the big money to be made from desktop computing would come from the business world. Apple needed to get into offices; they needed a business computer. And so they launched the Apple III. But it, like the Apple I, was a bomb – it ran hot and frequently crashed and was soon overtaken in sales by IBM's recently launched PC. It was 1981 and Apple didn't know what to do next.

And so two years later Jobs called John Sculley, then at Pepsi, and asked him to become president of Apple. 'If you stay at Pepsi, five years from now all you'll have accomplished is selling a lot more sugar water to kids,' Jobs told him. 'If you come to Apple you can change the world.' So Sculley joined, leaving Jobs to obsess about creating the perfect low-cost computer. Jobs devoted all his time to this project, leaving Sculley to run the company, which, he soon discovered, was an organisational mess (rivals referred to Apple's Cupertino, California headquarters campus, as Camp Runamok). Jobs had not only met his nemesis, he'd employed him, and given him the power to fire him.

Jobs may have been erratic, but it was his passion that drove him on. By the early 1980s Apple had expanded to such an extent that it was scattered across over a dozen buildings in Cupertino, buildings that were full of engineers, designers, technicians, marketers, publicists, couriers, most of whom dressed in the regulation Silicon Valley uniform of T-shirt, jeans and trainers. As everyone looked the same – how could you tell if there was an IBM or Compaq spy in the house? – it was decided that ID badges should be introduced: Steve Wozniak was declared employee number 1, Steve Jobs was number 2, and so on. But Jobs didn't want to be number 2, in fact he didn't want to be number 2 in anything. And so he argued that it was he, and not Wozniak, who should have the sacred number 1, since they were co-founders of the company and J came before W in the alphabet. When the plan was rejected, he argued that as the number 0 was unassigned, he'd be quite happy to have it. Which he did, and as 0 came before 1, he was technically top dog. It didn't matter that Wozniak was the chief technician and designer; Jobs had his number. 'Steve Jobs created chaos because he would get an idea, start a project, then change his mind two or three times, until people were doing a kind of random walk, continually scrapping and starting over,' says one insider. 'Apple was confusing suppliers and wasting huge amounts of money doing initial manufacturing steps on products that never appeared.'

In 1986 Sculley relieved Jobs of his chairmanship, ironically just eighteen months after Apple had launched their break-through product, the Macintosh, a computer with a built-in screen and a mouse-and-click user interface (and called Macintosh after designer Jef Raskin's favourite type of apple). At last, computers were accessible to the average user, who no longer had to type in obscure demands to carry out simple tasks. They created screen icons, cleaned up the keyboard and successfully demystified the computing process. Jobs, always a master of marketing, had propelled sales with a TV ad directed by Ridley Scott featuring an athlete being chased by storm troopers past throngs of vacant-eyed workers, and hurling a sledgehammer at a menacing 'Big Brother' face staring out of a screen. The message was that 1984 would not be Orwell's but Apple's. Jobs said at the time, 'We started out to get a computer in the hands of everyday people, and we succeeded beyond our wildest dreams.' The Macintosh's technology was so advanced that the Pentagon banned all exports to the Soviet Union.

But Jobs was gone, a centimillionaire with no job. He'd been given his 'fuck-you money' from Apple, he'd been on the cover of *Time*, he was a pop-cultural icon for Chrissakes! – what was he going to do now? Like Dustin Hoffman's character Ben in *The Graduate*, he was a little unsure about his future. He pondered a few options: 1) He thought of asking NASA if he could fly on one of the space shuttles, maybe as soon as the following year on the Challenger. 2) He visited the Soviet Union with a view to selling school computers to Mikhail Gorbachev. 3) And, perhaps even more fancifully, he considered making a bid for a Senate seat in California. But then, after a bicycle trip through Tuscany, he decided to do something far more prosaic: he'd get together a few engineers and do it all over again – he'd launch another computer company. He called his software company NeXT ('the next big thing'), and also bought a fledgling animation firm from *Star Wars* director George Lucas 'that needed vision'. That company was Pixar, these days the digital animation studio behind *Toy Story, Monsters Inc., A Bug's Life, Finding Nemo* and *The Incredibles*, films which between them have grossed over $3bn.

He returned to Apple as 'interim CEO' in 1997 at the request of a board desperate for innovation and, says Jobs, 'to salvage its fortunes'. As the company nearly folded in 1995, this isn't as cocky as it sounds, and Jobs soon made his mark by cleaning house, streamlining the products, and jumping on the Internet bandwagon. He quickly launched the pastel-coloured iMac desktops – a hit with every design-obsessive from Cupertino to

Clerkenwell – and followed them with the PowerBook and the iBook laptops, the flatscreen iMac (with its fifteen inch LCD monitor and G4 processor), the OS X upgrade Panther operating system and the PowerMac G5, arguably the fastest desktop computer on the planet. Jobs also made peace with Microsoft, adapting many of his operating systems to be compatible with their Windows product.

Jobs was always obsessed with design and presentation, obsessed with how a product felt, how a product looked, as much as how it worked. If there's anything PC users should thank Apple for, it's that their PCs probably aren't quite as ugly as they used to be. Jobs brought the computer's looks to the forefront and made PC manufacturers step back, take a look at the ugly beige and 'greige' boxes on their desks, and try to create something a little more scintillating. As soon as he introduced the five coloured iMacs at the tail end of the Nineties, suddenly all computers, all white goods, every toaster, vacuum cleaner and CD player looked as though they had been sent to the ergonomic doctor (even Rolex introduced iMac-influenced watches with translucent plastic in pastel colours). Apple's design sensibility – which was driven almost exclusively by Jobs and Jonathan Ive – was now so much a part of the company's DNA that unless each new product line substantially improved upon its predecessor, it was considered a failure; the Zen-like simplicity of a product's functionality only worked in conjunction with the brutal simplicity of its design. And if the company didn't get it right, there was a small army of devotees to tell them so. The company subscribed to the inverse law that says supply generates its own demand. If they made stuff, people bought it.

Apple had become a cult that rewarded the loner, a badge of honour you could wear in your own home. Own an iMac, an iBook, or a PowerMac and you could be king without even getting dressed. Steve Jobs had not only steered one of Silicon Valley's greatest companies to fame and fortune by creating some of the most sought-after products of the age, he had also emancipated a generation of nerds. But, successful and as innovative as he was, who could have known Jobs would take Apple into digital music?

2 I Came, iPod, I Conquered

How I fell in love with the iPod

The first time I saw one I wanted to steal it. Martyn wouldn't mind, would he? He could jump on a plane back to LA and buy another one. This one – the one in my hand, smiling at me – was only a few weeks out of its box, having just recently endured the twelve-hour flight from California in Martyn's hold-all. I felt a bit desperate and rather giddy (which is odd, because I was sitting down). It was small, smaller than a cigarette packet, a white and chrome little thing measuring 2.43 inches wide by 4.02 tall by 0.78 thick. Its serial number was laser-etched on the back in the smallest, daintiest typeface, instead of being on a tacky-looking sticker. It was quite heavy, but not too heavy. It felt good in my hand, like some sort of squashed mobile phone. A squashed mobile phone that had shrunk my friend's record collection ('Honey, I shrunk my record collection!'), turning every musical moment of his life, every adolescent memory, every chorus of 'Hi Ho Silver Lining', every last dance, every memorable car journey into imperishable MP3 form. He'd only had it two weeks but had already squeezed several decades of his life into it, into this... this iPod.

It was the new one, the 3G, the one that would carry 10,000 songs, 10,000 MP3 files full of Pink Floyd, Kelis, Slaughter & the Dogs, anything he damn well liked. It had a tiny screen, like the sort you get on fancy mobiles – was he sure it wasn't a mobile? – four little buttons, and this lovely control wheel that seemed to do everything. I'd heard it described as a musical Tardis, and that's just what it was, a white plastic and chrome

Tardis. It had this great 'shuffle' facility that, when you pressed it, meant that the Roy Ayers track Martyn was playing could just as easily be followed by the Clash, Roberta Flack, Pilot or the Fugees. Mad. It mixed up his music with 'the thoroughness of a blackjack dealer'. Like I said, mad.

And the interface rocked: he could get to any song, artist, album or playlist in under three seconds. Did I want one? Does the Pope wear a silly hat? It was just lying there, daring me to fill it. All white, all new, all twenty-first century. Apple CEO Steve Jobs says he knows a machine is good if he wants to lick it, but with the iPod you might think about going a little bit further.

Could the iPod have come at a better time? I have been buying records, tapes and CDs for thirty years, a journey that began with my mum and dad's 7" singles before kick-starting proper with the Middle Of The Road's *Greatest Hits* ('Soley Soley', 'Chirpy Chirpy Cheep Cheep', 'Tweedle Dee Tweedle Dum', 'Sacremento' … and Alice Cooper's 'Elected'. A journey whose latest ports of call were two Libertines CDs, the Divine Comedy's 'Absent Friends' and a re-release of Jeff Buckley's *Grace.*

At home I have an entire wall of CDs, around ten feet of 12"s and vinyl albums, three boxes of singles (probably about three hundred), and approximately one hundred cassettes, mostly self-compiled (home taping didn't kill music in this house), kept in what looks like a purpose-built box that actually once housed a leopardskin Dolce & Gabbana cushion (which I was given, before you ask). I've also got a shelf full of mini-discs, which rub up against the mini-disc player my brother kindly gave me several Christmases ago. It's a great piece of kit, but gets about as much use as it would in anyone else's house, being a testament – like the Betamax video player or the cassette single – to the arbitrary nature of format wars. Having spent twenty years as a journalist, many of which have been spent listening to records professionally, I have acquired an astonishing amount of stuff I wouldn't necessarily have bought, but which has enriched my life immeasurably.

I also still spend a shed-load of money on CDs, and not a week goes by without a random purchase or two. I have records I've played five hundred times or more (Stevie Wonder's *Songs In The Key Of Life*, Steely Dan's *Aja*, David Bowie's *Ziggy Stardust* for starters), and records I've probably not played all the way through. Records I bought and kept because they were trendy (UK Electro anyone? The *Infected*? The *Holy Bible*? Any Lou Reed record made after 1973?), records I refused to throw away for sentimental reasons but were, are, quite obviously, rubbish. And although I usually ignore my wife's repeated claims that I have too many records, I do. I probably have too many books and magazines too (I definitely have too many clothes), but having just moved house, and having spent weeks putting records into boxes that I'm sure I hadn't looked at since the last time I took them out of a box, six years ago (the last time we moved), I thought maybe I should do something about it.

So I did. I bought an iPod.

It's all Martyn's fault really, and in my mind I'm still sitting in his garden in West London, holding the damn thing in my hand, wondering if l could find enough time in my life to fill it up. But after a few months I realized that you don't find time for the iPod, you make time.

It took me a while to make the decision to get one, though. Would I have enough time to use it? I have a job, a demanding job, and a wife and a family, and friends (honestly, I do), and a social life, and a pile of books by my bed that never seems to get any smaller, and a daily, weekly, monthly intake of newspapers, magazines, press releases, DVDs, CDs, book proofs, book cata- logues, videos of forthcoming TV shows, bribes blah blah blah. Then there are all the functions, the openings, the parties, the launches, the glad-handing and the nightly round of shaking the hand that feeds me. And then there is all the stuff on the

Internet, the news bulletins, the e-mails, the website trawling, the this and the that and the whatever. I don't have time to watch terrestrial television, so how was I going to fit an iPod into my life? 'Seriously,' said my friend John, 'how much free time do you really have?'

None, which is why I decided to buy an iPod. Or rather I asked my wife to buy me one for Christmas, a Mac-compatible 40 GB monster that would satisfy all my needs. Well, my desires anyway.

I already had the computer, a brand spanking new 12" PowerBook G4 that was capable of burning CDs as well as having the intriguing iTunes logo in the vertical panel bar. iTunes would soon become my best friend, my first software buddy, the new home for my soon-to-be-shrinking record collection. I had bought the computer precisely for this reason, so my iPod would have somewhere to call home. I was slightly irritated that the MP3 generation seemed to be having more fun than I was, and having spent the best part of three decades collecting records, I didn't see why I should be missing out. MP3s? Computers? Compressed files and t'ing? I can do that. Gizza n' iPod.

Which is what my wife did, wrapping it up just like she'd wrapped up last year's digital video camera, handing it over with a slight I-hope-you're-going-to-use-this-you-know-because-I-went-to-an-awful-lot-of-trouble-to-get-it-as-they're-practically-sold-out-over-here-and-it-wasn't-exactly-cheap-you-know look in her eye.

Well, I hadn't let her down last year – I have hours and hours of insane family expeditions – and I was determined to be as enthusiastic this year. I unpacked the beautiful black and white boxes, began fiddling about, plugged everything in, and then began planning the rest of my life.

And so I started filleting my record collection, ripping the guts out of my vinyl and then uploading them onto iTunes. I began spending every available minute rummaging through every CD, album, single and cassette, looking for songs worthy of my new baby's attention. On day two I discovered I had *Hunky Dory* not just on CD, but on cassette, and also on vinyl – three times! The original, a mid-1980s re-release with extra tracks and a gatefold sleeve, as well as a limited edition Japanese picture disc of unknown provenance. The album was one of Bowie's most formative, a cornerstone of early 1970s British singer-songwriting, but did I need five copies? The process of deciding what to upload involved listening to every song I'd ever bought. Some were imported immediately, but many more were forced to walk my PowerBook's metaphorical plank. Would I rip it into an MP3, or would I press eject and spin the CD out of its slit?

I fell in love with the process immediately. As soon as the song was uploaded, either by importing the whole CD, or individually dragging it across to my library, the file just lay there, nameless, blameless. And so I would type in the artist's name, the song title, the album it came from (as well as a host of other categories), and then watch it flip automatically into its rightful alphabetical place. And having spent a few nights doing this, my friend Robin said I should upload while connected to the Internet as the program would then download the information for you. Fantastic! Isn't the Internet brilliant? My own private radio station was being compiled right before my eyes – all I had to do was upload the content.

As soon as I got busy with my new toy, experts popped up everywhere, those know-alls who had been in Podland for some time now. Was I going to start burning CDs, 70 minutes of personalized taste to give to friends and family? Was I going to move up a gear and burn my first MP3 CD, a full eight and a half hours of compressed digital fun? How was I doing with smart playlists? Was I making my own CD covers yet? Had I downloaded anything from Limewire?

This was all before me, as what I was really enjoying was editing my life. I had spent far too much of my life compiling cassettes of my favourite music, either for myself or for friends – 120-minute juxtapositions of the cool and the corny: esoteric Springsteen or doo-wop compilations, the A-Z of Suede, Go-Go's greatest hits (actually this easily fitted onto a C-60 – four Trouble Funk tracks and, er, not much else) … In my late twenties I began a series of 'One Louder' cassettes, in homage to Spinal Tap, reaching 'Twenty One Louder' before running out of steam, but there were plenty of others too: 'Terminal 1970s Freeway Madness' (Side 1: Fast Lane, Side 2: Slow Lane, you get the picture), 'Disco Epiphany', 'Disco Nirvana', 'Now That's What I Call REM', '100 Minutes of the Clash', 'The Best Beach Boys Tape In The World', 'Everything She Wants' (a shed-load of Wham! for an ex-girlfriend), 'Metal Leg' (a shed-load of Steely Dan for myself), 'Aimee Mann+' (must have been a slow week), 'Christ it's the Chemical Bros!' and 'David Bowie' (rather inspirational title, I thought).

Albums ceased to matter, and I could edit with impunity. Why bother with REM's *New Adventures In Hi-Fi* when all you really want is 'Electrolite' and 'E-Bow The Letter'? Why continue to ruin *Pet Sounds*, the best album recorded by anyone in the 1960s, by suffering the absurdity of 'Sloop John B' when you can simply delete it? Having embraced iTunes I could now listen to the Beatles albums without any of the Ringo tracks. My version of The Clash's *Give Em Enough Rope* no longer included 'Julie's Been Working For The Drug Squad', while 'Stairway To Heaven' had miraculously vanished from my edition of *Led Zeppelin IV*. Shame. iTunes became a great leveller, butting Thelonious Monk up against the Carpenters, Mylo up against Dusty Springfield, Oasis up against Elvis. I rediscovered the joys of Miles Davis, and began questioning why I had ever liked Lenny Kravitz or drum'n'bass. ABBA? Check. The Cult? What had I seen in them in the first place (even though 'She Sells Sanctuary' was still worthy of uploading)?

The iPod not only changed the way I felt about music, it helped me re-establish relationships with records I hadn't heard in five, ten, twenty years. Bad Company's 'I Can't Get Enough Of Your Love' became a constant companion, as did Ace's 'How Long' and Cracker's 'Low'. Zero 7 became gods in my eyes, as did the Yellow Magic Orchestra, Eno, Phoenix, Bob Seger and the Bees. All of a sudden they were living in my house, along with dozens of other pop stars I hadn't had anything to do with for ages.

I kept at it, uploading as though tomorrow were going out of fashion (Mike Skinner? Genius! Rip him now!). In four months I'd uploaded over four thousand songs, using up nearly half of my 40 GB iPod, creating the sort of library that would frighten the life out of any BBC radio programmer. As I compiled my library I'd play back my acquisitions on shuffle, moving from Sugar to Nancy Sinatra to Scott Walker and Ryan Adams via the Beastie Boys and Beck. Perverse, accidental and idiosyncratic ... I'd never listened to music this way before. (Choice is meant to make you anxious, but not if someone else is doing the choosing.) I began to think: could I get my entire record collection onto this machine? Could I get an entire lifetime's experience into this little white rectangle? Could I compress a life's worth of CDs, tapes, albums, singles and mini discs onto my Pod? OK, I might not have many mini discs, but they're my mini discs. Surely I couldn't collect all the good stuff that had ever been recorded. Could I? Could I really? In one place? Really? Could I? Surely I couldn't ...

I wasn't consuming music so much as curating it, and the iPod had brought out the anorak in me; I was becoming an organiser, an alphabetiser. But then that was the point, I thought to myself. As I began compiling the library, as I worked my way through the hundreds of jewel cases in my den, the thought began occurring to me that I shouldn't just turn my machine into a virtual Greatest Hits collection. There would be nothing clever about including every great Oasis track, every great Who song, or the complete works of Marvin Gaye. Anybody could do that, so why would that make my iPod special? It wouldn't, would it? And so the editing process became even harder: how to upload my record collection without missing out the obvious bits but also making it interesting, making it an artefact in its own right. If all the iPod did was collect all your stuff in one place then I could simply ask someone else to upload it for me, and where would be the fun in that? I may as well have gone to one of those companies – a growth industry this – who compile bespoke iPods for you ... 15 GB 20 GB, 40 GB, you name it. Or else I could ask them to fill one full of stuff they thought I might like, making it a different sort of consumer purchase completely. The big thing about the iPod, I thought, was the way in which it forces you to listen to your life in a different way. If I wanted someone else's juxtaposition to accompany me on aeroplanes and taxi rides then I could have started doing that when I was fourteen and simply asked other people to buy my records for me. No, I had to put more effort into this. I had to begin to take it seriously.

And so the editing began in earnest. While I was uploading Air's *Moon Safari*, an album I thought I needed in its entirety, I started thinking I might not need all of it, which forced me to go back in and find if this were true. And as for *Walkie Talkie*, their follow-up, after repeated plays it turned out I only really liked three songs, 'Universal Traveler', 'Alpha Beta Gaga' and 'Alone In Kyoto' (and none of them is exactly crucial). And as for the canon, well, it just wasn't going to work. There are many so-called classic albums that I have never particularly seen the point of, and when I started filling my iPod realized I had been too lenient with them. *Electric Ladyland*? Two tracks, tops. *The Stone Roses*? Five tracks, and you're pushing it. *Exile On Main Street*? I know it's always voted the best Stones album by critics and consumers alike, but it's got six decent songs, max. *Nevermind*? Nothing at all, thank you very much (Kurt Cobain wasn't a spokesman for my generation and I hope he hasn't remained a spokesman for anyone else's). Same goes for

Pearl by Janis Joplin, a singer almost as untalented and as physically repellent as Sean Ryder. My Pod didn't care a fig for the canon, and it wasn't going to start liking records just because it ought to, just because *Rolling Stone* and *Q* and *Mojo* said it ought to. God knows, I did enough of that. How many hours, days, weeks probably, did I waste as a teenager trying to like Emerson, Lake and Palmer's *Pictures At An Exhibition* or Pere Ubu's 'difficult' second album? Why did I bother pretending to like Black Uhuru? I was never going to like them, no matter how many times the *NME* told me I ought to (although they were right about so much else, Nick Drake, the MC5 and the Stooges included). When you're filling up your toy, the only records you should concentrate on are the ones you love.

Anyway, I had my own canon, one built on experiences I had when I was back in my teens, when, if I chose to, I would play an album until I liked it, no matter how insubstantial it was. I'm sure this is why I still love *Ooh La La* by the Faces, a record the band not only struggled to finish (it doesn't even last thirty minutes), but was disowned by Rod Stewart before the thing was even released (as he didn't bother turning up to the studio the title track was eventually sung by Ron Wood). Because of my misplaced diligence I also have an unreasonable penchant for *Billion Dollar Babies* and *Muscle Of Love* by Alice Cooper as well as *It'll Shine When It Shines* by the Ozark Mountain Daredevils – I'm fairly certain the record isn't any good but I've loved it for thirty years and will probably love it until I die (I was fourteen for Chrissakes).

Not only this, but a lot of stuff has simply been ruined by repetition and overexposure. In my student days I used to love Motown – the classics, the rarer than hen's teeth B-sides, all of it – but now can hardly bear to listen to it. I played it so much in my youth, even played drums in a group that used regularly to butcher 'Dancing In The Street', 'Nowhere To Run' and 'Heatwave', that by the time the advertising industry caught up with it in the mid-1980s, using Marvin Gaye and the Supremes to sell jeans and T-shirts, for me it was already past its sell-by date. How much Motown did I upload? Six songs, none of which is indispensable: 'There's A Ghost In My House' by R. Dean Taylor, some Diana Ross, 'It's A Shame' by the Detroit Spinners (the semi-classic single they made before moving to Atlantic), and a couple of things by the Four Tops. I've got more Robbie Williams than I have Motown, which, I like to think, makes me feel more modern than I actually am. I also refused to appreciate the blues, something I've done since seeing B.B. King on *The Old Grey Whistle Test* when I was twelve. The blues are too depressing, too authentic, too rootsy for me, and the iPod wasn't going to change my mind.

I soon realized that the iPod is uniquely egalitarian, and in its eyes, especially through the prism of the shuffle facility, Alessi's 'Oh Lori', Nick Heyward's 'Whistle Down The Wind' and Brian Protheroe's 'Pinball' are equally as important as Led Zep's 'Immigrant Song', Primal Scream's 'Loaded' or the Fab Four's 'Hey Jude'. The shuffle facility became my own private energy source, my own electricity, running my life, accompanying my every move, choosing every song in my head. I'd chosen every song it played, I just hadn't told it when I wanted to hear it. Oh lordy. The shuffle meant my iPod could cut from Roland Kirk's 'Fly By Night' to Ce Ce Peniston's 'Finally' – as it did just now – as though it were the most natural thing in the world. I would never have made that choice, and I probably never will again, but my little chrome friend says it's perfectly OK. Algorithms gone crazy? You said it, guvnor.

Am I a better person? Well, I'm certainly a different person, an evangelist almost, for the pleasures of the chrome. Where once I was snotty and standoffish, I am now quite, quite devout. Ask me anything about the iPod and I will bore the pants off you. Ask me about 'My Top Rated' and 'Recently Played' or the pleasures of Smart Playlists and I won't shut up until you shove my iPod in my mouth. I have become someone to avoid at parties (even more so than usual), someone who can't be trusted with technical information. Why? Because I'm bound to retain it and pass it on. I might tell someone, and if you're unlucky it might be you. I am the iBore, the man who bought into Steve Jobs' dream as though it were his own. So, yes, you could say I've changed. For the better, I'm not sure. An obsession I have had since adolescence has been rekindled to the point where it's eating into my leisure time with Pacman-like intensity. I am not only beholden to a computerised jukebox no bigger than a mobile phone, but my expectations of it are exponential. The iPod is a bottomless well, a black hole of limitless dimensions, a hobby that knows no bounds. As a fellow devotee said after he'd passed his own initiation ceremony, which lasted for about the same time as mine, approximately six months, 'The role of the records themselves changes when you go digital. They shrink into the background. Your records and CDs were once the main event; now, in computer parlance, they are your backup, standing ready in case of catastrophic failure of your digital library. They're what you read while you listen and wait for a box big enough to store every song ever recorded.'

So, have I changed? Maybe, like John Lennon said, 'Forever, not for better.'

What I knew for sure was that I was hooked.

3 The Single: Seven Inches of Aural Sex

Teenage dreams, so hard to beat

I wish I could say that the first single I bought wasn't Gary Glitter's 'I Didn't Know I Loved You Till I Saw You Rock'n'Roll', but it was. I wish it had been David Bowie's 'Starman', but it wasn't (I already had that on cassette, having taped it from the radio, but I know that for the purposes of the exercise, that doesn't really count). I wish it had been Mott The Hoople's 'All The Young Dudes' (a much, much, much better record), but someone had already lent me that, so I didn't really feel like buying it. Even the previous Gary Glitter record – 'Rock'n'Roll Part 1' – would have been better, cooler (at the time, anyway), but there you are. When you're twelve you don't make history, you're just a victim of it. Still, as I bought it, handing over my hard-saved new pence, I felt as though I was moving from boyhood to adulthood, leaving shin pads and cub scouts behind, and embracing a world full of platform boots and chinchilla coats. The record sounded dangerous, Neanderthal, rough ... big boy stuff.

Before the CD – well before the CD – and just after shellac and the 78, came the 7" single, the greatest form of teenage expression since pre-marital sex. The 7" single helped invent the notion of the teenager, and helped the 1960s prepare itself for some extreme social mobility. And I, like everyone else I knew who was a twelve-year-old boy in 1973, was an extremely willing victim.

As a boy, singles were my life, they were what I lived for,

what I spent my pocket money on. I couldn't afford many LPs, but singles could be bought every week.[1] At school, every break time was spent discussing what was going to be Number One that week, and what singles we were going to buy at the weekend. Slade. Wizzard. Bowie. At that age, with puberty a constant companion, and inarticulacy a foregone conclusion, these records were how I spoke to the world. Largely I chose records that made the most noise, that had the most attitude, records that had the most pent-up emotion – Cockney Rebel, Bowie, Roxy, Golden Earring; Alice Cooper's 'Elected', for instance, was so totally full of provocation that I felt my whole life was being expressed by it: it only lasted a couple of minutes, yet it made me feel a little like I was performing myself simply by listening to it – acting out my tortured internal world in one short 150-second one-act play.

But I liked a lot of other stuff too. When I was young I was fairly indiscriminate about the records I bought; I bought them because I liked them, not because they were cool or fitted into a particular adolescent agenda. It seems ridiculous to think so now, when the world is remixed every five minutes to the sound of a recently acquired and no doubt soon-to-be-banished backbeat (could be garage, could be jungle, could be a garage in a jungle), but back in the early Seventies people tended to either like long-haired white music, or satin-swathed soul music. You went to gigs, or went to discos. Liked The Who, or Funkadelic, drank snakebite or cocktails. Me, I tended to like anything. In the first three years I spent buying records, from 1972 to 1975, I bought *everything*: glam rock, soul, disco, funk, heavy metal, folk, pub rock, the lot (I even had a David Cassidy

---

[1] My first LP purchase was Alice Cooper's *Billion Dollar Babies*, which I bought two weeks after it came out, in a small record shop in Deal, on the south coast, having paid for it in 50p instalments for the previous month. I've also got a fairly strong recollection of paying £2.11 for *Dark Side Of The Moon*, from Chiltern Sounds in Marlow, about a year after it was released.

single, 'I Am A Clown', on the silver Bell label; in fact I've still
got it). This was a period when an Acker Bilk record was as
important to me as a Queen 45. I was falling in love with music,
pure and simple, and while I knew I could easily be swayed by
style – Frank Sinatra and Dean Martin having already stolen
my heart – there were things I liked simply because I heard
them on the radio. Who knew what Medicine Head looked like?
I liked 'One And One Is One' anyway. And did it matter that
Lieutenant Pigeon were fronted by a pub pianist who looked
like Dick Emery in drag? Like Bob Dylan once said about the
Judy Garland song 'The Man That Got Away', 'This song always
did something to me, not in any stupefying, tremendous kind
of way. It didn't summon up any strange thoughts. It was just
nice to hear.'

We pick up music by osmosis when we're young, but we're
also the victims of indoctrination. There was always music in
the house, always Frank Sinatra and Dean Martin records on
the gramophone, always the Beatles on the radio. The first film
I ever saw was *A Hard Day's Night*, which my mother dutifully
took me to see when I was just four. She was also a brilliant
pianist, and whenever she found time – usually on a Sunday –
would work her way through old music hall standards, wartime
ballads, and 'current songs from the hit parade' (as they said
on the 'wireless' at the time). One of the many things she used
to play for me when I was young was a maudlin old standard
called 'So Deep Is The Night', which had been adapted from an
old Chopin piece (as opposed to a recent Chopin piece, that is).
I'd heard it accompany one of the many TV compilations of
classic silent movie scenes that always seemed to be playing
on Saturday mornings and asked Mum if she could play it; she
picked it up in less than five minutes.

My father also indoctrinated me by turning me on to Lou
Reed, and specifically 'Walk On The Wild Side', which he
thought was tantalisingly decadent. These days it's played
regularly on Radio 2, but back in 1972 it was about as *risqué*

as a record could be and still be commercially successful. My father always tried to push me, always wanted me to exploit my intellect, which is probably why he got so frustrated when I didn't come up to scratch.

Why did I fall in love with music so much? Why does any twelve-year-old boy fall in love with pop? It's predestined, in a weird kind of way, like it is with anyone. With me, maybe it was because music would have me, because it made it so obvious it wanted to fall in love with me ... ME! And at the time, I felt I needed something, someone, quite badly ...

If asked to identify the one little thing that has caused me the most hardship in my life, the one vexation that has brought me most grief, I would have to point not to a debilitating illness or handicap, but to the consonant that follows ABC.

D, how I hate you.

Of course Bs, Gs and Ss have occasionally wreaked havoc too, but it is Ds that have kept me awake at night, made me weak from anxiety and affected the way in which I see and talk to the world.

Stammering is not a particularly dignified affliction, tied in as it is with foppish dilettantes who wander around Waugh and Wodehouse novels like accidents waiting to happen. Stammerers are portrayed as crooks, perverts, idiotic chinless wonders, maladjusted members of the underclass, or, more usually, simply figures of fun: Michael Palin in *A Fish Called Wanda*, Ronnie Barker in *Open All Hours*. It is an affliction that rarely inspires anything but pity, or sarcasm. There is little solace in knowing that Marilyn Monroe had a discernible stammer; she also had appalling BO. No one likes to stammer. It has no kudos. It is the aural equivalent of being clumsy, disconnected, uncoordinated: the involuntary repetition of mistakes. A stammer never goes away. It can disappear for a while, and it's easy to think it's gone for good. Then, all of a sudden, it's back, worse than before, a malevolent quirk that refuses to make life any easier.

A stammer (which, for what it's worth, is still more desirable a word than 'stutter', though they mean exactly the same thing) is like a rash that invades your body at times of stress, a signal to the perpetually beleaguered that God hasn't quite forgotten, not just yet, anyway.

About one person in every 100 stammers, and it affects four times as many men as women. There is a 20 per cent greater chance of you stammering if a close relative has a speech problem, although the roots almost always lie in childhood. Stammerers often have some difficulty learning words at a very young age, and emotional and physical stress on a child plays a big part. Some kids begin stammering to draw attention to themselves and then find they can't stop, although the attention is usually of the wrong kind.

My stammer was largely caused by my father, something he now profoundly regrets. It haunts him, my mother says. And though I believe her, and bear him no malice (I still love him), it haunted me, too, for ages (my upbringing was brilliant in so many other ways, but no one likes being hit, and no one likes being hit when they're young, particularly when they're very young). The way I was treated as a small boy scared me off fatherhood for years (it took me that time to realise that I didn't necessarily have to repeat my father's bad habits). Nowadays I think my relationship with my father is better than it's ever been, and because of our shared history I think we've both been extra careful with each other, and maybe know each other a bit better than we might have done had things been different. And in certain ways my stammer has defined me, made me what I am, whether I like it or not. Heigh ho.

I have stammered since I was about five, and it was at school where it hurt the most. Children are remarkably resourceful when it comes to identifying someone's weak points, but with a stammer the ammunition is handed to them on a plate; with a stammer you are putting the bullets into their hands yourself. I don't remember much from those days, but I remember enough.

Few things are more worrying when you're young than standing in the middle of a playing field with twenty other boys waiting to call out their names, knowing that when your turn comes, your stammer is only going to be exacerbated by the anxiety of getting it right. I also remember standing in the dinner queue, knowing that I was going to have immense difficulty asking for whatever was on the menu that day, the pressure increasing second by second as my school friends swiftly barked their requests before turning away.

Unless you've experienced it yourself, it's difficult to imagine the abject depression of worrying about every single word that comes out of your mouth. Between the ages of about five and sixteen it was utter hell. Every request had to be worked out in advance, every joke required a run-up (and God help you if you fell at the punchline).

The tribulations of teenage angst are bad enough without literally being tongue-tied. Some women say they find a stammer attractive, an indication of sensitivity perhaps, or vulnerability. But no teenage girl ever finds a stammer attractive, at least not the ones I knew at thirteen.

Consequently, in my early teens, I started to become scared of speaking. At home I buried myself in my record collection, poring over my singles night after night, counting them just to make sure they were still there. I studied every nuance, every crackle, every scratch. Listening to my records on the radio, or at other people's houses, was never the same, as they didn't have the same jumps and skips (I knew my records so well that I once identified David Bowie's 'Rebel Rebel' from the run-in groove, before the riff comes in).

Pulling myself away from my classmates, distancing myself from reality, I would while away the hours at school carrying on entire conversations in my head. I became monosyllabic, as grunting was easier than trying to say something which involved words, sentences, punctuation, opinion, thought, feeling, anything. I gravitated towards words I knew well – or at least words I was able to pronounce. In another attempt at self-defence, I forced my middle-class accent 'downwards': a little curt, more working class, blunt. If I sounded rougher than I looked, then maybe people would leave me alone, stop laughing at me, or looking at me twice. My downwardly mobile accent worked to a certain extent, and soon my voice was indistinguishable from any other fourteen-year-old boy with a Home Counties lilt.

As I matured, I began taking my stammering for granted, and it became almost an integral part of my make-up. During my late teenage years, when a different youth cult seemed to invade my life every six months or so, my stammer became a badge of notoriety, a symbol – like an earring or a black leather jacket – of a certain type of 'otherness'. But then I really did grow up, and the stammer (or at least its importance) faded from my life like so many Buzzcocks records. It was never completely debilitating, but seeing that my main hindrance was always the dreaded 'D', one of the worst things for me had been announcing myself on the telephone. It had almost made me reluctant to introduce myself, which, as a journalist, caused all too palpable problems. I mastered it, though, and even grew to conquer public speaking, something I used to abhor.

But age fourteen, I opted out of society and threw myself into my music, taking solace in my record collection. Safe in my room, a small upstairs room in a quarter at the top of a hill on an RAF base just outside London (I had seriously peripatetic parents), I felt so removed my sense of isolation was almost comforting. If adolescence is meant to be all about joining in – trends, gangs, clubs – I was in my own tree, all alone and quite content (and ripe for the kind of glamorous neuroses peddled by David Bowie and Marc Bolan). As boys, it wasn't the *idea* of music that brought us together, it was the way it made us feel (and this we didn't particularly articulate to each other). If you could listen to the opening bars of 'Jean Jeanie' or 'All The Way From Memphis' without getting a whiff of immortality, there was obviously no hope for you. In those days I could sit and pore over a single as though it were a rare book, money, or pornography (which was extremely difficult to find in those days). A few years later I remember staring at a copy of the Damned's 'New Rose' (Britain's first punk single, released at the end of 1976 on Stiff Records) as though it had some secret powers, and that all I had to do to liberate those powers was to stare at it for hours on end. I stared at the damn thing as though it were a dead dog, fascinated and transfixed in equal measure.

I've still got some singles, 562 in all – some I've had all my life (they belonged to my parents), some since my teens, and a few I've even bought fairly recently. Many, like the first Public Image single (that came with its own spoof newspaper, designed by Terry Jones eighteen months before he launched *i-D*), ATV's 'Love Lies Limp' flexidisc and an original copy of the Who's 'Substitute' are sheathed in clear-plastic covers. I've had some of my singles since I was about thirteen, and a lot of them have had their covers kept together by gaffer tape, Sellotape, masking tape, glue ... Some are covered in biro and felt-tip, tiny little tell-tale signs of my past. Every fold and crease is a memory, every tear and scratch. (When the first digital music carriers came to market, many of them were called memory sticks, which I always thought was very appropriate.)[1] I've even got a

---

[1] I know someone who started to create a soundtrack to his life, a song for whatever situation he was in, there at the roll of his thumb. I think this is a perfectly legitimate exercise; after all, we play music when we're sad or in love, so why not when we're driving through Big Sur, or sitting in a traffic jam on the A40. In fact, everyone I know has started to compile a soundtrack to their life. When I asked Tony Parsons at lunch one day if he was doing the same thing, he said he tended to listen to stuff he'd never heard when he was young, stuff he'd never heard before, stuff like Bert Jansch, and started rattling off a list of the favourite songs on his iPod. 'I think that the best Beatles song is the one on my Best Songs file – "It's All Too Much", a George Harrison piss-take of hippy-London that appears on the *Yellow Submarine* soundtrack. I think that's another thing the iPod does – it keeps things fresh – for fifty years. I love "It's All Too Much" but without the iPod

copy of 'Dishevelment Blues' by the Faces, which was given away with the *NME* in 1973. When their album *Ooh La La* was released, the paper gave out a free flexidisc as a promotional

---

I think the Beatles would have burned out for me with over-familiarity.' A day later I received four pages of yellow lined foolscap with the following written in Tony's trademark capitals (note his almost total disdain for the definite article): 'Best Songs' file on Tony Parsons' iPod: 'Can't Find My Way Home' – Blind Faith, 'Sorry' – Easybeats, 'Reel Around The Fountain' – Smiths, 'Tennessee Plates' – John Hiatt, 'Middle of The Road' – Pretenders, 'Strangers When We Meet' – David Bowie, 'You Trip Me Up' – Jesus & Mary Chain, 'Delia' – David Johansen, 'Disappearing Act' – Shalamar, 'Mr Loverman' – Shabba Ranks, 'Whenever You're On My Mind' – Marshall Crenshaw, 'Can't Find My Way Home' – Blind Faith (again), 'Born At The Right Time' – Paul Simon, 'Can't Stand Me Now' – Libertines, 'Up The Junction' – Squeeze, 'In A Big Country' – Big Country, 'Paper Sun' – Traffic, 'May You Never' – John Martyn, 'I'm Gonna Love You Too' – Buddy Holly, 'Love's Made A Fool Of You' – Buddy Holly, 'This Is The One' – Stone Roses, 'Sara' – Bob Dylan, 'Billy The Kid' – Ry Cooder, 'Return Of Django' – Upsetters, 'Waterfall' – Stone Roses, 'Revolution Blues' – Neil Young, 'We Didn't Start The Fire' – Billy Joel, 'Highwater' – Bob Dylan, 'Slow Train' – Flanders & Swann, 'The Way We Mend A Broken Heart' – John Hiatt, 'The Great Nations Of Europe' – Randy Newman, 'Anyone Who Had A Heart' – Dionne Warwick, 'Home & Dry' – Pet Shop Boys, 'Cynical Girl' – Marshall Crenshaw, 'The Most Beautiful Girl In The World' – Prince, 'Tokyo Joe' – Bryan Ferry, 'Sidewalking' – Jesus & Mary Chain, 'Fields Of Gold' – Sting, 'Promised Land' – Elvis Presley, 'Tangerine' – Led Zeppelin, 'Greetings To The New Brunette' – Billy Bragg, 'Walk On By' – Dionne Warwick, 'I Get Alone' – Libertines, 'Somebody's Baby' – Jackson Browne, 'Wild Honey' – Beach Boys, 'Caroline No' – Beach Boys, 'Dead Giveaway' – Shalamar, 'Blues From A Gun' – Jesus & Mary Chain, 'Deeper Well' – Emmylou Harris, 'There's Always Something There To Remind Me' – Sandie Shaw, 'All Right For Now' – Tom Petty, 'The Time Has Come' – Bert Jansch and John Renbourn, 'Elvis Presley Blues' – Gilliam Welch, 'Jelly Roll Blues' – John Martyn, 'It's All Too Much' – the Beatles, 'Nobody's Fault But Mine' – Page and Plant, 'Brushed' – Paul Weller, 'That Certain Female' – Charlie Feathers, 'Death Letter' – White Stripes, 'Can't Keep From Crying' – John Renbourn, 'Mersey Paradise' – Stone Roses, 'Willin'' – Little Feat, 'Love's Unkind' – Donna Summer, 'Another Girl Another Planet' – Only Ones, 'Help Save The Youth Of America' – Billy Bragg, 'I Can Tell By The Way You Smell' – Ry Cooder, 'In The Streets' – Prince Charles, 'Transcendental Blues' – Steve Earle, 'Ball

tool. They put five tracks from the album on Side 1 and asked the band if they'd record something special for Side 2. I found out thirty years later that they deliberately recorded an 'abomination' in the hope that the paper wouldn't have the balls to use it. But they did, and I loved it. Love it still.

There are not just my memories in here, either, there are the semi-remembered memories of other people, the previous owners of my second-hand records, the ones with their names and obsessions felt-tipped onto the covers. Who was 'Sally', who drew her name in bubble-writing on the cover of my copy of 'Space Oddity'? Whose Rotring pen carved the harlequin shapes onto the cover of 'It's Different For Girls'?

These days I don't even look at sleeves – they're too small, and my life is too full. I've played Coldplay's *Parachutes* album over a hundred times but if you held a gun to my head and asked me what is on the cover, I'm not sure I would be able to tell you. It's some sort of yellow circle, a sun-like sphere sitting on a bed of black of Spinal Tap-like intensity. Back then, between the ages of twelve and eighteen, I knew everything about my singles: what was on the B-side, whether or not there was a note of its length, the colour and provenance of the label, whether it was a re-release (never a good thing), and – during punk – whether there was anything scratched into the run-out groove. I've still got all my Bowie singles – 32 in all – all my T. Rex, all my Donna Summer, all my Clash ... and dozens of Elvis Costello singles. I've got John Handy's 'Hard Work' (Impulse, 1976), the Brothers Johnson's 'Stomp' (A&M, 1980, picture sleeve), the Fall's 'Bingo-Master's Break-Out!' (Step

---

And Biscuit' – White Stripes, 'Pretty Flamingo' – Manfred Mann, 'I Fought The Law' – Hank Williams Junior, 'Little Red Hen Blues' – Taj Mahal, 'I'm So Glad' – Cream, 'All Summer Long' – Beach Boys, 'Fishing Blues' – Taj Mahal, '7 Nation Army' – White Stripes, 'Finally' – Ce Ce Peniston, 'Crying Won't Bring You Back' – Peter Green, 'Learning To Fly' – Tom Petty, 'Damn, I Wish I Was Your Lover' – Sophie B Hawkins, 'Rudi Can't Fail' – the Clash, 'Who Are You?' – The Who, 'Real Real Gone' – Van Morrison.

Forward, 1977, picture sleeve), Larry Wallis's 'Police Car', still in its original Stiff sleeve, complete with two – count 'em! – catchphrases: 'Today's sound today', and 'If it means everything to everyone it must be a Stiff'.

The 45 rpm single was introduced by RCA Victor in America on 31 March 1949 and lasted forty years before being replaced by the compact disc. It started life as a replacement for the shellac 78s which had just been superseded by Columbia Records' latest invention, the $33\frac{1}{3}$ LP. But as everyone preferred the Columbia version for 'longer programming', the 45 became the standard for singles. The speed was based on calculations that proved that the best compromise between adequate signal-to-noise ratio and playing time was three minutes per radial inch (and not, as has become myth, that a spiteful RCA executive simply arbitrarily subtracted 33 from 78). According to the National Sound Archive, 'Calculus was used to show that the optimum use of a disc of constant rotational speed occurs when the innermost recorded diameter is half the outermost recorded diameter.' Which is why a 7" single has a label $3\frac{1}{2}$" in diameter. It took seven years for 78s to completely die out, but by 1956, and the dawn of Elvis, of rock'n'roll itself, the 45 had the market to itself. That year, Columbia – RCA's 'speed war' nemesis – developed in-car stereos, which played custom-built 16 rpm discs with forty-five minutes of music pressed onto each side. RCA responded with a 45 rpm version, but who wanted to change singles every three minutes in the fast lane?

In the hodgepodge of my singles collection you will find many things (and a lot of which looks like it's been sandpapered within an inch of its life): Brook Benton's 'Walk On The Wild Side', Culture Club's 'I'm Afraid Of Me', the first three Pigbag singles, Run DMC's 'Walk This Way', the Edgar Winter Group's 'Frankenstein', Marianne Faithfull's 'As Tears Go By' ('I want a song with brick walls all around it, high windows and no sex,' said Rolling Stones manager Andrew Loog Oldham when he commissioned Jagger and Richards to write it for her), Oasis's

'Wibbling Rivalry' (the 1995 recording of Noel and Liam Gallagher fucking arguing with each other), the Human League's 'The Sound Of The Crowd', Boz Scaggs' 'What Can I Say', Sly & the Family Stone's 'Life'. War's 'Low Rider', that annoying Peter Frampton vocoder record ('Everybody in the world had *Frampton Comes Alive,*' says Wayne in *Wayne's World*. 'If you lived in the suburbs you were issued it. It came in the mail with samples of Tide.'), Crowded House's 'Don't Dream It's Over', Elvis Costello's 'Alison' ('Forty-year-old stereo' it says on the A-side!) and Thomas Leer's 'International' (a record that was, is, like the old Bob Dylan saying, 'Cool as pie, hip from head to toe') ... And because I am as much of a completist and a fetishist as the next man, there are my complete collections of Buzzcocks singles (punk brought back picture sleeves with a vengeance), T. Rex singles, Clash singles, Madness singles, Specials singles, all of them lovingly collated and neatly filed. Lovely.

For years I thought all I needed to compartmentalise my collection was a jukebox, although since the iPod I don't need one. The singles playlist I've been compiling is a soundtrack to my life, from 1972 to 1980, a soundtrack that can, in a flick of the wheel, conjure up any salient part of my youth.

And if I flick to the right place, I'll land on David Bowie's 'Rebel Rebel', as good an adolescent rallying cry as you're ever likely to hear, and a record that convinced me, at the tender age of thirteen, that life wasn't so bad after all. Who knows, I thought to myself, maybe this could be the life for me.

Maybe I could be a Space Face too.

4 A Glamour Profession

How Bryan Ferry and Roxy Music turned
my head

At the age of twelve, cocooned in my room, in an attempt to create a respite from the domestic situation downstairs – there are signs that the incessant buzz of argument is going to ignite at any second – I am alone with my turntable, as I always am. It is about four years old, made in 1969 by Pye, a nondescript mass-market brand that never had Bang & Olufsen aspirations, and bought by my dad around the same time. It's flat and low and looks like one of those 00-scale models of new towns you used to see in civic centres in the early 1970s. Its plastic lid is smoked, and folds down over the turntable with a reassuringly inaudible thump (it has strips of felt glued to its edges, which always make for a soft landing).

Even to my unnurtured mind I can tell it's a strange beast because instead of lifting itself up and returning to its seat, when the cue arm finishes playing a record it simply follows the run-off groove to the centre of the record, to the label, and then just dies, stops, and lies there limp, as though the seismic notions contained within, say, Sly & The Family Stone's 'Family Affair' or Dean Martin's 'Volare' have caused it to collapse, exhausted by the emotional intensity of it all. When I was given the deck by my parents – I think they realised I needed solace and somewhere to go and play the odd-sounding records I was beginning to bring into the house and so bought themselves a state-of-the-art stereogram – and began mucking about with it, I began thinking they had just palmed it off on me because it was broken, but then quite quickly realised that this was probably the greatest record player ever invented. Why? Because it meant that at night I could play a record and not have to worry about getting up and turning the damn thing off before I went to sleep. I could drift away listening to *The Man Who Sold The World* or *Dark Side Of The Moon* or Bo Hansson's *Lord Of The Rings* and imagine I was in the Wild West End of London or Middle Earth, or indeed the dark side of the moon, and not have to worry about coming home to switch the stereo off. I can tell you, at the age of twelve this was tantamount to living in a Case Study bachelor pad with sliding doors in the bathrooms, wall-mounted televisions in the bedroom and wall-to-wall shag pile in the den.

(As for my parents' stereogram, it cost them £89 5s – five shillings, about 25p – which, according to a formula provided by the Office of National Statistics, is the equivalent of £1141 in today's money. It was a Ferguson, with durable satin teak veneer and a 4-waveband radio including VHF and an all-transistor chassis. It had twin 8"x5" speakers, delivering a total of 6 watts of sound. Not only that, it had the latest four-speed record changer unit with a ceramic cartridge. 'Luxury to look at, and luxury to listen to,' went the PR stuff.)

But I'm not going to bed just yet as it's only 8.30 p.m. My seven-year-old brother is in bed next door and my mum and dad are still glowering silently at each other downstairs. It is a Saturday evening and they have just been watching *The Generation Game*. And I am alone, although not really. Like many a middle-class Air Force brat, having moved every eighteen months since I was born, my friends, my peers, are not like-minded twelve-year-olds, but circular pieces of black vinyl, 7" and 12" in diameter, some of them with orange labels, some of them purple, green, yellow, but all of them as important to me as members of my immediate family. In fact, considering the fights that have been going on all week, a lot more important, and certainly a lot more consistent (they don't shout at me, and what they do say is always exactly, *exactly* the same). These records are my brothers and my sisters, the nieces and nephews I don't have. And I love them (not that I don't love my real brother, of course, it's just that he's not, you know, a record).

Last night it was Sinatra-esque dreamscapes of John Barry, Sergio Mendes and Georgie Fame, although tonight I'm behaving like any twelve-year-old would be in 1973, playing the records of David Bowie, Alice Cooper and T. Rex. Sure, I have become unduly fond of Dean Martin, Frank Sinatra and an odd, possibly Scandinavian folk duo called Nina & Frederick (the sort of polo-neck-wearing couple who in my naivety I imagine enjoy threesomes and strong liquor rather than gimp masks and amyl nitrate), but on a purely visceral level I am obsessed by Kohl eyeliner, technicolor quiffs, space age platform boots and sloganeering glam rock.

Sixty-seven songs in my iPod library are largely the work of one man, Bryan Ferry, the Tyneside lounge lizard who, along with David Bowie and Marc Bolan, helped invent the 1970s. Right now – just now, as you're reading this – it's the future, but back then it was too. Mixing the glamour of nostalgia with edgy modernity is now the order of the day, an unavoidable rite of passage for any self-respecting entertainer, no matter where they fit in the food chain. Sci-fi retro styling? Make mine a large one, and quick with it. Bryan Ferry knew this thirty years ago, when he decided to launch himself as the most glamorous playboy in pop. Not only a radical architect of glam rock back in the early 1970s, for the last three decades Ferry has been King Cool, an effortless ambassador of the good life. When Ferry's Roxy Music first appeared, at the very start of the 1970s, they were so different from their peers that they may as well have been from outer space.

Was this the man who was going to help me escape suburbia?

Roxy's music was certainly arresting – pop art Americana mixed with searing R&B and avant-garde electronics – but it was their clothes that really turned heads. Leopard and snake-skin. Gold lamé. Pastel pink leather. At a time when most pop groups thought long hair, cowboy boots and denim were the height of sartorial elegance, Ferry and his band walked into the world looking like renegade spacemen. Boys loved them, and eventually girls did too. The right boys, and the right girls, of course. The first Roxy Music album – cunningly called *Roxy Music* – is like a whirlwind of playful decadence, a members-only nightclub with Ferry as the quintessential playboy making a bumblebee exit, buzzing from table to table on his way out.

Roxy were a montage of hot music, giddy drunken laughter, stoic posing and nightclub reverie. The music took the old sweet rock'n'roll melodies and twisted them like hairpins. It was symphony strictly from artifice, and all the better for it. If you happened to grow up in the 1970s then you couldn't ignore Roxy. You could adore them or resist them, but never ignore them. As a teenager in the early 1970s, Roxy were my world. It wasn't a world I particularly understood, and certainly not one I could decipher, yet I knew I wanted it badly. It was a seemingly classless world full of bright lights and dark alleys, of loose women wearing tight dresses, and very bad men wearing very good suits. This was a glamorous world etched with danger, a full-scale escape from reality, a world full of rich people pretending to be poor, and poor people pretending to be rich. And Roxy were its fulcrum, the very zenith of Style Centrale. I spent a lot of time with Bryan Ferry when I was young, and although his words described things I had never experienced, and thought I probably never would, I felt close to him, close enough to share gum.

My friend Alix went overboard in describing them, but I knew what he meant: '. . . crossing the greasy campness of 1950s Teddy Boy narcissism with the satin-tat and feather boas of the Charleston-era 1930s, mixed up with a dash of 1970s androgyny and 1920s sci-fi, and fired through some kind of Ken High

Street drag queen particle accelerator, so that it positively glowed like fluorescent Biba lip gloss.'

Yep, that's what I wanted alright.

It was another ten years before I met my hero. I was twenty-four and thought I was over compliments, whether from men, women or pop stars. Especially pop stars. The year was 1985 and I had been commissioned to interview Ferry, to publicise his first solo LP since the 1970s. Even though I was fast approaching my mid-twenties, I still had a crushed velvet soft spot for the man who had turned an affected, withdrawn thirteen-year-old into an affected, withdrawn thirteen-year-old with an unhealthy interest in snakeskin jackets and 1950s American kitsch. And at the time I might not have been able to copy his jet black, duck's tail quiff, but I could pretend to sing in French as well as anyone in my class ('*Jamais, jamais, jamais!*').

Rather annoyingly, it had been arranged that I would meet the ageing crooner at his Chelsea offices early one Sunday morning. For some reason, which I have far too much hindsight to recall, I had spent the previous evening in a seedy Mayfair nightclub wearing a bright red velvet drape coat, a garish pink shirt with elaborate ruffles, and a pair of voluminous custom-built trousers made from dozens of different pieces of violently clashing tartan. At three o'clock in the morning I no doubt looked as presentable as anyone else in a seedy Mayfair night-club, but at nine the following day, stumbling down the King's Road, having spent the night God knows where, I must have looked an absolute fright (come on, I know I did).

But dear old Bryan didn't think so, and if he did he didn't let on. Oh no. After a few polite exchanges he looked down at the material covering my legs and said, in an incredulous whisper I have never forgotten, 'My God, those are the most amazing trousers I have ever seen.'

Now, even though I know that this could have been just another example of Ferry's notorious charm, I was quite shocked at my reaction. The singer had disarmed me so much that the interview was a mere formality. (Even by this stage of my career I had interviewed a lot of famous people, but Ferry was the only one who had caused the hairs on the back of my neck to spring up when he walked in the room.) There was no way I could ask him anything remotely challenging (why had he bothered ruining 'Jealous Guy'? Why had he emasculated Roxy?) as I was still beaming at the memory of these casually delivered words of praise.

Much like me, as a boy Ferry had longed for escape. Having grown up in the north-east of England in a fairly impoverished mining village called Washington, near Durham, Ferry was desperate to travel south, to London, where everyone goes, to metropolitan excess. He was helped in his cause by the legendary pop artist Richard Hamilton, who taught Ferry at Newcastle University. I got taught by a mad French woman in green fishnet tights – and Bryan Ferry gets Richard Hamilton! Hamilton not only inspired the Roxy Music 'cover girl' album covers, he also inspired the music itself, a mixture of sci-fi aspiration and 1950s Americana. 'To go that route seemed the only option,' says Ferry. 'I mean, we could've had a picture of a band, looking rather glum, which was normal, standing on a cobbled street or something. But I didn't fancy that. The pin-up was a great way to sell things traditionally, whether it was a Cadillac or a Coke bottle or a packet of cigarettes.'

Or even Roxy Music, come to that.

In 1957, Hamilton came up with a definitive description of Pop Art, one that could easily apply to Roxy itself, and one that Ferry took to heart: 'Popular (designed for a mass audience), transient (short-term solution), expendable (easily forgotten), low cost, mass-produced, young (aimed at youth), sexy, gimmicky, glamorous, big business.' Throw in some 1950s balladry, white noise and synthesiser treatments, plus some futuristic teddy boys, and there you have Ferry's vision. Even their name was pop: 'We made a list of about twenty names for groups,' says Ferry. 'We thought it should be magical or mystical but not mean anything, like cinema names, Locarno, Gaumont, Rialto ...' According to Andy MacKay, Roxy's redoubtable sax player, 'If Roxy Music had been like cooking, it would be like a dish in Marinetti's futurist cookbook, *Car Crash*: a hemisphere of pureed dates and a hemisphere of pureed anchovies, which are then stuck together in a ball and served in a pool of raspberry juice. I mean, it's virtually inedible, but it can be done.' A fashion grenade rather than a fashion parade (Roxy were roughly analogous to a Gucci or a Chanel, only with a yard of fake leopardskin and a sachet of sequins thrown in for good measure), without them there would have been no Prince, no Culture Club, no Duran Duran, no Suede, no Pulp, no Blur, no Franz Ferdinand. And probably no me.

From the age of thirteen all I ever wanted to do was go to art school. These days I sometimes wish I'd actually paid attention at school, applied myself more to business studies, and ended up in the City. But I didn't. I was obsessed with David Hockney, Andy Warhol, David Bowie, *Interview* magazine, and all those travel books I found in the local library full of photographs of Main Street America. Billboards, Coca-Cola signs, Las Vegas swimming pools, palm trees, traffic lights, backlit Perspex shop signs, the cluttered skylines of Los Angeles and Detroit. Americana, that was what I was in love with, an Americana seen through the quizzical eyes of Pop Art and trashy pop, Tom Wolfe and Vance Packard.

And what I loved about the whole idea of Roxy Music was the fact that it wasn't the sound of bedroom doors being slammed, it wasn't the sound of youthful market-town angst or adolescent frustration ... it was the sound of aspiration, travel, power ... sex. It was a modern-day love letter to an anglicised America, a 1970s idea of 1950s space nobility. They – we! – were conquering the new frontier. In silver jumpsuits! Playing guitars! In front of girls!

To an adolescent boy in south-east suburban England, Roxy's B-movie dreams were unbelievably glamorous, and as my father got posted from nondescript small town to nondescript small town – in Norfolk, Suffolk, Buckinghamshire, Lincolnshire, Cambridgeshire, Berkshire, Kent, from RAF quarter to half-timbered bungalow to pebbledash semi – my itinerant existence (which is what we all had before we had a lifestyle) was accompanied at all times by Bryan Ferry, David Bowie and the extravagant fantasies of my future life. I painted, I drew, I meticulously designed cities, cars and magazines with felt tips and Sellotape. And I played records, all the time, from the moment I got up to the moment I went to sleep. I'd fall asleep listening to Roxy's 'Virginia Plain' or Frank Sinatra's 'Night & Day'. I was one of those twelve-year-olds who saw Bowie perform 'Starman' on *Top of the Pops*, one of those twelve-year-olds who, having seen this, would forever be in love with the idea of pop music, whose idea of glamour and sophistication was bound up in a flame-haired rock'n'roller in thigh-high boots and wonky teeth.

Spurred on by Bowie and Ferry, I got my hair cut in an approximation of Ziggy Stardust's, bought half a dozen pairs of glitter socks (I can still remember them: red, yellow, black, pale blue, purple and silver), and got into tank tops, butterfly-collared shirts, Oxford Bags and velvet jackets with aircraft-carrier lapels. Suddenly I was a space-age juvenile delinquent with knobs on.

Although we didn't know it at the time, we were the first post-modern generation, while Roxy Music – obviously, dumb-o! – were the first post-modern pop group. Before Roxy Music, fashion hated rock and rock hated fashion. Ferry courted the art school crowd and paid lip service to the fashion industry, while never forgetting the denim-clad punters who paid his wages. Clever move, but one that never endeared the band to America. Although America informed pretty much everything they did, Roxy never made it there, as the great swathes between

New York and Los Angeles didn't get their home-grown art school camp, didn't get their weird songs or their get-up. What the hell was a 'Pyjamarama' anyway? For Roxy, success in America was like trying to catch a fly with chopsticks. Why would they understand Bryan Ferry when they were obsessed with the Eagles?

Essentially Ferry discovered his own identity via the assumption of false ones, in a bid, perhaps, to spend the rest of his life in a world full of Roxy Music album covers. Using a little bit of Billy Fury, a little bit of Biba and a soupçon of good old-fashioned music hall, Ferry reinvented himself as a glittering, larger-than-need-be playboy. And boy did he love his job. He was brazen in his lust for a life that was never really meant to be his. He wanted not just the fast cars and the fast women, but the kudos that came with them. It wasn't enough for him to be seen to be enjoying himself, people had to believe that he meant it, that these things for him were not merely confetti – they were food and drink.

Roxy, meanwhile, were the perfect vehicle, a hard-edged, driving rock band who understood the importance of flash. If Ferry was the fruit and flowers, Roxy themselves were the bricks and mortar, a bunch of talented musos who were prepared to let Ferry take them where he wanted to go. Of course there was also Brian Eno, the frenzied genius who famously left the band after their second album *For Your Pleasure*; and while many critics say the fire went out of Roxy's engine when he moved on, their third album, *Stranded*, from 1973, is their one true masterpiece, containing Ferry's very best three songs, the three my iPod is never, ever without: 'Serenade', 'A Song For Europe' and 'Mother Of Pearl' (a song which perfectly encapsulates his ambivalent feelings towards the world he had invented for himself).

Having dissolved Roxy in 1975, and then again in the early 1980s, Ferry has been solo for twenty years. He has made albums that are so polished they practically rubbed him away, albums of cover versions, movie soundtracks, and had the occasional hit. He still plays gigs at stately homes, sometimes with Roxy, sometimes alone. He now wears little but Savile Row, flits around the fringes of London society and enjoys the company of young women. Still something of a role model, he is a fiftysomething roué, and at an age when many men are considering just exactly where to lay their laurels, and wondering where they left their slippers, the elder statesman of glam rock still dusts off his Antony Price tuxedo, musses up his considerable raven black thatch and takes himself to town.

I last saw him a year or so ago, in the front row at a Gucci fashion show in Milan. He was sitting, quietly, crouched in a heavy cashmere overcoat, as though he wasn't especially bothered about attracting the attention of the photographers. The front row has huge redemptive powers, and can grab a celebrity back from the clutches of obscurity in the time it takes to take a picture with a mobile phone. It's also the yardstick by which a designer's show is measured, although Ferry didn't seem interested in either possibility. He is, after all, now a fully paid-up English gent, with manners to match. As I took my place next to him and turned to introduce myself, he gently touched my knee and said, 'I know, Dylan, we've met. In 1985. You were wearing the most amazing pair of trousers. You didn't think I'd forget, did you?'

5 Build It and They Will Come

How Jonathan Ive and Steve Jobs made
the iPod

It's only a small, three-panel cartoon, yet it speaks volumes about its subject.

Panel one is captioned 'The road to Cupertino' and features two spiky-haired religious devotees, dressed appropriately in Buddhist-like garb, trudging through the forest. 'We're almost there, mate!' says the first. 'Almost *where*, Ivan? You said we were going to a conference.'

In the second panel our two compadres are sitting in a crowd of similarly dressed geeks listening to an address from a fellow disciple. 'We're going to do way more than that!' says our first friend. 'We've come to pay homage to "The One" ... and I would appreciate if you referred to me as iVan with a small i from now on.' 'The One?' replies his friend.

Panel three is captioned 'The One they call Ive' and features a picture of the designer sitting in the lotus position, arms folded, dressed only in a robe, levitating over one of his creations.

For many of his generation, and for most of the one behind him, Jonathan Ive is nothing less than a deity. Ostensibly he spends most of his time sticking bits of metal and plastic together, but he is treated as something of a demigod. Ive is the most revered designer of the modern age, a sort of Warhol for the digital generation, if Warhol had been a shorn-haired muscle-bound industrial designer from Essex, that is. As vice president of industrial design at Apple, Jonathan Ive has combined what he describes as 'fanatical care beyond the obvious stuff' with relentless experiments into new tools, materials and production processes, to design such groundbreaking products as the iMac, the iBook and the PowerBook G4. It is perhaps fitting for the man whom the *New York Times* described as 'perhaps the most influential designer in the computer world' to have achieved media ubiquity before the age of forty, but what is slightly more unusual is the list of nicknames he's become known by: he has more than your average pop star: the Armani of Apple, the Beckham of design, Mr Mac ... Apple Man. Even Bono – a fan for years before Ive created a special black U2 iPod for the launch of *How To Dismantle An Atomic Bomb* – created one for him: Johnny iPod.

'Jonathan's designs have touched millions of people's lives and transformed the workplace,' says the fashion designer Paul Smith, echoing what many in the entertainment, technology and fashion industries think of him. His products are not just the same old things packaged to look new; they actually are new. They are objects no one would have imagined ten years ago, which reach beyond the technical and aesthetic constraints of the twentieth century. Which is why Jonathan Ive is the first great designer of the twenty-first century.

Born in Chingford in Essex in 1967 ('please tell people it's not Chigwell ... they always say it's Chigwell,' he says with a smile), Ive was the son of a silversmith who became a teacher and then an Ofsted inspector for design and technology. It wasn't just indoctrination which caused Ive to be interested in design, though; from an early age he was pulling things to pieces to see how they fitted back together again – toys, radios, cassette machines, anything to do with music.

'By the age of thirteen or fourteen I was pretty certain that I wanted to draw and make stuff,' he says. 'I knew that I wanted to design but I had no idea what I'd design as I was interested in everything: cars, furniture, jewellery, boats, products of all kinds. After visiting a few design consultancies, I eventually decided that product design would be a pretty good foundation as it seemed the most general.'

When he left school he had wanted to design cars and enrolled on a course at Central St Martins in London but found it too challenging. The other students were 'too weird. They were making "vroom vroom" noises as they did their drawings.' And so he ended up at Newcastle Polytechnic, studying product design. Newcastle was slower than London, less frenetic, less transient (no one making 'vroom vroom' noises); it was a place he could think, a place he could forge a career.

Which he did. Towards the end of the Eighties he came south to co-founded the London-based industrial design consultancy Tangerine, where he helped develop everything from TVs and VCRs to sanitaryware and combs. One grey day, Ive drove up to Hull to present a new toilet to Ideal Standard. It happened to be Comic Relief Day and the firm's head of marketing sat through the entire presentation wearing a big red plastic nose. Ive's designs were rejected.

At Tangerine he also worked on the development of the 1991 PowerBook for Apple (who had hired the company as external consultants), the earliest version of the machine this book is written on. While working on it he became frustrated at the arbitrary nature of the intended design; he thought the industry was suffering from 'creative bankruptcy', and that Apple should take the lead by spending more time developing the external forms of their products. Apple listened, and a year later he was working for them as director of design. Initially reluctant to embrace them, he slowly started to fall in love with Apple, a company that at least appeared to know what good design was, even if it wasn't always so good at using it.

'I started to learn more about the company, how it had been founded, its values and its structure,' says Ive. 'The more I learnt about this cheeky, almost rebellious company the more it appealed to me, as it unapologetically pointed to an alternative in a complacent industry.

'I hated computers when I was at Poly, but I assumed it was my problem, that I was somehow inept. But in my last year there I discovered Macs and they spoke to me, they said so much about the company, and about the product itself. Essentially it wasn't a crappy computer, which is what I had been used to up until then.'

When he says, 'Apple really was born to innovate,' you get the feeling he's really talking about himself.

However, it wasn't until Steve Jobs returned to the company that Ive was given the freedom to concentrate on the 'pursuit of nothing other than good design'. Now steering a company – his company – that had been diluted by a 'design by focus group' mentality, Jobs realised that he needed people like Ive to reinvent Apple. And so began the iMac project.

The translucent turquoise iMac was launched in 1998, and on its first weekend Apple sold over 150,000 of them. With its unified curvaceous organic form, it looked as though it had been shipped in from a nearby film-lot, maybe from the set of a digital-retro remake of *2001: A Space Odyssey.* Not only did it break all conventions in terms of what a computer should actually look like, it had a character all of its own, one that shouted cool. It wasn't a PC, it wasn't made by Microsoft ... and yes, it *was* cool. Spurred on by a high-profile ad campaign – 'Chic, not Geek' – the iMac became the best-selling computer in America. When Steve Jobs launched the first Apple computer, it was not supplied with a case, so hobbyists had to construct their own, many from wood. The iMac was nothing *but* case.[1]

---

[1] There is a popular urban design myth indulged by the camouflage trouser-wearing boffins of Silicon Valley that plagues both Jobs and Ive. The gist is that Apple had actually designed the iMac years earlier but that the existing design chiefs were not interested, so it was put away, in one of the many ante rooms that snake around Cupertino's giant glass atrium. When Jobs returned from the wilderness and asked what ideas they had been working on – what stillborn computers, what design tabulations – Ive is alleged to have pulled it out of the iBin, and the rest is iHistory.

Not only did it help shore up Apple by selling more than two million units in its first year, the iMac transformed product design by introducing colour and light to the drab 'greige' world of computing where, until its arrival, new products were routinely encased in opaque grey or beige plastic.

'There's no other product that changes function like the computer,' says Ive. 'The iMac can be a jukebox, a tool for editing video, a way to organise photographs. You can design on it, write on it. Because what it does is so new, so changeable, it allows us to use new materials, to create new forms. The possibilities are endless. I love that.'

Computers used to sit behind plate glass windows in specially refrigerated purpose-built offices tended to by bespectacled boffins in white overcoats. They were cumbersome and expensive and were used principally to crunch numbers. But when IBM ignored the demand for 'minicomputers' – what we basically think of now as a computer – it opened the floodgates to a generation of young, long-haired entrepreneurs. Like Steve Jobs. Jobs wasn't interested in producing mainframes, as these big computers were called, he wanted to concentrate on minis, exploiting transistor technology by making smaller and smaller machines. Machines that looked like they belonged in the home, machines that looked happy to be at home.

Jonathan Ive wanted similar things.

The first modern computers arrived in the late 1940s, with IBM quickly establishing themselves as the main players on the commercial side. They were so successful, so omnipotent, and so far ahead of their rivals that in the early 1950s the industry was defined as 'IBM and the seven dwarfs'. It was a hegemony that survived until Microsoft began to spread its tentacles. And it was Microsoft that Apple needed to attack. If they couldn't do it by critical mass – in the Eighties Microsoft began to dominate the PC market in a way no company had ever before – then they would have to do it with design, which, to a certain extent, they had always done. In the Seventies,

Apple started telling anyone who would listen that the company was at the intersection of technology and the arts – that's how they liked to describe themselves; a company with one foot in the Sixties and one in the Eighties. Their manifestos were sprinkled around like confetti on the Thanksgiving parade: 1) Ease and simplicity, simplicity and ease. 2) Caring beyond the functional imperative. 3) Acknowledging that products have a significance way beyond the traditional views of function.

But Ive is not just a decorator, which is why he has always had such a problem with those who simply imitate the form of his designs. Ive is an industrial designer, and the inner-workings of his machines are as fundamental to his peace of mind as the arched back of the iBook or the translucent glow of his jelly iMacs. How could he make things quicker, simpler, smaller? He thought back to how things used to be, back in the days when the success of a computer was determined by how small it was (much like calculators and mobile phones). If an integrated circuit of transistors looked like the wiring diagram of an office building inscribed on the nail of your little toe, then surely (the boffins would heatedly exclaim) circuits could soon be found inside everything from rocket ships to stereos … ? Surely it would soon be possible to make one – well, maybe more than one, maybe a million – small enough to fit on the head of a pin!

Ive's brain works in similar, steadfast ways, making the art of the impossible the only game in town.

This Essex boy made good doesn't look much like a talismanic figure. His seventy-hour working weeks mean his pallor is largely untouched by the Californian sun, and in his tight gunmetal grey T-shirt, indigo jeans, hybrid running shoes and swarthy all-over head-stubble, Ive looks less like a techie nerd and more like a mid-Western jock. His only concession to the designer fetishism he has helped foster since he has been at Apple is his watch: a smart piece of precision engineering on a white natural-rubber strap designed by his friend, the similarly enigmatic Marc Newson. Walking down the street in his adopted home of San Francisco, Ive could easily be mistaken for one of the city's omnipresent bike messengers (either that, or a tourist from Hoxton). But his casual appearance belies his hallowed position at the very heart of corporate America, or at least what passes for corporate America in the twenty-first century. One should never forget that while Ive is a hero to the combat-pant-wearing Internet generation, he is a New Media executive who pulls down over $2m a year.

A reluctant speaker, Ive comes across as deadpan and rather droll. He is self-deprecating to the point of absurdity, and the only time you'll hear him use the word 'I' is when he's talking about one of the products he helped make famous. Ask him a simple question and he can launch off into a monologue, giving you a passionate twenty-minute tour of a new computer's design, or how the lid closes on a particular model of the PowerBook, or how the intensity of the backlight affects your mood.

Ive lives in a pretty but small two-bedroom house in the Twin Peaks district of San Francisco with his wife Heather – a writer and aspiring novelist he met while at college in Newcastle – and their young family. He devours the British TV comedies his friends send him (when it was first broadcast he became an obsessive fan of *The Office*), although most of his down time is spent either listening to or making music. Affectations seem to bore him, and while he loves the sushi here, he misses the curries in London's Brick Lane. Free time is spent 'living a serene life'. This consists of dabbling with techno-pop, computer-generated music, and relaxing with colleagues (a collaborator at work, his music allows him to work fastidiously on things alone). And after a string of sensible Saabs, and vintage Jaguars, Ive's current toy is a £150,000 Aston Martin DB7, his only really ostentatious possession. He uses it principally for the daily fifty-mile commute to the Apple HQ in Cupertino, although he says he bought it largely because of his longstanding interest in car design rather than any attempt to be a show-off.

He is obsessed by details, or at least the prospect of eliminating them. To wit: no screws around the edge of any computer screen, no hook interfering with the view of the display on Apple laptops, and as few knobs, buttons and lights as possible. Ive and his team take great pride in simplifying their products, getting rid of extraneous clutter and solving prosaic problems so that the consumer doesn't have to. Attention to minutiae is his metier: the suspended 'sleeping' state on a Mac was once indicated by a slowly flashing light, but Ive changed that. Soon, the light was pulsing slowly, as though the machine were actually breathing.

Clive Grinyer, a former colleague at Tangerine who now works for telecoms giant Orange, first met Ive in 1988. 'We hit it off immediately and he invited me to Newcastle. He built one hundred models for his final project at the Poly, a system of hearing aids for teachers and deaf pupils in schools. Normally, students would make five or six models at most. He had refined it so much that you realised he was totally dedicated to his art.'

When he built a pen for a Japanese company, he built in what he called a 'fiddle factor' because he knew that was what people liked to do with their pens. In an anecdote that rivals Spinal Tap in its madness, at Tangerine he once spent an afternoon choosing between fifteen shades of black for a computer. He even consulted sweet manufacturers to discover how to make the plastic casing for the iMac both blue and transparent.

Ive pours invention and elegance into his products. 1) The first iMac was a gumdrop-inspired solution to making an all-in-one machine. 2) The second, with its movable flat screen, alluded to a sunflower. 3) The popular transparent Apple mouse came from thinking about how drops of water sit on a flat surface. 4) An angle-poise desk lamp helped inspire one version of the iMac. 5) The see-through outer casing of the iBook came from the look that food has when wrapped in Clingfilm.

And none of them are gimmicks. 'I don't want to design things that the world doesn't need,' he says. Because he has been so plagiarised, he has a heightened sense of purpose, and dislikes designers who use 'swoopy shapes to look good, stuff that is so aggressively designed, just to catch the eye. I think that's arrogance, it's not done for the benefit of the user.'

To almost everything he touches, Jonathan Ive attaches his prefix, the i. It infers modernity, cool, edge, and has now been appropriated by a generation of carpetbaggers who use it in much the same way they used .com in the late Nineties. Ive's transparent plastic iMac, the iBook, the G4 Cube and the Titanium PowerBook are cultural icons. They single-handedly remind us of the power of sophisticated, sexy design. With the original iMac, launched in 1998, he created the first object of desire and affection, in effect feminising what had hitherto been a masculine product. Suddenly, computers were no longer defined in terms of process and speed, but also in terms of colour, form and tactility. If you own any household items in jelly-coloured plastic, for instance, or have bought into the fad of household goods made of heavy, transparent plastic, you own something influenced by him. But staying one step ahead of the competition isn't just a part of his design brief, it's part of the Apple DNA. The breathing 'On' button is not the sort of thing Microsoft does.

But it is Jonathan Ive through and through. Towards the end of the Nineties, he started to get serious acclaim, began to be heralded as this 'signifier', this beacon of applied creativity, a veritable guru of the age. He was voted the best this, the most influential that, the man most likely to ... do ... whatever it was we expected of him. As soon as consumers started to realise that design was now sexy, and that, with the application of technology, was about to project us into this brave new world (one decorated in all the trendy ergonomic nonsense you could possibly want), we all started wondering who was going to show us around. It didn't seem right to embrace the social commentators and media consultants we had trusted for the last couple of decades. Surely we should put our faith in the sort of people who actually got their hands dirty, who actually knew how all this worked, who actually had a hand in making this stuff? People ... someone ... like Jonathan Ive.

He wasn't just a PoMo geek either – he'd been awarded the highest British design honour with his appointment to the RSA's Faculty of Royal Designers for Industry. How could you beat that? There were only two hundred members, and Ive was right up there with architect Norman Foster, furniture designer Ron Arad and fashion designers Paul Smith and John Galliano. Not bad, eh? He was a rock'n'roll tech-head, if that wasn't a contradiction in terms. How cool!

Up until the beginning of 2001, Ive had fundamentally been playing around – successfully – with form. He hadn't been reinventing the wheel, he'd simply been making it smaller, trendier, and in a bunch of weird colours. He had yet to turn his hand to something that actually invented, or defined, a product genre. An impossibly brilliant man, not even he knew what was around the corner, not even he knew that the devotion he inspired in his disciples was going to get even more intense.

Not even Jonathan Ive knew he was going to have a hand in designing the first and maybe most important music carrier of the twenty-first century – and, in the process, change the music industry for ever.

February 2001: a freelance engineer called Tony Fadell is skiing in Vail. As he carefully prepares to attack another black run, his mobile rings. On the other end is Apple's hardware czar, Jon Rubinstein, who isn't calling about Fadell's welfare. Rubinstein has just been charged by Steve Jobs to create a groundbreaking music player and to get it to market by Christmas that year. A groundbreaking music player ... in ten months. Rubinstein had a list in front of him and Fadell listened intently. There are certain requirements: it has to look original, it has to have acute functionality (i.e., it has to work a hell of a lot better than all the other digital music players out there, the ones that aren't really working at all according to the feedback the technicians are getting), it has to have an extremely fast connection to your computer (via Apple's super-fine high-speed FireWire standard) so songs can be quickly uploaded, it has to have downloading capability, it has to dovetail with the company's recently introduced iTunes software, and, most importantly, it has to look, feel and act exactly like every other successful Apple product. It has to be hot and cool at the same time. Very hot and very, very cool.

It was, in short, a challenge, but then Fadell was on top of a mountain, and things looked pretty good. 'Why can't I build a digital music player?' he thought to himself as he stared across the sky, feeling quietly invincible. Everyone else was launching digital music players, so why weren't Apple? It was easy now, now that the industry was getting to grips with MP3s. We've known about them for ages – let's use 'em.

MP3s were invented by a group of German scientists in 1987 as a way of shrinking video files so they could be run on computers. By stripping away as much data as possible – all the stuff that theoretically listeners and viewers don't notice – they created manageable files which contained less information but which were perfectly acceptable to the human eye and ear, files that were usually one twelfth of the original file size (roughly, one minute of audio data equals 1MB of space at 128kbs – kilobits, the measurement of audio data storage space used by a piece of music per second of its downloading). As the technology actually compressed files, they were obviously not CD quality, in fact in some cases they were not even cassette quality, even though everyone said they were; the loss of quality was discernible when the files were amplified, but on headphones? No problem. On headphones MP3s were just fine, more than just fine in fact, they were fucking fantastic! I mean, have you heard this stuff! Hear, take a listen!

And after the code was approved by the International Standards Organisation, these files became known as ISO-MPEG Audio Layer-3s, or MP3s for short. And there they stayed, waiting to be exploited by Steve Jobs.

Fadell didn't make his decision there and then, but by the time he was at the foot of the mountain, even though he was feeling slightly less invincible, he could see the possibilities. He had been given carte blanche to draw on all of Apple's senior staff, including Jobs himself, so what was there to lose? That day Fadell skipped his après ski, called Rubinstein back and started thinking. Two months later, back in his glass bunker in Infinitive Loop, the Apple HQ in Cupertino, he was well on his way. Crucially, Apple Vice President Phil Schiller came up with the idea of a scroll wheel that accelerated as your finger spun it, making it easier for you to work your way through the menus and playlists and song titles. As for its memory, a few hard-drive players already existed, but most were large and bulky. To develop the iPod, Apple initially bought the entire inventory of a new generation of smaller drives from Toshiba, making the iPod the smallest and sleekest hard-drive player in the market. This also had the added bonus of preventing Apple's rivals from offering the smaller players for months afterwards. They were quick to reject flash memory chips, the most common technology used in music players, as they were only able to hold a few dozen songs. They may have been cheap, but weren't of interest to Jobs – he wanted a machine that could hold *thousands* of tunes.

Then Jonathan Ive came up with the case, a piece of kit that was smaller than anything else on the market. 'From early on we wanted a product that would seem so natural and so inevitable and so simple you almost wouldn't think of it as having been designed,' said Ive. And he insisted it be white,

Apple white: 'It's neutral, but it is a bold neutral, just shockingly neutral.'

The design, or rather, the shape, was incidental ... it just happened that way. 'It could have been shaped like a banana if we'd wanted,' says Ive.

Instead it looked like a cigarette pack for those addicted to music instead of tobacco. A cigarette pack in cocaine white.

It was made, crucially, from twin-shot plastic: from a processing point of view it became possible to do things with plastic that had never been done before. Twin shooting materials – moulding different plastics together or co-moulding plastic to metal – gave the engineers a range of functional and formal opportunities that didn't really exist before. The machine had no fasteners and no battery doors, making it possible to create something that was completely sealed.

According to Ive, the product had a natural birth. 'We are unique that we have an OS [operating system] as well as hardware,' he says. 'On top of this, the components were coming into alignment. We had jukebox software, and hard drives were getting smaller, so it was design and technology coming together in a perfect way. We made the iPod as simple as we possibly could, especially on the inside. It really annoys me when people say that simplicity is a style, because it's not, it's not a veneer. Simplification is one of the most difficult things to do. Also, for the iPod to be successful it has to be part of a large complicated system – it has to be hooked up to a computer of some sort, plus it needs all the software. The iPod just navigates and retrieves data.

'In a way, the interface became the icon of the product.'

Naturally, most of the initial drawings and designs for the iPod were produced on a Mac. How could it be any other way?

Jobs was being evangelical about this product, a product that was still in the earliest stages of design. He was running around telling everyone how good it was going to be, even though he knew little about it. When quizzed beyond his knowledge he would give a withering look and quote Darwin: 'It is not the strongest of the species that survive, nor the most intelligent, but the one most responsive to change.' Jobs wanted a machine that defined the market, a machine that was able to handle all the music you wanted to hear (just how much could you really squeeze onto a portable?), something that was simple to use (the competition's machines were ugly and confusing), and something that was quintessentially Apple. Which is what he got. Jobs has a tendency to send his pet projects back to the drawing board as they're nearing completion, a sign, perhaps, of his perfectionism or his inability to let go. 'It's happened on every Pixar movie,' Jobs confesses. But when Jobs finally saw the prototype several months later, he said, 'It's as Apple as anything Apple has ever done.'

And it wasn't just a portable jukebox for all your music (Jesus, have you seen this, it can Hoover up all your CDs, it's like listening to your own greatest hits! I just fed my entire music collection into this thing and I can't believe it ate the whole thing! It's like *Little Shop Of Horrors*! You just gotta get one!), it did loads of other neat stuff too: it could be used as a clock, a diary for synchronising appointments, for digital voice recording ('Hello Cleveland!'), for downloading data and for photo storage. The iPod was a true breakthrough product. Other MP3-playback devices took for ever to load with music since they used relatively slow USB (Universal Serial Bus) for data transfer, had limited capacity since they used solid state memory, and were clunky and ungainly since they weren't crafted by Ive's Industrial Design Group (Ive may like to say otherwise but his job has always been to curve edges and miniaturise). They were ugly, ugly, ugly! The 6.5-ounce machine's huge 5 GB hard drive could be filled with approximately one thousand near-CD quality songs in ten minutes through its fast FireWire port, and seamless integration with iTunes 2.0 made synchronising music libraries a snap. Backed by a ten-hour battery life, the iPod was essentially an all-day record shop you could fold neatly into your pocket. It had an equaliser to adjust the volume of anything you downloaded. You could have all the instructions in Spanish, French or Italian. It had twenty minutes of skip protection. Hell, you could even listen to it on your stereo – all you had to do was buy a headphone plug to composite audio cable (the white and yellow and red pronged cord you use to connect your TV and DVD together) and just sit back and wallow. How fucking cool was that! It was just so damned neat. Even the scroll wheel guy Philip Schiller said so: 'iPod is going to change the way people listen to music.'

As for its name, this new beast had been christened before it was born – the i was for Internet, plus 'Portable open database' – the i and the Pod fused together, in keeping with the fashion for jamming names together with an UPPER CASE letter sticking up in the middle ('as if creating some hyperhard alloy for the twenty-first century,' said Tom Wolfe).

And then they launched it, on 10 November, a month after 9/11. Not only was it birthed into a country already deep in mourning, but the bottom had fallen out of the tech market (hell, for months the bottom fell out of all markets). The iPod was criticised for being expensive – $399 – and for the fact that it was only compatible with Macintosh, a computer owned by less than a twentieth of consumers. And it didn't hold that many songs (wasn't one thousand enough guys?), or have a compatible online music store to download from. Apart from that it was perfect.

'We applied a design philosophy to a product we didn't have, to a product we wanted desperately,' says Jonathan Ive. 'You have to remember – and this is very important – that there's a lot of us at Apple who like music, who actually like music a lot – it's as simple as that. Although we had a brief to make a music player, at Apple things are not always as premeditated as they appear. Another thing you have to remember is that our goal is not to make money, our goal is to make the very best consumer products so that we can then make a lot of money. That might sound naive, but that's why I go to work every day.'

The advertising of the product was crucial, and needed to set the machine apart from everything else in the market. Apple's brief to New York-based ad agency Chiat Day was simple: empower the individual. Unlike every other aspect of the computer world, the iPod had little to do with togetherness, had little to do with community spirit. The iPod was all about individuality and personal space, and its marketing would soon reflect that. Chiat Day's most successful ads for the machine revolved around 'iPodWorld', a place that you and only you could visit: bright, pop-coloured backgrounds, and in the foreground individuals seen only in silhouette (so as not to alienate the consumer – you, them, us!). And curling through the posters were those little tell-tale white headphones, the tiny signifiers of a secret society, that only we, and we alone, knew about. Where were we? We were in our own little worlds, listening to our own private soundtracks in our own particular way. To reinforce the idea that Apple were selling an idea rather than a product, the ads appeared on fly-posters, bus-sites and billboards, as though they were advertising a band. Clever, that.

Design aficionados and Apple geeks loved the iPod, and as soon as Apple got their act together and began upgrading it – which they did almost immediately – interest began to grow and grow. Apple then produced a version that was able to run on Windows, successfully launched an online version of iTunes, and in under a year had secured a whopping 70 per cent market share. Jobs had done it. This wasn't just another ruby in the crown, this was the crown itself. Quarterly sales soon reached 250,000 units, and then just eighteen months later ballooned to over 800,000, making the iPod the most successful digital music player in the world. In under three years. Soon people were calling it the Walkman of the twenty-first century, the

Walkman of the digital generation, the Walkman that Sony forgot, and critical mass began to spread.

According to U2's manager Paul McGuinness, 'The iPod is to music what penicillin was to medicine.'

Ask Jobs, and he will tell you we're about to enter the third phase of personal computing. The first era was all about utility – people using their thinking machines to do word processing, run spreadsheets, create desktop graphics and the like. The second phase was about wiring all those machines together on the Internet and getting them to talk to each other. The third phase involves those same people using computers to orchestrate all the new digital gear that has steadily crept into their lives.

'We are surrounded by camcorders, digital cameras, MP3 players, Palms, cell phones, DVD players,' says Jobs. 'Some of these things are plenty useful without a personal computer. But a personal computer definitely enhances their value. And several are completely unusable without a PC – a PC meaning a Mac, in our case. We believe the next great era is for the personal computer to be the hub of all these devices.'

This is all about 'owning the whole widget', and it is the vertical integration between iTunes (the software) and the iPod (the hardware) that has been the key to Apple's success. Because it owns 'the widget' (all of it), Apple can control the user experience from beginning to end.

'There are lots of examples where not the best product wins,' says Jobs. 'Windows would be one of those, but there are examples where the best product wins. And the iPod is a great example of that.'

6 ¡Bondage, Up Yours! It's Time for Punk!

The Sex Pistols make a man of me

It's 1977, I'm seventeen, and I'm not allowed to like Isaac Hayes. I'm on the top floor of a huge squat in Camberwell, just about the least salubrious postcode in all of south London, and there's a party going on downstairs. It's 4 a.m. on a Sunday morning, and there are still about a hundred people in the basement, dancing away to the first two Ramones albums as though their lives depended on it.

Up here there are about a dozen punks, all lying on the floor, all smoking this amazingly strong grass and nodding sullenly at the ceiling. There's a small record player in the corner, which has just finished playing Patti Smith's *Horses*. And as no one appears to be the least bit bothered about replacing it, I root around in the stack of LPs lying against the wall, dig out Isaac Hayes's *Live At The Sahara Tahoe* and put it on.

It lasts for approximately eight seconds before a medium-sized, ox-blood Doc Marten boot kicks it off.

'Take that shit off and put on the Stranglers!' says a short, sharp girl with bloodshot eyes and peroxide feather-cut. 'Disco sucks. Soul music is for fucking robots!'

Which is just about where we are in 1977.

Punk was as much of an apocalyptic catalyst for me as it was for many of my generation, and it shook me around, threw me up in the air, and – when I bounced back down again – forced me to confront my preconceptions about life, the universe and everything in it. Well, at least the records I bought and the clothes I wore.

I had been in love with punk for exactly eighteen months, when I first heard the Ramones' 'Beat On The Brat' at a house party in High Wycombe (one of those Home Counties towns that wishes it were a little bit closer to London). The next day I decided to turn myself into Johnny Ramone, and for the last year and a half have been walking around with a floppy, pudding-bowl haircut, drainpipe jeans, plimsoles, a matelot top and a (plastic) leather jacket. Overnight I turned from a neurotic boy outsider in an oversized overcoat and a hooded brow (clutching my Bob Dylan, Robert Wyatt and Dean Martin albums under my arm), into the personification of a Bowery punk. Tell me this: how could you not fall in love with a group who displayed such a blatant disregard for sophistication as the Ramones? Whose bare-boned playing was matched only by their idiotic singing (the lyrics to their song 'I Don't Wanna Walk Around With You' are four lines long, three of which are the same)? When Joe Strummer, the lead singer of the Clash, approached the Ramones after seeing them play live in London in 1976, he was worried that his band's musicianship was still too rough for them to start recording. 'Are you kidding?' Johnny said. 'We're lousy, we can't play. If you wait until you can play, you'll be too old to get up there. We stink, really. But it's great.'

But I am already living as though iTunes had already been invented. I believe that Frank Sinatra is just as important as the Sex Pistols, although no one agrees with me. In 1977 you either like the Clash and the Sex Pistols or you're the enemy. But can't you like everything? I do.

It's September and I've been in London for exactly six weeks, having left High Wycombe for Chelsea School of Art and the Ralph West Halls of Residence just south of the King's Road, opposite Battersea Park. It is home to two hundred students, all of them studying some sort of arts degree at one of the big London art schools, and most of them in London for the first time. My room in Ralph West is another sanctuary, a place I can pretend is anywhere in the world. I am seventeen, and music is the most important thing in my life: more important than work, sex, family, everything. The Clash's next single (we've read in the *NME* it's 'Clash City Rockers'!) is what's keeping me going. I know I've got some sort of practical exam next week but to be honest I'm more interested in the Throbbing Gristle gig I'm going to on Sunday (in the end it was scary: they used dry ice and I thought they were gassing us). Last night we went to the Roxy for the first time, and although it wasn't very memorable (there was a no-mark punk band on who made the Dickies look like Sham 69), it was about as exciting as a gig can be. My life is defined by punk rock: I'm meant to be stretching some canvasses tomorrow morning but I'm actually cadging a lift and going to buy some tickets for the festival at the 100 Club (the Jam, Adam & the Ants, etc.).

My sanctuary is all-denominational, and having spent an evening with Iggy Pop, the Ramones or the Talking Heads (I remember one night in Linda Shearsby's room we played their '77 album six times in a row), I'd slink back to my room and play Joni Mitchell, Steely Dan or Van Morrison. I didn't feel embarrassed, didn't feel as though I were letting the side down; for me it was perfectly natural. My room may have been covered with Sex Pistols posters, but my heart was elsewhere, in California, the deserts of Arizona, the West Coast of Ireland ... Notting Hill in the late 1950s. On the perimeter of sleep I would lie there and imagine myself living the lives in those songs, believing my own life to be full of the same possibilities.

What no one ever renembers – or admits – about punk was the fact that we all liked other stuff too, and while it may have been convenient and cute and cool to pretend otherwise – 'Hi, my name's Dylan and I am from the planet Year Zero and the first record I ever bought was "Anarchy In The UK"' – none of us arrived in London fully formed. We all had baggage, all had a cupboard full of rattling, decaying skeletons. And my skeletons were holding about two dozen Frank Sinatra albums. Punk may have been the manifestation of disenfranchised youthful defiance, lathering up our seditious tendencies, but it was also a simple expression of adolescence: we liked it because we were young. Walking down the King's Road on my way to Chelsea every morning, my head wasn't full of anarchy, it was full of hope. I wanted music to remind me of prosperity, not oppression, which is probably why I've never liked the blues.

The thing I remember most about punk was the violence, the fights: being barricaded by skinheads in the back of a church hall in Beaconsfield after a concert by a band called Deathwish; pint glasses being thrown at the Nashville; fist fights in the doorway of the Marquee (the Jam again – weren't we always going to see the Jam?).

And there is one evening I remember more than most. I was in the upstairs toilets of the Rainbow, Finsbury Park, some time in late 1977, as the Ramones thundered furiously through their blitzkrieg bop downstairs. And up here, in the relatively tranquil surroundings of the Gents, Sid Vicious was exchanging punches and the occasional kick with one of the Slits (Viv, Ari, Tessa? Who knew? Not me) whilst I, with a relative nonchalance which was becoming dramatically less nonchalant with every well-aimed punch, was trying to get rid of four pints of hastily-consumed, lukewarm, over-priced lager.

They had tumbled in just as I was unzipping myself and, after a few choice exchanges in vintage Anglo-Saxon (which is what the pop fraternity used before discovering Estuarial English), had set about each other with a ferocity reserved only for the very passionate or the very drunk. I couldn't tell which, and had no intention of finding out.

Oh my God, I thought, there he is, in all his feisty glory – the trademark bog-brush hairdo, the sneer, the lovingly distressed biker's jacket, the drainpipe jeans, the intricately torn Vivienne Westwood T-shirt, the bloody big boots ... and sooner or later, I thought, he is going to notice me.

When you're young the famous are different. As you get older you quickly realise that they're unnervingly like normal people, with all the same banal fears and anxieties (only with rather more engorged egos and expectations), but in one's youth the famous have the capacity to become unwieldy icons. Vicious was one such star. Punks might have publicly eschewed the trappings of celebrity, but they were still stars to us (they were still stars to themselves, if truth be known), particularly if they happened to be a Sex Pistol. *Especially* if they were a Sex Pistol.

I'd had brushes with fame before: Adam Ant once spilled my pint as he pushed past me on his way to join the Ants on stage at the 100 Club; a year earlier I'd helped roadie for Generation X at the Nag's Head in High Wycombe; and the man who played drums on Johnny Wakelin's 'In Zaire' (no, I don't remember it either) apparently lived three streets away from my mother.

But this was different. This was Sid Vicious, a genuine angry – and none too bright – young man. Of course I'd heard that he was a bit of a jerk (now and then he had the misfortune to come across as The Fonz's stupider cousin, usually when he opened his mouth), but he was still the bass player – and I use the term advisedly – with the most notorious bunch of ne'er-do-wells in the Western world. And he was standing four feet away from me.

The fight continued apace. It never occurred to me to try and interfere; in my eyes this would have been tantamount to suicide, and this particular Slit looked like she could punch and kick her way out of any altercation, even with a Sex Pistol. She certainly looked like she could knock the living daylights out of me.

Suddenly it was all over, and Sid's eyes turned in my direction. Oh my God! Surely he would suss me now, I thought (I was doing a lot of thinking that night). Surely he would see that I was nothing but a poseur, an art school plastic punk who'd only recently thrown away his Tonto's Expanding Head Band albums (which I would have to buy again – at great expense – years later), and his flares (which I wouldn't).[1]

My fear was palpable. Would he see me for what I was, pick me up by the lapels of my black leather (OK, OK, *plastic*) jacket, spit in my eye and throw me against the wall, snorting in disgust whilst condemning me for once owning a Jackson Browne LP? Would I have an extraordinary tale to tell the next day at college, or become a news item in the tabloids. ('Foul-mouthed punk rocker Sid razors Chelsea art student in nightclub toilet!')? No. I wasn't famous, you see, just another paranoid spotty seventeen-year-old with a silly haircut, blank expression, and inflated sense of his own importance. He didn't know me from Adam Ant. Having extricated himself from his opponent's clutches, the great Sid Vicious simply marched past me, and went on his merry (read: tired and emotional) way, to see the Ramones finish their set. He didn't even look at me, let alone pass judgement.

Disappointed? You bet I was.

The Pistols very quickly turned into caricatures, and they make a poor showing on my ATF (All Time Favourites) punk playlist. This is probably the most proscriptive playlist I've got, and contains everything from early Velvet Underground right up to the Hives. Opinions differ about the provenance of punk, although the counterblast really began on 16 August 1974, in front of a tiny crowd in a seedy New York bar called CBGB, when four monosyllabic nerds from suburban New York walked on stage – Johnny, Joey, Dee Dee and Tommy Ramone. As they

---

[1] Two pairs of flares I remember vividly: the first was a pair of baggy, high-waisted green pinstripe trousers with three buttons above the fly and a patch pocket on the left thigh (I obviously thought that I looked pretty cool at the time – like Bryan Ferry perhaps, or Adam Faith during his *Budgie* period – but in hindsight I must have seemed like a circus clown who'd been forced into alternative employment – accountancy, perhaps). The second was a pair of patchwork denim pants, which I foolishly thought made me look as though I'd just stepped off a plane from LA, having spent the last three years hanging out with the Eagles. Ha, what did I know?

spent as much time shouting at each other as playing, the concert was shambolic, but they improved rapidly, and it soon became clear they had hit on something.

Punk, basically.

Before this there was the Velvet Underground (1966), the Stooges (1968), the MC5 (1969), Jonathan Richman (the first Modern Lovers album was recorded in 1973 even though it wasn't released until four years later), Richard Hell ('Blank Generation' was written in 1974), and then Patti Smith, with *Horses* (1975). The Ramones' first album was released in 1976, swiftly followed by the Damned's 'New Rose' (November 1976), the Sex Pistols ('Anarchy In The UK', November 1976), the Buzzcocks, ('Spiral Scratch', January 1977) and the Clash ('White Riot', March 1977). The lineage then goes all the way through the Jam, ATV, the Stranglers, Television and the rest, right up to the release of the belated Siouxsie & The Banshees single 'Hong Kong Garden' (which to these ears always sounded like an adrenalised advertisement for a particularly enterprising Chinese takeaway) in August 1978. Punk then begat new wave which begat power pop which begat mod (pathetic!), 2-Tone (genius!), electropop and the cult with no name (which is what Spandau Ballet and Culture Club were called before they became new romantics). By the end of the decade, punk had fizzled out, leaving in its wake a new generation of acts whose thirst for success far outweighed any absent-minded idealism (it was fitting that the first British No. 1 of the 1980s was 'Brass In Pocket' by the Pretenders).

Anyway, my punk playlist has 216 songs on it, by no means complete but including the Clash, the Buzzcocks, Generation X, Thomas Leer, Ian Dury, Spherical Objects, the Slits, everything from the Undertones to the Gang of Four and from X-Ray Spex to 999 (I know they were crap but 'Emergency' is still one of my favourite records). The big problem with punk is that not all of it sounds that wonderful anymore. Extraordinarily exciting and almost visceral at the time (the opening chords of the Clash's 'Complete Control' are probably the most electrifying moments ever committed to vinyl, a call to arms that has only increased in stature over the years), much of it sounds compartmentalised, almost as though it exists only in a time capsule. Out of context stuff like ATV, Chelsea, the Damned and the Saints – even a lot of the Jam, come to that – sounds tinny and dated. And when you've got people like the Hives and the Libertines and the Strokes and Franz Ferdinand making punk with twenty-first century production techniques as well as a twenty-first century sensibility (tempered, knowing, smart), they make a lot of late-1970s punk sound old-fashioned and ill-considered. Music we hear when we're a teenager tends to define us for life, and although we might think that the stuff made when we were that age surpasses anything that came after it (or before it), these days people think exactly the same, claiming 'old' pop – i.e., the stuff made in the 1960s and 1970s sounds 'unfinished'. (To my ears Queens of the Stone Age don't sound better than Led Zeppelin, but to a lot of people they do, and why not?)

I loved punk when I was sixteen, and at the time probably felt more passionately about it than I have ever felt about anything in my life. I dressed like a punk, bought punk records – hundreds of the damn things – and went to dozens and dozens of gigs: the Damned and the Jam at the 100 Club, Elvis Costello & the Attractions at the Nag's Head in High Wycombe, the Stranglers at the Rainbow, the Clash at the Rock Against Racism concert in London's Victoria Park, the Ramones at Aylesbury Friars, the Buzzcocks at the Hammersmith Odeon, Chelsea, Generation X, X-Ray Spex, Public Image, the lot – but I can't listen to a lot of it these days, as it grates too much. It reminds me of tower blocks, being beaten up on the nightbus, walking six miles home, having beer for breakfast, and chips for tea. A lot of punk reminds me of being poor, being a student, being an outcast. Punk produced some of the best music in the world, music that, from mid-1976 to early 1979 reinvented itself every five minutes, and yet ... and yet, the sky is black, the speed is cut, all the girls have peroxide hair, and everyone disguises their accent.

Having moved to London I quickly became obsessed with it, became obsessed with finding out where everything was, how everything linked together (how did you get from Sloane Square to the Holloway Road?), where everyone lived (John Lydon lived in Chelsea, I'd read that, but where exactly?) ... I wanted to know everything about everywhere. Why was East Ham miles away from West Hampstead? Why wasn't Stamford Hill really a hill? Where exactly was Abbey Road? (I was one of those thousands of Bowie-freaks who needed to know where the cover of *Ziggy Stardust* was shot, and, after living in London for a few months, discovered it was done in Heddon Street, just off Regent Street.) Where were all those places that Ian Dury talked about? How could you really get to grips with punk unless you knew all the references, unless you knew what Billericay Dickie was all about?

London has been eulogized in books, in plays, films and poems, and not least in song. But the city has no real anthem, nothing to compare with Frank Sinatra's 'New York New York', few things as evocative as 'Paris In The Spring' or Dean Martin's 'Napoli'. Songs about London are not usually moments of epiphany; they tend to be colloquial, sentimental, cosy – sort of British.

During the late nineteenth century, music hall gave rise to many London songs such as 'Burlington Bertie From Bow' and 'If It Wasn't For The 'Ouses In Between'; in fact, most eulogies to London have a music hall quality about them, from 'Maybe It's Because I'm A Londoner' right through to 'Up The Junction' (Squeeze). There have been others, songs like 'A Nightingale Sang In Berkeley Square' (from the 1920s), Noël Coward's 'London Pride' (popular during the Blitz), 'Chim Chim, Cheree' and 'Portobello Road' (both from Disney films), and of course the appalling 'Streets Of London' by Ralph McTell. But by and large it has been left to pop music to supply the soundtrack to the city.

During the late 1950s London was a magnet for burgeoning pop stars, and Soho coffee bars like the 2Is, the House Of Sam Widges, the Heaven & Hell and Le Macabre became the focus of British pop culture. But few decent London songs emerged from the era. By the early 1960s the success of the Beatles and Merseybeat had shifted attention from London so much that groups from the South would pretend to be Liverpudlian in order to attract record company attention.

The Kinks changed all that.

More so than the Beatles, the Stones or the Who, the Kinks have an enduring association with the capital. Ray Davies, the group's songwriter, spent his formative years in Muswell Hill, and many of the band's songs were set in the city; among them 'Dedicated Follower Of Fashion' (which I think should still be played in every 'quirky' little Japanese jeans shop in Soho or NoLiTa), 'Berkeley Mews', 'Willesden Green', the 1971 LP *Muswell Hillbillies* (the cover of which shows the band drinking in the Archway Tavern, Holloway), 'See My Friends', and of course the classic 'Waterloo Sunset' – some would say the quintessential London record, and a song to rival 'Lullaby Of Birdland' or 'Under The Bridges Of Paris' for evocative mood and power. Davies wrote the song in memory of the time he spent in St Thomas's Hospital opposite the Houses of Parliament as a youth. 'Two nurses wheeled me out on to the balcony, where I could see the Thames. It was just a very poetic moment for me. Ever since it's [been] my centre.'

And then there was 'Swinging London', those few brief years in the mid-1960s when London was the most fashionable place in the world; all of a sudden the capital had attitude. And there were songs, too: 'Itchycoo Park' by the Small Faces, 'Play With Fire' by the Rolling Stones, 'The London Boys' by David Bowie. Inevitably there was also some extraordinary bandwagon-jumping, this time by the likes of Roger Miller ('England

Swings') and the New Vaudeville Band ('Finchley Central').

London next became a focus for pop during punk. The cult was born in London and the city became a metaphor for the whole movement: urban decay, anarchic fashion, backstreet violence, fast drugs, silly hair. The town became vaguely mythical, a honeypot for the future punk royalty: the Jam's Paul Weller was so obsessed with the city he would travel from Woking up to the West End just to record the traffic (one of the band's earliest songs was called 'Sounds From The Street', and their first two albums are so poorly produced they don't sound much better than Oxford Circus in the rush hour). The group's urban fixation showed in 'Down in The Tube Station At Midnight', 'In The City', 'A Bomb In Wardour Street' and bassist Bruce Foxton's dreadful 'London Traffic' (': . . going nowhere' – nice one, Bruce!) – all of them little snapshots of tough city life. Pop has always needed the city's shroud to make it cool – how could you be a market town punk or an East Anglian mod? One of punk's defining rationales was reinvention; when we arrived in London none of us wanted to admit we had actually been brought up in Henley or Swindon. And Woking? Puh-lease . . .

The Clash also made a point of writing about London, often writing about little else, although they tended to concentrate on Notting Hill and all points west. Pop archaeologist Jon Savage once called *the Clash* 'virtually a concept album about North Kensington and Ladbroke Grove', containing 'White Riot', 'London's Burning', '48 Hours' and all the rest. While they soon cast their concerned eyes over the Middle East, South America and any imploding quasi-Stalinist state they could find, for a while London was their world, inspiring their two finest songs: 'White Man (in Hammersmith Palais)' and, of course, 'London Calling' (about which Joe Strummer said, 'I want it to sound like it's coming through fog over the Thames').

Punk's Gilbert & Sullivans couldn't leave the place alone, and every one of them – Ian Dury, Elvis Costello, Jimmy Pursey, whoever wrote the songs in Chelsea, Bethnal, London and 999 – felt they had to say *something* about the damn place.

Then came Madness. Most good pop has an air of melancholy about it, and Madness's paeans to north London are no exception. 'Our House', 'Grey Day' and 'Cardiac Arrest', in fact most of their songs, evoke the pathos and bathos of small lives in the big city. Their songs are both euphoric and maudlin, odd little tales of woe spilling out of Camden Town, the back-streets of Somerstown and the fields of Hampstead Heath. Madness were the consummate colloquial pop group, and their London is full of grey skies and Routemaster buses, small-time crooks and barstool philosophers. Sharp-witted, eccentric and often staggeringly blunt, their songs are much like Londoners themselves.

The West End became trendy again in the mid-1980s, when the rejuvenation and gentrification of Soho coincided with style culture's obsession with the pop mythology of the 1950s and 1960s. This culminated in *Absolute Beginners*, Julien Temple's fairly awful attempt at recreating the Soho of hipsters, beatniks and cappuccino kids. Elsewhere this relentless pursuit of a mythical postcode manifested itself in coffee bars, style magazines, nightclubs ... and hardly any good songs about London. The one group to wring anything out of this period were a long-forgotten band called Boys Wonder, who wrote the occasional great London song but who never had a hit – in itself the perfect metaphor for the time. The only truly great London song from the 1980s remains the Pet Shop Boys' 'West End Girls'. (Ironically, the best song to celebrate the town as the after-dark glamour capital of the world is Roxy Music's 'Street Life', made in 1973, when London wasn't especially cool at all.)

Faux cockney has been the hip lingua franca of British pop for half a century, exploited by stars like David Bowie, Cockney Rebel's Steve Harley and Suede's Brett Anderson (not to mention Dame Mick Jagger, whose implausibly theatrical cock-er-ney drawl remains one of the greatest inventions of the late twentieth century). But during the Britpop years (roughly 1994–6) mockney's finest exponent was Blur's Damon Albarn, whose occupational slumming involved professing a penchant for greyhound racing and fairgrounds. And while most people's fondest memories of the period are probably bound up in Oasis's 'Wonderwall', Albarn's 'Parklife' – the ultimate tongue-in-cheek celebration of London lad-culture – is the defining record of the time.

Today's estuarial emperor is the Streets' Mike Skinner, the street poet laureate who is justly celebrated from Elephant & Castle to Seattle, although the world that Skinner celebrates – a chavster's world full of blow, booze, Sky TV, mobiles and fast food – is one found in every city in Britain, not just London.

Perhaps the reason there are so few songs written about the metropolis anymore is because (a) there is no single homogenous image of the city and (b) all the old images are redundant clichés. London today is just another urban sprawl, a Dickensian theme park without its own culture, a city full of fragmented communities and half a dozen Starbucks, much like any other Western city. For years the only music coming out of the city which has had a sense of locality is rap, but dance music is now so global it seems old-fashioned to sing about old London Town.

So I guess, unless you're happy to include Ralph McTell on your playlist, that anthem is 'London Calling'.

7 Steve Jobs Approximately

It's Steve Jobs, not me, who's in love with
Bob Dylan

The land of Apple lies fifty miles south of San Francisco, in Cupertino, at the southern end of the bay, smack bang in the middle of Silicon Valley. The company arrived here in the late 1970s and has remained in the same lush location through all its ups and downs, through all its trials, tribulations and changes of CEO. It's now spread over dozens of buildings off De Anza Boulevard, not far from where Steve Jobs went to school. The town is home to sixty high-tech companies, including Hewlett-Packard, IBM and Sun Microsystems.

The entrance to the Apple HQ bears a simple nameplate – 'Infinite Loop', along with a colossal Apple logo, a logo – *the* logo, now one of the most recognised in the world – that is echoed throughout the complex, appearing on everything from door handles to notepaper. Its design, which will always be indebted to the Beatles, no matter what, is now nearly as identifiable as those belonging to Coca-Cola, McDonald's and Nike, the holy trinity of internationally recognisable symbols, part of the everyday landscape of popular consumerism, and one of the few brands that can be identified solely by its logo. Jean-Louis Gassee, who founded Apple France before moving to Cupertino as chief technical wizard, thinks the logo is one of the defining symbols of its age: 'You have the apple – the symbol of knowledge. It is bitten – the symbol of desire. You have the rainbow – but the colours are in the wrong order.

Knowledge, lust, hope, and anarchy: any company with all that cannot help being mythic.'

Infinite Loop is a seriously impressive corporate centre, a sprawling, multi-acre site with beautifully manicured lawns featuring enormous pixilated sculptures, a gym, and one of the most amazing cafeterias in California: chef-prepared salads, a sushi bar, made-to-order wood-fired pizzas, a pasta counter, salad desk, burrito counter, smoothies, the lot. Smoking is not allowed anywhere on Apple property, not even away from the buildings.

Years ago, in the early 1980s, when the computer industry was really still in its infancy, there was no reason to be ostentatious – in fact it was detrimental. If you wanted to convince customers and investors that you were a lean, thrifty outfit, you had to appear that way. But not any more. Nowadays, unless you have a vaulted ceiling, a glass atrium or an I.M. Pei conservatory, then you're really nothing. (In a eulogy to his former company, and with the deftness of a corporate publicist, ex-Apple CEO John Sculley said, 'Everything at Apple is as much about perception as reality.') With its green-glass windows and curved metal atrium, Infinite Loop feels like any other Eighties-inspired post-modern office block that has dared itself to be different, and its strict geometries of stone and glass feel as conventional as a Doric column. It is certainly not Silicon Valley's finest architectural achievement, and looks as though it should house an advertising agency that specialises in corporate affairs. But it is grand. And the difference here is security. There is a lot of it.

Apple's research and development facilities are some of the most secure buildings on the Apple campus. Here, shredding machines are considered old hat, and confidential papers (which these days are usually printed e-mails) are discarded into locked waste-paper baskets that are emptied at least twice a day. There are guards on every corner, while the electronic ID badges worn by the staff are used to monitor personnel movement as well as to simply allow entry to restricted areas.

This is less to do with corporate paranoia and more to do with the fact that industrial espionage in the technology industry is as rife today as it used to be in the secret services. Because of this, and because Apple is the sort of company that enjoys stuff like this, new products and processes tend to be known internally by code words. These are usually coined by the engineers and designers responsible for producing them, although there are certain trends that are popular. First came girls' names (rather unimaginatively named after girlfriends, wives, offspring, etc.), then fruit (as well as the Macintosh variety of apple, Pippin and Jonathan were also popular), and more recently the sort of ironic retro-perceptive names that litter the Pixar movies (the original five coloured iMacs were known both internally and externally as Life Savers). Others include Smeagol (Mac OS X 10.2.7), Jackson Pollack (QuickDraw), Gelato (the Newton MessagePad came in two flavours, 1 MB or 2 MB), Onyx (PowerBook G4), etc. As far as anyone can remember, the iPod was always just known as that.

Engineering miracles are an everyday occurrence here.

Jonathan Ive works in a huge open studio containing a number of communal design areas. A certain amount of transparency is required here, as it is at other high-tech companies (Nike springs to mind, up in Portland, Oregon). The rationale effectively means that if your rank allows you to walk through glass, then you should be allowed to see everything on the other side. Here, everyone can see what everyone else is doing. 'We have little exclusively personal space,' says Ive. 'In fact, the memory of how we work will endure beyond the products of our work.' The physical environment reflects and enables the collaborative process. 'We have assembled a heavenly design team,' Ive continues. 'By keeping the core team small and investing significantly in tools and process we can work with a level of collaboration that seems particularly rare.'

Apple's design guru is obsessed with music – liking everything from ironic nu-metal to computer-generated chill-out –

and he's proud that the design workshop possesses by far the loudest sound system on the Apple campus, a sound system fed by his iPod. 'If I hadn't made it,' he says, 'I would have bought one as soon as I'd understood what it was.'

The designers in the workshop are an eclectic bunch, and come from all over: the UK, Japan, Australia, New Zealand, and – of course – California. Most of them have been together for over a decade, and Ive still calls them his closest friends. He likes to say that what they share is the ability to look at old objects anew, even if it's something they use every day, or even something that they've designed themselves.

This is where Jonathan Ive sends his e-mails to Sir Paul Smith in London. The fashion designer is one of the first people Ive sought out when he moved to California in the early Nineties, even though Paul lives in Holland Park, in London.

'He was visiting London and just rang up and asked to see me,' said Smith, in his Covent Garden HQ. 'I think he thought I was one of the few people who could understand what he was trying to do at Apple. And I was. When we eventually met we just devoured each other. We've met dozens of times since, and whenever we have supper we'll talk about the joys of aluminium or the fibre of a particular sort of plastic. I remember once we were in this restaurant in Tokyo with some of his team and we spent the evening discussing the relationship between the paving stones outside and the wooden door frame of the entrance.'

Smith is Ive's designer soul mate, and having happened upon someone who shared the same design values, who had the same passions and excitements, Ive sent him one of the first iPod prototypes.

'One morning this ... box arrived, and in it was this pod-type thing. I didn't know what it was, I thought it was some sort of new mini-disc or something, and to be honest with you it stayed in its box for nearly a week until I could get round to working out exactly what it was and what it did.'

But when he did finally get it working, Smith was hooked, and over the space of a few weeks got various members of his staff to upload his vast CD collection onto it (everything from Van Morrison, U2 and Bjork to – nowadays – the White Stripes, Franz Ferdinand and Coldplay). He was the proverbial early adopter. Since then Smith has received dozens of food parcels from Ive, and just an hour before I spoke with him had taken receipt of a brand new 20" G5 iMac, one of the first in the UK. It came with a handwritten note from Ive himself, signed 'Jony'.

'I think Jonathan and his team are just the best designers there are, and talking to them about design is like talking to Paul Weller about fabric – they totally know what they're talking about. They all have this incredibly boyish enthusiasm. And as for the iPod, it's just the most amazing piece of kit there is. It just feels so good in your hand, it's so ergonomic. I love the wheel, as it's basically a circular mouse. How clever is that! He sits all day in his office inventing stuff like this ...'

Formal gatherings at Infinite Loop, or at least the important ones, are always held in the boardroom, which is in the only high-rise building on Apple's low-slung campus. The long wooden table can seat up to three dozen people, and allows a panoramic view of the expanse of Silicon Valley. This is where Jobs held court when he returned to Apple in the mid-Nineties, asking his designers to bring their 'projects', to see what they were working on.

Jobs' office on the fourth floor is a room with a less than spectacular view of the Valley than you might expect: you see the shrubby treetops extending out towards San Francisco Bay, and the distant rush of the traffic on the freeway below. This is where Jobs comes when he isn't taking his corporate helicopter/baronial perk over to Pixar, across the Bay Bridge up the coast in Emeryville, or using his Gulfstream V jet (given to him by Apple when he accepted the role of CEO) to fly off to New York, LA or Europe. This is where he sits when he's pontificating on the reconfiguration of content delivery systems. When he is in this mood, Jobs is not just an evangelist for his company and his products, he is an evangelist for the whole notion of digital revolution. In the flesh Jobs is the same as he ever was: jeans, New Balance trainers, and the trademark black polo-neck jumper. If he were a Simpsons character he would be a trendy New Age priest, espousing the delights of digital technology as though it were a new religion.

This is also where Jobs is rumoured to tinker with a prototype 110 GB iPod, enough surely, to hold all of his beloved Bob Dylan collection. Jobs has been listening to Bob Dylan since he hit puberty. Jobs is a Dylan freak. In his teens he obsessed over Dylan's lyrics, and he spent hours and hours deciphering them. He'd get LSD fresh from his pals over in Stanford, take a fistful, and then spend the night on the beach with his girlfriend. 'California has a sense of experimentation and a sense of openness,' said Jobs – 'openness to new possibilities.' And in the early days of Apple, Jobs would play Dylan tunes on his guitar in his backyard while his mother, Clara, washed his baby nephew in the kitchen sink. He played the same songs when he took breaks from constructing the first Apple in the family garage, and would spend hours listening to bootleg Dylan recordings on his reel-to-reel tape player in his room (it was once noted by some wag that, such was fans' fascination with the singer, bootleg obsessives would be willing to buy a recording of Bob Dylan breathing heavily – which to some people is what he does anyway). And once – wearing, incidentally, a double-breasted jacket and a bright red bow-tie – Jobs quoted the entire second verse of 'The Times They Are A-Changin'' at a 1984 shareholders' meeting ('I'd like to begin by reading part of an old poem by Dylan, that's Bob Dylan ...'). In later life Jobs actually dated Joan Baez, and it's been suggested by some that the only reason he did so is because she was famously Dylan's lover.

'Steve Wozniak turned me on to him,' said Jobs. 'I was

probably ... oh ... maybe thirteen, fourteen. We ended up meeting this guy who had every bootleg tape in the world. He was a guy that actually put out a newsletter on Dylan. He was really into it – his whole life was about Dylan. But he had the best bootlegs, even better stuff than you can get today that's been released. He had amazing stuff. And we had our room full of tapes of Bob Dylan that we copied.

'He was a very clear thinker and he was a poet. I think he wrote about what he saw and thought. The early stuff is very precise. But, as he matured, you had to unravel it a little bit. But once you did, it was just as clear as a bell. I was listening the other day to "Only A Pawn In Their Game" and that stuff's as good today as when he penned it.'

One of Apple's first employees, Daniel Kottke, said, 'That's how I became friends with Steve Jobs. We used to take psychedelics together and talk about Buddhist philosophy. I had no idea he was connected with Woz [Steve Wozniak] or selling blue boxes [telephone dialers that allow you to make free calls] at the time. We just talked about transcendentalism and Buddhism and listened to Bob Dylan.'

Jobs even created a piece of programming language software that he called Dylan (which stood for 'dynamic language'). For months after its launch in May 1994, Bob Dylan sued Apple for trademark infringement, although they later settled out of court, with Apple obtaining the rights to use his name. 'It is our intention to license the Dylan trademark to any implementation which passes a standard test suite,' said the press release, somewhat pompously. The software didn't set the computer world alight, although they continued to use Dylan's name, even using the singer's image in its Emmy award-winning 1997 'Think Different' ad campaign. For this they appropriated images of icons like Dylan, Einstein, Gandhi and John Lennon and Yoko Ono. 'Here's to the misfits, the rebels, the trouble-makers ... While some may see them as the crazy ones, we see genius.' Jobs personally called Dylan and Yoko at home to use their image. He wanted to emulate the success of Nike's 'Just Do It' and to a certain extent he did.

Dylan is one of the best-represented artists on iTunes, and there are 51 of his albums available for download, including two different versions of his *Biograph* compilation and three 'exclusive' tracks. At the launch of iTunes in the US Jobs started building a playlist beginning with 'Simple Twist Of Fate' and also showed how you could view videos, using Dylan's 'Tangled Up In Blue'. Like the rest of us, Jobs believes *Blood On The Tracks* to be Bob's finest work. Until recently he thought his hero hadn't done anything of worth since then, and when a *Business Week* journalist tried to turn him on to *Empire Burlesque* in the mid-Eighties, Jobs asked the record to be taken off after the first song, reiterating his negative opinion of recent Dylan.[1]

'As I grew up, I learned the lyrics to all his songs and watched him never stand still. If you look at the artists, if they get really

---

[1] I've seen Dylan in concert a few times, but never with any great success. I always thought he took too much of a perverse delight in deliberately abstracting his most enjoyable songs. The last time I saw him, not only did the audience often have no idea what he was playing, but it was plain to see that his band didn't either. I once watched Dylan fluff his lines approximately twenty times in the mid-Eighties: I'd gone down to Heaven, the gay disco near Charing Cross in London, to see him film a scene in the shockingly bad 'rock' biopic *Hearts of Fire*, directed by the previously redoubtable Richard Marquand (he's directed *The Return of the Jedi*; *Jagged Edge*). Along with Rupert Everett and someone called Fiona (as she wasn't a fully-functioning actress or singer I can only assume she felt it right to only claim half a name), Dylan had to pretend to be at a press conference, fielding questions from a bunch of hacks, which he did with a spectacular lack of enthusiasm, application and skill. He had to simply *hurrumph*, in a monosyllabic, dismissive kind-of-a-way and then walk off to the bar. Rather easy, one would have thought. But Bob found it so difficult that after every take Marquand would walk down and say something like: 'Bob, that was absolutely fine, really fine, but I think you should try it with a little less shrug and a little more, you know, "hurrump". Do you see? I need to see you emote.'

good, it always occurs to them at some point that they can do this one thing for the rest of their lives, and they can be really successful to the outside world but not really be successful to themselves. That's the moment that an artist really decides who he or she is. If they keep on risking failure, they're still artists. Dylan and Picasso were always risking failure. This Apple thing is that way for me ... If I try my best and fail, well, I tried my best.'

Steve Jobs' adventures in the music industry have had a profound effect on his relationship with music in general and with his iPod in particular. Posing with Sheryl Crow for an article in *Fortune* in 2003, he said to the singer that he had never really understood the relevance of rap. But while mucking about with a prototype of the iTunes Music Store on his Mac he began to download some of Eminem's tracks.

'You know, he really is a great poet,' Crow said.

To which Jobs replied, 'Yeah, he's starting to grow on me.'

8 Yowsah Yowsah Yowsah: Disco, Soul & Sex!

Oh yes, lots and lots of sex . . .

I spent much of my teenage years pretending to be someone else. Dressing up is a particularly British affliction, and, on discovering punk at the tender age of sixteen, I was similarly afflicted. Like the Edwardians who roamed north London council estates in the late 1940s, the teddy boys who donned brothel-creepers and drape suits in the 1950s, or the mods of the 1960s with their mohair jackets and loafers, for me the 1970s was a decade of fancy dress.

I arrived in London in 1977 at the height of punk, fresh from school, wide-eyed and penniless (with billowing trousers and cheesecloth shirts), to start an arts foundation course at Chelsea School of Art, only to find a city awash with not so much musical anarchy as fashion insurrection; in short, style wars.

It wasn't the fact that London was full of punks that surprised me, it was the fact that everyone at my art school seemed to think that life was one big coming-out party. There was a smattering of punks and hippies, of course, but there were also urban paratroopers, flame-haired girls masquerading as Rita Hayworth or Clara Bow, and half-a-dozen young turks trying to look like Bryan Ferry. Narcissism plumbed new depths as haircuts reached new heights; everyone had an alias, an ambition and an aerodynamic coiffure to match.

Like a lot of people from my generation who came to London in the late Seventies, it was reinvention I was looking for. I was also looking for fun, an education and a career, but fundamentally I wanted to escape my past. 'Everyone will hate you when you grow up because you're middle class,' said my mother when I was about fourteen. 'The upper class will hate you because you're encroaching upon them; the working class will hate you because you're trying to leave them behind; and the middle class will hate you because they see themselves in you, and don't want to be reminded of where they came from.' Thanks, Mum. The subtext was always, 'Deal with it.'

Having spent a year at Chelsea School of Art, in the summer of 1978 I applied to St Martins, the crucible of sex, art, fashion and music, to study photography and graphic design. What could be more fun? An art school in the middle of Soho! The centre of the known universe! And although St Martins was the first place the Sex Pistols played, supporting Bazooka Joe in 1975, it was already experiencing another sea change. It was in 1978 that the Eighties first arrived, and they arrived first at St Martins.

Being at art school in the late 1970s meant living in a playpen, a pop-cultural whirlpool of nightclubs, gigs and parties, a world where punks mixed with public schoolboys, where soul boys danced with drag queens, where barrow boys dressed up to look like wing commanders. I'd only been there for five minutes before I realized I could be anyone! I didn't need to just dress like a punk, I could look like a pirate, a cocktail barman, a 1940s torch singer, a stevedore, anyone.

In many ways the late 1970s was the period when style culture really began to blossom in this country, when a generation of socially mobile boys and girls first began to understand – *en masse* – that their aspirations could be realised simply by looking the part. It was also the dawn of what became the New Romantic movement, when sartorial elegance became the easiest way to make your way in the world. And, like many of my peers, it was a time when I changed my look at the drop of a wide-band trilby; one minute we were Lower East Side punks in plastic leather jackets and baseball boots; the next we were

Soho secret agents, stalking moodily around West Wonderland in cheap raincoats and floppy fringes – a different haircut for every day of the week.

During the late Seventies and early Eighties there were occasions when I suppose I would admit to being a fashion victim, but then I always hated myself in the morning. There were, though, lots and lots of those mornings. And evenings, too; evenings when I wore my black velvet bomber jacket with a fake-fur collar complete with imitation tigers appliquéd in silver plastic on the back. Then there was the three-quarter-length two-piece Prince of Wales check drape suit made for me by a little man in Harrow (which I first wore, if I remember rightly, to the Bri-Nylon retrospective at the V&A).

And how can I forget my 'Hard Times' distressed jeans which by the time I was finished with them had more holes than a decent Emmenthal and smelt like one, too? My own particular favourite was my 'punk matelot' look: motorcycle jacket, striped T-shirt, earring, white navy fatigues and winkle-pickers – with hindsight I must have looked like a Latin American rent boy.

Style culture in those days was rather a clandestine endeavour: groups of friends who thought and looked alike, giddy in the knowledge that they – we – were somehow different from the crowd. These days style culture is all pervasive; it surrounds us like the air we breathe, but back then it was elitist in the extreme.

On Charing Cross Road there was a pub called the Cambridge, just a Sid Vicious spit from St Martins, and the trendiest bar in all London, whose upstairs bar was always full of art students, former punks, pop stars and fashion designers. Malcolm McLaren had his own stool, the Sex Pistols seemed to be there every Friday night, and Siouxsie and the Banshees took up residency by the jukebox. Jamie Reid was the coolest man there. He designed everything for the Sex Pistols (the single sleeves, the posters, the ads), and to a seventeen-year-old graphics student was a genuine, 24-carat, bonafide hero. He always wore a tight, thigh-length black leather suit jacket, his hair was always fashioned into this greasy, truck-driver quiff, and he had a bottle of Pils seemingly grafted to his left hand. Pils was the only thing that anyone drank, making us think it was the only thing they sold.

Everything happened at the Cambridge: a girl was decapitated by a lorry after she bet her friend she could crawl underneath it before it pulled away outside; a St Martins fine art student called Alan was beaten senseless because he persisted in dressing like Hitler (floppy fringe, jackboots, leather trenchcoat and tell-tale moustache). The first time we saw him we immediately took bets on how long it would take before someone kicked the living daylights out of him. And just two weeks later he stumbled into the Cambridge covered in the most fearsome bruises. Alan had, to quote an old Nick Lowe song, been nutted by reality, and soon left the college.

Most people congregated at the Cambridge before moving off into the night, to the latest tranche of nightclubs sprouting up all over the city. With the fancy-dress parade at its height, a generation of young entrepreneurs were taking over nightclubs for one night a week, installing their own DJs and creating a phenomenon out of nothing. The only condition was: you had to dress up. I lived in nightclubs for nine years solid, from 1979 to 1988, starting with the Blitz, St Moritz and Hell, right through Le Beat Route, Club For Heroes, the Wag Club and the Camden Palace, right up to White Trash, Do-Dos, Café de Paris and Taboo. These clubs were the breeding ground of the Eighties, the clubs that produced a new generation of pop stars (Boy George, Spandau Ballet, Wham!), fashion designers (John Galliano, Katharine Hamnett, Bodymap), film stars (Tim Roth, Daniel Day Lewis, Sadie Frost), journalists, photographers, designers, and the club entrepreneurs themselves, many of whom would go on to launch restaurants, hotels and the like. These were not the discos of my youth, not the sweaty rugby clubs where we used to stick our thumbs in the pockets of our high-waisted trousers and head-bang away to 'Hi-Ho Silver Lining' and 'Brown Sugar', not the youth clubs where, at the end of the evening, you'd find yourself with your arms around an inappropriate girl, smooching along to the Chi-Lites' 'Have You Seen Her?' or 10cc's 'I'm Not In Love'. No, these places were somewhere else completely, serious dens of iniquity where the main preoccupations were fashion, sex, drugs ... and dancing.

If there's one thing that helped turn me from a neurotic boy-outsider to a relatively gregarious grown-up it was learning to dance. Really dance. My self-administered emancipation was found on the dance floors of nightclubs all over central London, dancing to the sort of music that, would, for a few years at least, become my alternative DNA.

After all the raw emotion and unsullied rock of the Seventies, the Eighties were all about cold conformity, unabashed ambition and surface smarts, and all of it standardised by a metronomic back beat. Essentially, dance music has always been driven by fashion and technology, so it's no surprise that much of it concerns itself with the notion of perfection, and variations thereof. As soon as drum machines began taking over dance in the mid-Seventies, the art of the impossible became the only reason to make records: what exactly was the perfect beat? First we had click tracks, rhythm boxes (samba, mambo, bossa nova, etc.) and robotic synths; and then, in 1978 Roland launched the CR78 (famously heard three years later on Phil Collins' 'In The Air Tonight'), and a year later Roger Linn launched the world's first mass-market drum machine. As soon as the Linn Drum appeared it had a huge effect on the way records were put together, and for months afterwards the charts were full of songs underscored by the metallic thud of the Linn Mark I. Drummers liked to say the sound was reminiscent of damp cardboard being struck by a large fish, although this begs the question: how did they know? Roland then came up with the TR808 (heard on Marvin Gaye's 'Sexual Healing'), then the 909, which was the drum box of Chicago house, and the TB303, the sound of acid house. Since then, digital recording equipment has become so advanced that all you need to make a record is a laptop and a bunch of bad ideas.

The three records that cartographically defined the start of the new decade were 'The Adventures Of Grandmaster Flash On The Wheels Of Steel' by Grandmaster Flash (Sugarhill, 1981), 'The Message' by Grandmaster Flash and the Furious Five (Sugarhill, 1982) and 'Last Night A DJ Saved My Life' by Indeep (Sound Of New York, 1982). The first personified the scratching and sampling and stop-start techniques that would affect every record in some way for the next twenty-five years; the second was a forerunner of gangster rap and the whole culture of complaint; and the third is a coronation of the DJ as the axe hero of the Eighties.

As soon as I descended into clubland, I began accumulating the best collection of disco records the world has ever seen. I bought them, danced to them, and then stuck them in boxes under the stairs. And then twenty years later I bought an iPod and they all came to life again. And they're all here, collated with love. There are 301 dance tracks on my 'Ibiza' playlist, the oldest of which dates from 1971, while the most recent was uploaded about an hour ago. For the last fifteen years or so, dance has been embroiled in such a widespread and mediocre compilation frenzy that barely a week goes by without the release of another *Disco Fever* collection, usually featuring Kool & the Gang, Gloria Gaynor and any number of badly remixed Bee Gees tracks. But that hasn't stopped the genre from developing its own 'canon', an acknowledged litany of world-famous karaoke-friendly floor-fillers. And I own quite a few of them.

In my meticulously created vacuum-sealed simulacrum of the best disco in town, these are the records you'll hear in the first hour or so, the twenty greatest 'disco' records in the world: 1) 'Don't Stop 'Til You Get Enough' by Michael Jackson (*Off The Wall*, Epic), 1979; 2) 'One More Time' by Daft Punk (*Discovery*, Virgin), 2001; 3) 'TSOP (The Sound Of Philadelphia)' by MFSB

(*The Sound Of Philadelphia*, Philadelphia International), 1973;[1]
4) 'Slave To The Rhythm' by Grace Jones (ZTT), 1985; 5) 'Music
Sounds Better With You' by Stardust (Roule), 1998; 6) 'Lola's
Theme' by Shapeshifters (Positiva), 2004; 7) 'Spacer' by Sheila &
B. Devotion (Carrere), 1979; 8) 'Crazy In Love' by Beyonce
(*Dangerously In Love*, Columbia), 2003; 9) 'Shake Your Body
(Down To The Ground)' by the Jacksons (Epic), 1978; 10) 'Going
Back To My Roots' by Odyssey (RCA), 1981; 11) 'I Want Your
Love' by Chic (Atlantic), 1981;[2] 12) 'Lady' by Modjo (Polydor),
2000; 13) 'Let The Music Play' by Shannon (Warehouse), 1983;
14) 'Hey Ya!' by Outkast (*The Love Below*, Arista), 2003; 15)
'Rock Your Baby' by George McCrae (*Rock Your Baby*, Jay Boy),
1974; 16) 'Staying Alive' by the Bee Gees (*Saturday Night Fever*,
RSO), 1977; 17) 'Hey Fellas' by Trouble Funk (Sugarhill), 1982;[3]

---

[1] MFSB stands for Mother Father Sister Brother, or, alternatively, Mother-
fuckin' son of a Bitch, and this song features the Three Degrees on backing
vocals. It was also the theme of the American TV show *Soul Train*.

[2] Some of Chic's songs have unlikely origins. Group leader Nile Rodgers
initially wrote 'We Are Family' (eventually recorded by Sister Sledge) at the
Woodstock festival in 1969, while he wrote 'Le Freak' after being refused
entry to the very club it celebrated, Studio 54: the original chorus centred
around a bouncer-directed 'aah ... fuck off!' which was soon changed to
'freak out!'.

[3] Go-Go: Dance music, now almost defunct. Washington DC's percussive
double-funk began loping through the arteries of European club culture
during 1983. Two years later it was the hippest groove on the globe. The
origins of Chocolate City Go-Go begin in the Seventies, when all-night
parties rocked to the Neanderthal rhythms of Trouble Funk, Chuck Brown &
The Soul Searchers and Redds & The Boys. Go-Go proved more popular in
Britain than anywhere else outside DC, Trouble Funk's 'Good To Go' and
Chuck Brown's 'We Need Some Money' becoming mini-anthems. With their
'86 European gigs, Trouble Funk provided some of the decade's finest shows,
and some of those who saw them say they were the best gigs of the decade.
(My best gigs ever? Well, definitely Trouble Funk at the Town & Country
Club in London in '86; Elvis Costello, & The Attractions the same year at
London's Bloomsbury Theatre; the Talking Heads and the Ramones at
Aylesbury Friars in '77, the Jam at the London punk Mecca, the 100 Club,
also in '77; Prince in the round at Wembley, '88; every U2 gig I've ever

18) 'Rock Your Body' by Justin Timberlake (*Justified*, BMG), 2002; 19) 'I Feel Love' by Donna Summer (GTO), 1977; 20) 'Trick Me' by Kelis (*Tasty*, Arista), 2003.

The best club music of the early Eighties tended to be gay disco – Coffee's 'Casanova', Lime's 'Your Love', 'I Can't Take My Eyes Off You' by the Boys Town Gang, and any Hi-Energy record you care to mention. How could it not be? Dance music during this time was all about transgression and euphoria. Gay discos also tended to be where the most interesting people went after dark. Taboo was one such place, a Leicester Square nightclub that looked like the bar in Star Wars, full of weird, alien beats with intergalactic haircuts and tin-foil tunics. The woodwork squeaked, and out came the freaks. This is what I imagined the last days of Rome to be like – if the Romans had had discos, that is. Everyone dressed up, everyone danced, everyone had sex. Lots of sex. Fucking in the toilets, blow jobs at the bar, girls doing girls, boys doing boys, everyone doing each other.

There was one infamous female journalist (who later turned into a quasi-pop star), who used to trade blow-jobs for coke, and could regularly be seen traipsing off to the toilets accompanied by a boy with a hard-on and a rolled-up fiver. Another night there, two famous fashion designers, one feted contemporary artist and the lead singer of an enormously popular rock band, were huddled together in a cubicle in the men's loo, hoovering up cocaine as though it was going out of fashion (fat chance). As they piled out I overheard one of the designers say, to nobody in particular: 'I do so much these days that when I go to the cashpoint the notes come out ready rolled.'

---

seen – Boston in '88 was especially good, as were the Earl's Court gigs in 2001; David Bowie at Wembley Arena in 2003 and Dr Feelgood at the Nag's Head in High Wycombe in 1975 when I was still at school.) Go-Go cooled off quickly, and the movement suffered through negligent radio, a disastrous blaxploitation movie (*Good To Go*, with Art Garfunkel!), and the musicians' growing dissatisfaction with their lack of worldwide success. In the Chocolate City itself, Happy Feet are still dancing, albeit quietly, and not very often.

Sex was everywhere in those days. One night in Skin II (a fetish club you couldn't get into unless you were dressed head to cock in leather) I saw a bald-headed, leather-clad boy slowly push a big, black rubber dildo up a similarly bald, leather-clad girl's backside, as she bent lasciviously over the bar, quietly pleading with him to push it harder. This sight certainly kept me occupied while I waited for my beer. Another night I pushed open a cubicle door in Club For Heroes to find the lead singer of one of the most successful girl groups Britain has ever produced being taken from behind while she was throwing up into the bowl. She didn't seem to mind (nor did her bass player, who was snorting a line of coke on the window sill).

Everyone fucked themselves stupid. After Taboo, the truly heroic would retire to an unprepossessing hotel behind Marble Arch, where one night one of London's most notorious cover girls serviced nine men at once. Around four in the morning, this is where you'd often find the six Daisy Chain girls, who would decamp from Taboo or the Wag Club, bringing with them any available DJ/minor pop star/journalist/club runner/dealer who had a bag of user-friendly coke. Their party trick was lying naked in a circle, giving each other head, writhing around to the beat-box strains of the Beastie Boys, Schooly D and Soul Sonic Force.

As club culture became more sophisticated, or at least more homogenous, the records started to get more uniform. DJs would alter the bpm in order to slide seamlessly from one track to another, so that in effect what you got was one long song with various highs and lows. And as art tends to imitate life, so records started to get longer and longer – first five minutes, then six, seven, eight, then ten, then – unbelievably – sixteen or seventeen. In DJ booths the world over, the question was: how long can you keep it up for? In the laser-beamed, mirror-balled, smoked-mirrored Eighties, the 12" remix wasn't so much king as an all-singing, all-dancing insomniac emperor with a propensity for fast drugs and a libidinous streak as wide as the dance floor at Studio 54. Remixes started off as simple repagination, reassembling the constituent parts in a novel but comprehensible manner. Soon though, remixes were doubling in length, trebling, quadrupling. Patrick Cowley's 1982 remix of Donna Summer's 'I Feel Love' – quite probably the most architecturally sound dance record ever constructed – is over fifteen minutes long, and for a while became the benchmark of dance remixes. It changed the way we played music at home, too: I once played the SOS Band's 'Just Be Good To Me' for over two hours. The three 12" remixes I had were around eight minutes each, and I kept switching them around on my decks at home, the drums descending on my head like paving stones, the heavy-handed robotic synths marching forward with no particular place to go. It's an Amazonian record, as big and as sexy as you like – even today, when it's much easier to create songs on this scale – an absolutely compulsive piece of music from fanfare to finale. And making it longer only prolongs its licentiousness.

With digital technology, there's no reason why someone couldn't remix it so it's an hour long, a day long, or three and a half weeks long. With just a 40 GB iPod, Donna could be girding her loins for well over two weeks. And with Smart Playlists you can turn your playlist into one long seamless BPM-approximate soundtrack, an accompaniment that could see you through the whole night, from the early evening rush hour ('Does this cod-piece go with my tie?') to the 2 a.m. paparazzi stagger, when you're falling out of the cab. In fact, with my iPod my party can last for weeks, a never-ending one-night stand.

In a rather back-to-front fashion, disco made me treat soul music with more respect. Even though I had a box full of soul singles from my early teens, by the age of twenty-one I thought I had moved on, thought that soul was for adolescent girls, not boys who desperately wanted to be trendy. But I came round quickly. After all, I soon realised that soul was the music of love. If 12" remixes were one-night stands, then soul, and soul albums in particular, were fully-fledged affairs. Soul music was fundamentally about love, L-U-V, about finding it, loving it, losing it, and missing it. That's what soul did best, and that's what you bought it for, especially if you were a man. If you'd broken up with your girlfriend, then it was perfectly OK to wallow in the soulful soliloquies you found on Motown or Atlantic. Shit, if Otis Redding and Marvin Gaye were both man enough to say this stuff, then what was wrong with listening to it?

There are those who, in an attempt to keep soul music special, and to distance it from the never-ending cycle of Motown/Atlantic/Stax/Kent/Northern Soul compilations, only champion the most esoteric, obscure stuff, but while I'm also sick of what have now become ubiquitous Motown advertising jingles, I think there is an extremely fertile middle ground. And so, after careful consideration, I would volunteer the following as the twenty greatest soul songs of all time: 1) 'Ship Ahoy' by The O'Jays (*Ship Ahoy*, Philadelphia International), 1973; 2) 'All Day Music' by War (*Greatest Hits*, Island), 1976; 3) 'Sweet Soul Music' by Arthur Conley (Atlantic), 1967; 4) 'Joy And Pain' by Maze (MCA),1981; 5) 'I'll Be Around' by the Detroit Spinners (Atlantic), 1973; 6) Fa-Fa-Fa-Fa-Fa (Sad Song)' by Otis Redding (Atlantic), 1966; 7) 'Dancing in the Street' by Martha and the Vandellas (Motown), 1964;[1] 8) 'Tired Of Being

---

[1] In 1978/79 I played drums in a fairly 'adventurous' Sixties band called the Dads, and this song was in our repertoire. One night we played on a boat on the Thames, and as my kit wasn't fastened to the deck, I started the evening playing on the port side, and ended up on starboard. The Dads played mostly ska and soul, although we did have an 'experimental' song called 'Red Bus' which was, as you might suppose, about the prosaic delights of riding on a London bus (our singer was the extraordinarily lovely Corinne Drewery, my oldest friend, who later went on to have hits with Swing Out Sister). I was also in another group, the Timing Association, with several other Neurotic Boy Outsiders with short hair and black clothes from St Martins. We made a self-financed single called 'It's Magic' which, I hasten to add, wasn't. On receiving our first copy, we took it down to Broadcasting

Alone' by Al Green (*Al Green Gets Next To You*, Hi Records), 1971; 9) 'Me And Mrs Jones' by Billy Paul (Philadelphia International), 1972, and the first dance at my wedding in 1997; 10) 'Ain't No Sunshine' by Bill Withers (CBS), 1971; 11) 'Be Thankful For What You Got' by William DeVaughn (Chelsea), 1974; 12) 'Why Can't We Live Together' by Timmy Thomas (EMI), 1972; 13) ' Harlem Shuffle' by Bob & Earl (OSE), 1963; 14) 'I Can't Stand The Rain' by Ann Peebles (Info), 1973; 15) 'At Last I Am Free' by Chic (*C'est Chic*, Atlantic), 1978;[1] 16) 'Don't Make Me Wait Too Long' by Roberta Flack and Donny Hathaway (*Roberta Flack featuring Donny Hathaway*, Atlantic), 1979; 17) 'You Might Need Somebody' by Randy Crawford (*Now We May Begin*, Warner Brothers), 1981; 18) 'Nights Over Egypt' by the Jones Girls (*The Best Of Philadelphia*, Philadelphia International), 1983; 19) 'Too High' by Stevie Wonder (*Innervisions*, Motown), 1973; 20) 'I'm Doin' Fine Now' by New York City (Epic), 1973.

It was also soul music that expedited the loss of my virginity, or plastic soul, anyway. *Young Americans* is the album David Bowie made after finally ditching his Ziggy Stardust alter-ego, and all the variations thereafter (*Aladdin Sane*, *Diamond Dogs*, etc.), an attempt at cracking the US soul market which he

---

House to wait for John Peel, in the hope we could convince him to play it on his radio show. As we approached him he stepped back a couple of paces, and, when we produced our record, said, 'Jesus Christ boys, I thought you were going to mug me.' He played it three days later. When the Buzzcocks split up in 1981, their guitarist Steve Diggle took me to a pub in Victoria, just behind Buckingham Palace, and asked if I wanted to join his new group, Flag Of Convenience. I said I couldn't, not just because I would be replacing the irreplaceable John Maher (one of the greatest drummers to ever sit on a stool), but also because I'd just sold my drum kit.

[1] '... I can hardly see in front of me ...' Although the song describes a woman who can hardly see because she is crying, when Nile Rodgers originally wrote it, he was describing his own experiences tripping on acid at a Black Panther demonstration in New York's Central Park in the early 1970s. He'd just been tear-gassed.

recorded with such crack session musicians as guitarist Carlos Alomar and saxophonist David Sanborn. It's my favourite Bowie album, and remains his most underrated, full of heart-rending strings, searing sax, and enough minor chords to melt the coldest of cold hearts (and even though he made it on cocaine – one of the coldest of all drugs, it has an enduring warmth to it). Bowie calls it 'plastic soul', 'blue-eyed soul' and 'the squashed remains of ethnic music as it survives in the age of muzak rock, written and sung by a white limey'.

Unlike most people my age, dressing up wasn't just a means to an end, it was a vocation. I didn't dress up to get sex. I dressed up to dress up. But they say that luck favours the prepared, and at the very tail end of 1977 – when punk was at its height, nightclubs were eighteen months away, and the Eighties were still choosing what clothes to wear – I had sex anyway. For the first time. We had been drinking in the upstairs bar at the Cambridge, and got talking as we were drinking up. We both lied about having a fondness for the Stranglers (who happened to be on the jukebox at the time – is there nothing people won't say in order to convince someone they're nice enough to have sex with?), walked each other home, down the King's Road, and eventually to Ralph West (my place, not hers). I still maintain it was the clothes that did it: a leather jacket (real this time) covered in punk button badges ('Blockhead', 'Gabba Gabba Hey!', 'If It Ain't Stiff It Ain't Worth A Fuck'), black T-shirt, black leggings, baseball boots, shaved head. And while I obviously know who was with me that night, I'm not certain she knows that she was responsible for dragging me (with hindsight, rather well) into manhood. In fact, given the extraordinarily comprehensive seduction techniques I displayed that night, I would imagine that she thought I had had sex, oh, exactly no times. But, and in the grand scheme of things, this is a pretty big but, I can't truthfully recall what we were listening to while we were actually 'doing it' (and we would have been listening to something, because that's what you did when you were seventeen). I have a fairly good idea that it would have been *Young Americans*; I say this because I would have probably put on Side 1 the minute we got back to my room, and as we were listening to the title track I would have poured two glasses of cheap white wine and spent rather too long ostentatiously rolling a joint on an LP sleeve (and the choice was always crucially important – I reckon at this juncture I would have used '*Heroes*' or my 'Psycho Killer' 12"). Then, just as the coagulating fug of intoxicants was beginning to envelope us, I would have flipped the record over so we could both wallow in the luscious delights of 'Somebody Up There Likes Me' and 'Can You Hear Me' as the snow steadily fell over Battersea Park).[1]

But I'm not sure. It could just as easily have been '77 or *Horses* or *The Idiot* or any number of Roxy Music albums I had lying around. Music To Seduce Women By is a whirling hosepipe of a subject (so to speak), and unless handled properly will flail about you, causing havoc and confusion as you inch your way along the sofa. When I was seventeen the records you played whilst seducing a woman were simply a way of showing off, of proving you'd actually bought the new Blondie album or an Elvis Costello bootleg. As I got older I became more cynical, and acquired a failsafe collection of CDs that were absolutely a means to an end: Marvin Gaye's *I Want You* (this is without question his best record, although for seduction purposes you should always try and skip the opening track, as you might come across as a little, er, forward), Ennio Morricone's *Once Upon A Time In America*,

---

[1] 'Fascination', another song on the album, was originally called 'Funky Music', and had been written by Luther Vandross, who had been hired by Bowie to sing on *Young Americans*. When Bowie asked if he could change the lyrics, Vandross replied, bending to his employer's exhalation like a reed, 'You're David Bowie. I live with my mother. Of course you can change the lyrics.'

Tom Waits & Crystal Gayle's *One From The Heart*, and any half-decent Nick Drake compilation. In my experience you don't really need more than three or four records because if she hasn't 'bought it' (in the words of Woody Allen) by then, you may as well call her a cab.

Then of course there was always subject-specific targeting – using Simon & Garfunkel because you knew she liked them, and suggesting Depeche Mode for the same reason (although I'm not sure that any relationship based on a shared passion for Depeche Mode is destined to last, frankly).

Just as I was finishing the last paragraph I got a call from Alix in Paris, who happened to be playing Kool and the Gang through his iMac as he was finishing a piece for *Dazed & Confused*. When I told him what I was doing he called me an amateur (par for the course I'm afraid), and said that the best record for seducing women is Captain Beefheart's 1972 album *Clear Spot*, a record I only knew because one of its tracks, the wilfully obtuse 'Big Eyed Beans From Venus', was played on *The Old Grey Whistle Test* in the early 1970s, and helped convince me that I should stop buying *Popswap* and start buying the *NME* immediately. Alix reckons it's the most romantic record ever made, and played me some of it over the phone. The three salient tracks are 'Too Much Time', 'My Head Is My Only House Unless It Rains' and 'Her Eyes Are A Million Miles', where the Captain sounds like Otis Redding on acid, which is sort of how Beefheart sounded at the best of times, I suppose. He was infamous for corrupting the blues, although his unhinged 'anti-music sound sculptures' were never commercially viable. Hence Doobie Brothers producer Ted Templeman, who was brought in to add some radio sheen to *Clear Spot*. It didn't trouble the charts of course, but the record was astonishing. And while Alix's choices are spot on, I think the object of your desire might question your intentions after listening to track two: 'Nowadays A Woman's Gotta Hit A Man' (which, as a seduction tool, I think is right up there with Blink-182's 'I Wanna F*** A Dog In The A$$').

In the pantheon of great lotharios, Captain Beefheart makes for an unlikely figure, although seduction is subjective territory, and one man's 'Hot In Herre' is another's 'My Ding-a-Ling'. If I had the choice of taking tips from Nelly or Chuck Berry (who was famously arrested for secretly filming female guests using the toilets at his ranch), I would probably opt instead for Marvin Gaye, Prince or Mick Jagger. Or, having seen him in action, maybe Jack Nicholson.

I met Jack in the early Nineties at a party for *Vogue* at San Lorenzo, the perpetually Eurocentric trattoria in London. He arrived at the party by chauffeur-driven Porsche, of all things, resplendent in his trademark *Reservoir Poodles* ensemble: crumpled suit, black suede shoes, white shirt and impenetrable black Wayfarers. He loped down the stairs, puffing incessantly on an obviously beleaguered Marlboro Light, where he inadvertently joined the queue for the buffet immediately behind me. Assuming it would be rude not to, I engaged him in conversation and, for approximately six minutes, we discussed the quality of the champagne, the long night ahead and the pros and cons of various members' clubs in London (the Groucho won hands down, principally – according to Jack – 'because there you can walk around on your hands and knees and no one bats a damn eyelid'). You can cover a lot of ground in six minutes.

Then, as he finished surveying the sumptuous but strictly vegetarian fare laid out in front of him, he slowly turned his head to mine, lowered his sunglasses by the merest fraction, and whispered in his unmistakeable drawl, 'Are the women here as bad as the food?'

He proceeded to find out for himself, for over the course of the next two hours Jack hit on every woman in the room, that's e-v-e-r-y w-o-m-a-n, or at least every woman who wasn't nailed down or handcuffed to her husband. His technique was priceless: he'd simply sidle up to them, puffing on his gasper, and then lean into them so his head was directly in front of theirs. This would quickly be followed by a 'Hellooo baby' or a

'Hi, I'm Jack ...', which, I have to say, had most of the girls melting into their banana daiquiris.

His technique is the subject of a surely apocryphal story I heard a few years ago from an LA-based screenwriter: it's around midday in Los Angeles and Jack's new agent picks him up from his Mulholland Drive home in a huge black stretch with tinted windows. They're on their way to meet a prospective director for one of Jack's projects, and his agent wants to make sure the big man is there on cue. On the way, they stop in West Hollywood to pick up the agent's new assistant, an e-x-t-r-e-m-e-l-y leggy blonde called Michelle. As she climbs in the back of the limo, Jack – who hasn't met her before – makes with the hellos and the pleased-to-meet-yous and the rest of his Runyonesque patois, giving it plenty of smirk and flying eyebrow as he goes. He then starts humming the Beatles' 'Michelle' while complimenting her on her clothes and jewellery (Jack is by this time giving the impression that he might have had an early morning beer). Then the humming turns into singing and the compliments get more specific as Jack starts gliding his hand up the inside of Michelle's very long, very lovely legs. As he begins stroking the top of her thigh, she slaps him across the face, tells him to get his hands off her and then demands to be let out of the car.

'What the fuck do you think you're doing, you asshole?' she screams, as she climbs out.

As the stretch moves on, without Michelle, Jack's agent leans across and says, 'Jack, why'd you do that? She's new, she's good, and now I gotta go and get another one.'

'Weeellll,' says Jack, managing to elongate the word to three syllables. 'You know what? I play the numbers game. I reckon there are two types of girls in the world: those who wanna fuck me, and those who wanna tell their friends they knocked me back.

'And I reckon it's about 50/50 ...'

9 Digital Dreams: It's a CD!

Why Prince was the King of swinging London

As a metaphor for the Eighties, the CD is as good as any. Like Madonna, the Filofax, MTV, privatisation, shoulder pads or post-modern architecture, the CD is a defining symbol of the age, an age where presentation was paramount. The compact disc compartmentalised its contents; cleaned it up, washed behind its ears, and then dressed it up for market; it digitally improved it, shrunk it and then enshrined it in a pocked-sized jewel case. Like the designer decade it would soon become synonymous with, the CD was an emblem of burnished success – a smarter, more upmarket version of everything that had gone before it. The CD was new school, cool. Not hip, not yet anyway, not totally, but certainly modern.

And the Eighties were all about modernity ... designer modernity.

Like Duran Duran, 'designer' was big in the Eighties. First it became an adjective and then a prefix, applied to everything from vacuum cleaners (the Dyson) to pop groups (the Black Crowes being a designer Rolling Stones, for instance). From adland's ideal home (Mont Blanc fountain pen, Braun calculator, Tizio lamp) to Tesco's fresh food counter (why buy radicchio rather than iceberg? Kos it says much more about you than ordinary lettuce can!), in the designer decade, design was everything and everything was design: designer deaths on your television screens, designer water next to designer beer in your fridge, designer labels in your wardrobe (lots and lots of those), designer condoms between your sheets, designer stubble on your face (worn by designer actors like Mickey Rourke and Bruce Willis).[1] And – how could we forget – designer sounds on the stereo. The CD was a designer product like no other, and heralded an era where music became codified. Almost overnight, music became a lifestyle accessory, a background fizz to be played at designer dinner parties in designer lofts in designer postcodes. 'CD music' became pejorative, as did the likes of Sade, Anita Baker, Dire Straits and Simply Red. Critics said this was music with the edges rubbed off, with the soul extracted ('Crystal-clear sound for the couch potato generation!' they sneered). Aspirational in essence, if you didn't have the wherewithal to surround yourself with the occupational hazards of yuppiedom – the waterfront conversion, the Breuer chairs, the cappuccino machine, the Golf GTi with the personalised number-plate – then a few CDs left casually lying on the sub-Matthew Hilton coffee table would suffice. And whereas in the Seventies we had rolled joints on LP sleeves, in the Eighties our CDs were used for snorting cocaine. Simple as that. If, during the Sixties and Seventies, music was developed as revolution, in the Eighties it was enjoyed as a lifestyle soundtrack.

It had a sound, the Eighties, manifested in the Fairlight synthesizer, the Australian-manufactured machine used by Peter Gabriel, Thomas Dolby, Alan Parsons, Herbie Hancock and *Miami Vice* producer Jan Hammer. If you wanted to sound futuristic, modern, then the Fairlight was your baby. And let's

---

[1] 'Designer' was originally used adjectivally to describe the notionally elitist designer jeans produced by Murjani, Gloria Vanderbilt Jeans, in the Seventies. It is said that the company wanted Jackie Onassis to lend the brand her name (and thus added value), but when it could not get the former first lady, it called in the New York socialite. The garments were advertised on the sides of buses with the slogan, 'The end justifies the jeans,' alongside photos of a line-up of Vanderbilt-clad (signed) bottoms. The prefix 'designer' is now redundant as everything is designed: OutKast are the new Funkadelic; IKEA is the new MFI; the iPod is the designer Walkman.

face it – at the time we all wanted to sound modern, whether we were pop stars or not. In the Eighties, every established pop star from Bob Dylan to the Rolling Stones began using drum-machines on their records, in the hope of being embraced by the new MTV Generation. Listen to anything from the Eighties today – Madonna, Michael Jackson, Bon Jovi, the Eurythmics, Steve Winwood, the Pet Shop Boys, Sting – and you'll hear the time-capsule *clank* of over-produced synthesized drums.

For a while, music on CD all sounded like CD music, every track swathed in atmospheric synthesized swirls, every hook punctuated by piping sampled horns, and every crescendo building on banks of overlaid keyboards. And then there were the drums, the dreaded computerized drums. Music on CD sounded cleaner, leaner, less down and dirty. Initially it suited soul, heavily organised rock and gentle singer-songwriter stuff, but wasn't so good at replicating the noise and squabble of punk, or the energy and naivety of rockabilly, or early rock'n'roll. And while digital recording technology offered the opportunity to add clarity to old recordings (sprucing up muddy recordings by everyone from the Shangri-Las to Sonny Boy Williamson with no scratches, clicks or surface noise), it wasn't always suitable. Even the copying process felt impressively modern, clean and computer-friendly. As the studio computer turned the music into separate binary codes – 44,000 codes per second of sound! – you'd see the music in visual form, on a screen divided horizontally by bars (reflecting the frequency spectrum) with rising and falling levels following the bass, drums, guitar, singer, etc. If you watched this for long you'd begin to think you were living in some sort of perpetual Kraftwerk remix.

There are many records that defined the era, although not all of them stand up now (Tracy Chapman, anyone? Erasure? Foreigner?). It was the decade when David Bowie (trying to please his fans) made his worst records, when the Stones (trying to please themselves) made their worst records; when Terence Trent D'Arby's debut LP (*Introducing The Hardline According*

To...) spent eight weeks at number one, and the follow-up (*Neither Fish Nor Flesh*) died a designer death. Prince's 1987 opus *Sign Of The Times* was the best album of the Eighties (the Clash's much-lauded *London Calling* was actually released in 1979), a sexy smorgasbord of a record, the buffet at the porno-party of your dreams. It's all here: love, sex, religion, drugs, politics (sexual and otherwise), and a homemade sense of fun. It's a record that couldn't have been made in any other decade, layered as it is, with drum machines, samples, and modern studio wizardry. (It's the record studio maverick Todd Rundgren would have made if he'd been born ten years later and knew how to dance.) And while it has the trademark studio sheen of any record made in the Eighties, compositionally it is about as eclectic as it's possible to be and still retain a substantial fan base. Not only that, but he did everything himself: he wrote the songs, played most of the instruments himself, recorded and produced the record himself, and delivered the final product to the record company, who then distributed and marketed it.

Although he was American, Prince's entrepreneurial spirit was indicative of what was happening in Britain at the time. As society's safety net was swiftly reeled in and folded up, the pioneering spirit became the order of the day, and whether we went to work in banks or in nightclubs, going to work was what we tried to do. The Eighties was the decade of dressing up and looking busy. All over the country the post-punk generation were dressing up to get ahead. Britain's obsession with youth culture seemed to intensify during the last few months of the Seventies, and it was only natural that it would soon start to be reflected in the media. Up until that time our reading matter was principally American, and our perceived sense of style came from magazines such as *Interview, New York* or the now defunct *Punk*. We might take a lead from something in *New Musical Express*, or maybe *Tatler* or *Vogue*, but there was no magazine for us.

Until 1980, that is, when Nick Logan and Terry Jones started a small publishing revolution by launching, respectively, *The Face* and *i-D*. Logan, former editor of the phenomenally successful *NME* and creator of *Smash Hits*, and Jones, a former art director of British *Vogue*, both independently realised that style culture, or what was then simply known as 'street style', was being ignored by much of the mainstream press. So they launched their own magazines, not only to catalogue this new explosion of style, but also to cater for it. *i-D* and *The Face*, which were aimed at both men and women, reflected not only our increasing appetite for street style and fashion, but also for ancillary subjects such as movies, music, television, art and zeitgeisty things in general – everything that was deemed to have some sort of influence on the emerging culture. They soon became style bibles. Cutting-edge manuals of all that was deemed to be cool. Fashion, nightclubs, art, pop – if it clicked, it went in.

Pop music was vital in disseminating this new culture, and the emergence of the new pop groups such as Duran Duran, Frankie Goes To Hollywood, the Eurythmics, Spandau Ballet and Culture Club – who, in a move away from the punk ethos (more like a volte-face, actually), began spending their vast royalty cheques in the designer boutiques along Bond Street and the King's Road – gave rise to a new-found tabloid interest in anything to do with pop.

Suddenly the red-tops latched onto the idea that pop was fashionable again. The lives and loves of Boy George, and Simon Le Bon, Annie Lennox, Holly Johnson and the Kemp brothers became front-page news.[1] The pop stars believed their

---

[1] As pop became big business, the tabloids began to encourage readers to phone in with stories about celebrities. Had they seen one misbehaving? Had they grown up with one? Consequently, the features teams of the nationals became less averse to the telephonic ramblings of over-excited readers. One night at the *Daily Mirror*, one of the phones on the news desk rang. The night editor picks it up, only to find a loony on the other end.

'Hello, is that the *Daily Mirror*? It is? Oh good. I just wanted to let you know that I've invented a time machine,' said the loony.

own publicity, too, and many – particularly Duran Duran – began living the life of dilettantes and new-moneyed aristocrats, poncing about on boats and dating catwalk models. They had taken reinvention to its natural conclusion. Five years before their huge success, they had looked as though they were made of money even though their pockets were empty; now the good life was theirs for the taking. And they took it, each with both hands. Greed was good, after all, and credit so easy to come by, while dreams and wishes seemed so easily obtainable. In a way, success became democratised, and worlds that had once been available only to certain sets of people became accessible to, if not everyone, then at least anyone with enough luck and tenacity.

The pop world wasn't just fashionable, it was sexy, too, and the arrival of androgynous celebrities such as Boy George and Annie Lennox put a whole new spin on Swinging London (British pop was then such a potent export commodity that in 1983 more than a third of all American chart places were taken by British acts). Pop stars began hanging out with fashion designers and frequenting the many nightclubs that were springing up all over the capital; PR agencies were beginning to exploit this new-found confluence of art and commerce, and the high street began taking notice of all the new money.

Affluence played an enormous part in the designer lifestyle

'Aha, a time machine. I see …' said the night editor, with a heavy heart.

'Yes, it's a rather good time machine as it goes forward in time, backwards in time, and sideways in time. It really is the most amazing thing you've ever seen.'

'Well, that certainly does sound interesting. What would you like us to do about it? How about you bring it in to show us here at the paper?'

The loony can't believe his luck, and stammers for a while before answering, in a typically breathless fashion, 'Yes, absolutely. When would you like me to bring it in?'

Just a split second before he quietly replaces the receiver, the night editor says, 'Yesterday.'

boom of the early to mid-Eighties, creating a divisive culture in which the yuppie dream was allowed to thrive. If you were on the right side of the fence then the party went on all night.

In the mid-Eighties, when style journalism hit its first peak, hedonism was de rigueur. I joined *i-D* magazine in the early Eighties,[1] and I soon realised that my social life was as important to my employers as what I actually did in the office. In fact, I realised it was more important. It wasn't good enough to replicate the high points of Swinging London in the pages of the magazine, you actually had to live the life.

And live the life we did, in every nightclub and bar, at every ball and private view, 365 days a year. And usually for free (nobody paid for anything in those days). The mainstream media became so obsessed with the social habits of the five hundred or so 'designer butterflies' who constituted the London scene, that we were invited to everything. You went everywhere and you met everyone. These were the days when you'd bump into George Michael in the Wag Club dancing to his own records, or stand behind David Bowie in the queue for the gents' at the Mud Club.

I remember one particular party, in Harrods in 1985, where I was standing with a group of luminaries that included former Labour leader Neil Kinnock – slumming it for a bit of tabloid exposure – Duran Duran's Simon Le Bon, PR guru Lynne Franks, Boy George, fashion designers Jean Paul Gaultier and Katharine Hamnett, the American artist Julian Schnabel and

---

[1] The 'Dry-Clean Only' decade essentially gave me a career, and after leaving St Martins, my designer lifestyle got me a job working for the style press, and afforded me the opportunity to write about fashion and music with enthusiasm if not authority. I was hired at *i-D* by Terry Jones in 1983, becoming editor in 1985, when I was twenty-four. I stayed there for four years before moving across to *The Face* and *Arena*, which I edited for another four years, until 1992, before going off to work for the *Observer* and the *Sunday Times* as the Eighties put away its drum machine and succumbed to grunge, Britpop and ecstasy.

one of London's most notorious transsexual prostitutes. It was as if social boundaries had yet to be invented, as though social mobility was the birthright of anyone in a loud jacket and a pair of patent leather shoes.

Pop stars were everywhere, propping up the bars and piling into toilet cubicles. Walk into Club For Heroes, Heaven or the Wag Club and you'd see someone from Spandau Ballet or Duran Duran, Madonna, Shane McGowan, Depeche Mode, August Darnell, the Pet Shop Boys, Boy George, Kirk Brandon, Pete Townshend, George Michael and Andrew Ridgeley. (You went to Rio, Monte Carlo, New York, LA, Tokyo and Toronto, and they were all there too, propping up the bar and nodding as you walked in as though they were still drinking cocktails in Soho.) Wham! personified the new decade, a designer duo that exemplified controlled exuberance. Suburban boys with West End aspirations, they were high street through and through, appealing to twelve-year-old girls, estate agents and art students alike. They were also a welcome antidote to the hordes of shoe-gazers filling the pages of the music press. Who wanted to listen to some doleful Bolshevik ballad of oppression when you could be cutting a rug to 'Club Tropicana'?

I first saw them in July 1983 at the launch of their debut LP *Fantastic* (such confidence!), in a small suite of offices just behind Fulham Broadway tube station. While dozens of sneering music journalists and record-company bigwigs stood about working at being brilliant, these two nineteen-year-old soul boys, dressed in Hawaiian shirts, cutaway jeans and deck shoes, jived together on the dance floor, jitterbugging along to their own version of the Miracles' 'Love Machine'. Rarely had I seen two men enjoying themselves so much. To be dancing to one of their own records! At their own party! In front of other people!

After they became famous they still went out, and it was not unusual to see Andy on display at the Limelight or George down at Taboo. For about eighteen months 'Everything She Wants' (No. 2, December 1984) was the hippest record to be seen dancing to, and George could often be seen doing just that, right in front of the DJ booth. It was a common sight, yet still disconcerting, and while you might have shared a space at the bar and adjacent spots on the dance floor, there was George the next night, glistening with fame, on *Top of the Pops*. Even at 3 a.m. in the bowels of some sweaty West End nightclub (usually the Wag), dancing by himself to Phyllis Nelson's 'Move Closer', he looked as though he'd just stepped off the plane from Ibiza: tandoori tan, summer whites, designer stubble (something he invented) and perfect Princess Diana hair: 'Some days I made the covers of the tabloids. Some days Princess Di made the covers of the tabloids,' he said. 'Some days I think they just got us mixed up.'

For a while we even shared a tailor, Wham! and me. From his shop in Kentish Town, an ex-boxer called Chris Ruocco would knock up suits and stage costumes for the boys, and you'd occasionally see them trying on a new pair of trousers, their hot hatchbacks double-parked outside. I once went for a fitting only to find Chris surrounded by thirty custom-built tartan suits, in readiness for the boys' upcoming tour of China. Needless to say, it was the Black Watch for me that summer.

It's possible to illustrate the mercenary tendencies of the decade by the simple fact that they were spent going to shop openings; not 'happenings', not art events, and not always concerts. We collectively paid homage to consumerism. I went to thousands of parties in the Eighties in many parts of the world, but oddly the ones I remember most took place in shops – the openings of Tower Records in Piccadilly, the Next store in Kensington, the Katharine Hamnett store in Brompton Cross, the HMV store in Oxford Street, the relaunch of Harvey Nichols, the relaunch of Way-In at Harrods, the opening of everything everywhere. And the thing that all these parties had in common is the fact that at each and every one of them I saw famous people thieving – walking off with magnums of champagne, CDs, jackets, bottles of perfume, silver trays full of uneaten canapés, other people's girlfriends. Everything was free in the Eighties, even the things that weren't meant to be (especially the things that weren't meant to be).

During the Eighties the media went fashion crazy as London became a crucible of self-expression, the centre of anything and everything. Everyone wanted to buy into the dream, even pop stars. In 1986 I wrote a long and rather inflammatory piece in *i-D* about a silly Italian youth cult called the Paninari. In a style that now seems excited (actually, to be fair, it's a lot worse than that), I catalogued the Paninari obsession with casual sportswear, their predilection for riding little motorbikes through the streets of Milan and hanging out in sandwich bars (hence the name, a *panino* is a bread roll), and of course their reactionary pre-pubescent machismo. Acting on disinformation, I also wrote that the Pet Shop Boys – who were apparently big fans of Paninari fashion – had even recorded their own paean to the cult, called, simply enough, 'Paninaro'. As the song eventually appeared a few months later, I thought nothing of it. Until about three years later, that is, when I read an interview with the Pet Shop Boys in *Rolling Stone* magazine. They had read my piece: 'We read that we'd recorded this song,' said Pet Shop Boy Chris Lowe. 'Of course we hadn't but we thought it was such a good idea that we soon did.'

Style culture became the binding agent of all that was supposed to be cool. Catwalk models were no longer simply clothes-horses, they were rechristened supermodels. Fashion designers were no longer just considered gay iconoclasts or hatchet-faced prima donnas. They became solid-gold celebrities to be fawned over and profiled. Designers who had previously been demonised for their outrageous abuse of models and staff were now being sanitised for everyday consumption. Pop stars were no longer considered to be council-house Neanderthals, they were suddenly elevated to front-page sex symbols, whose every word was copied down, amplified and endlessly repeated in the gossip columns of the national press. It was a sartorial melting pot, a visual melange of crushed velvet miniskirts, high heels and lipstick. And that was just the men.

In previous periods of intense fashionability in London – namely in the Sixties, when class divisions in society first began breaking down – the consumer aspects were largely confined to the female market: trendy women's magazines, trendy women's shops, trendy female icons. But in the Eighties it was different, and if the decade can be remembered for anything, it should be remembered as the decade in which the post-industrial man finally became liberated. If women found their sexual liberation in the Sixties, men discovered their social mobility in the Eighties – as consumers.

The lifestyle explosion has reached saturation point. And as for street style, it doesn't really exist any more. Doc Martens are no longer the boots of the disenfranchised but are worn by everyone from seventeen-year-old-bricklayers to forty-five-year-old architects, from schoolgirls to ageing rock stars. Distressed leather jackets are just as likely to be found on the backs of advertising executives as they are on biker boys. People have done just about everything with their hair, with their clothes and with their bodies, piercing all the parts it is possible to skewer.

As the American performer and comedian Sandra Bernhard said, there is not much more people can do to themselves, 'unless they start wearing lumber'. Recycled nostalgia is now the thing, and in this post-modern age of arbitrary gesture and kitsch'n'sink subculture, urban tribes are ten a penny.

Everyone's a trendy now, everyone codified and hip to the modern world, while elitism is becoming increasingly fetishistic. Odd. Weird. Uncalled for. Why be wilfully different when you can consume with impunity? For those of us who have come through the Eighties unscathed, and successfully negotiated the perilous contours of the new face of consumerism and the free-market economy, life is good. Very, very good indeed. And now many of us are the people we pretended to be all those years ago.

As it happened, I didn't entirely survive the Eighties unscathed. I can still remember the music in my head as I was being stabbed. As the switchblade cut through my zoot suit into my back, blood pouring out of me onto my crisp white poplin shirt, ABC's 'Tears Are Not Enough' ricocheted inside my skull. By rights it should have been 'Poison Arrow', but then that would have been too ironic to be true. I've still got the scars to prove it, a two and a half inch cut just behind my ear, just above the nape, and a six-inch gash that crosses my spine, a scar that seems to get bigger and more burgundy with each passing year.

As a boy I'd always wanted a little Action Man scar, a straight one-inch cut lying diagonally across the cheek. Nothing scary or particularly disfiguring, just a small battle scar, something to indicate I'd been around.

Later, I considered a tattoo, but realised that self-inflicted scars didn't carry the same cachet. By the time I was twenty, I didn't want either.

Then, suddenly, I didn't have any choice.

It happened towards the end of 1981, on a cold November Saturday night (everything seemed to happen on a Saturday night back then) in a London dead zone. There was Pascal, Corinne, Jill and Stella, plus some other girls whose names I forget.

It was around 11.30 p.m., chucking-out time. We'd just come out of a pub in a run-down part of Islington, and were on our way to a party down the road. All night the jukebox had been playing ABC – well, all night we'd been playing ABC on the jukebox. We alternated between 'Tears …' and Elvis Costello and Pigbag, but it was ABC who we were all not-so-quietly obsessed with. They were modern, they had soul, they under-stood ironic fashion. How could a gang of smarty-pants art students not like them? Also, they were not yet famous, so they were p-e-r-f-e-c-t.

1981 was a vintage year for pop, a year when the confluence

of radical disco, post punk and white funk produced the likes of Was Not Was, the Human League, Kid Creole and the Tom Tom Club, and when every good new record seemed directed at the same mythical dancefloor. But while the year was best italicised by Grace Jones's *Nightclubbing*, ABC evinced the perfect mix of celebration and irony. A few months later we'd be charmed by the delights of 'The Look Of Love' and 'All Of My Heart', but for now we were content to career around King's Cross singing 'Tears Are Not Enough.'

I've no idea whose party it was we were en route to – no one ever knew in those days; you just pitched up and clocked in, a six-pack of something or other swinging in a plastic carrier bag.

As we strode along, five girls and two boys, searching for street numbers, seven or eight lads in their late teens came towards us, shuffling along the pavement. They were wearing tracksuits and floppy fringes: soft shapes disguising hard fists, hearts and minds.

When they got parallel, one of them punched Pascal hard and full in the side of the face. I turned around and started running towards him as the girls stood in fright. But before I'd taken two paces I was kicked from behind and fell on to the road. Someone jumped on my back.

I was too drunk to be scared, and the adrenalin was pumping so much that I didn't much care what was going on. I knew the situation was dangerous, but the only logical thing to do seemed to be to punch and kick as hard and as often as I could.

But then I felt something sharp and wet in the back of my neck, swiftly followed by something similar in the middle of my back. I was being cut – slashed, stabbed, call it what you like – with what felt like a cut-throat razor (having never been stabbed before I wasn't sure about this – but I soon found out). I didn't feel pain, as such, just shock. And my mind raced as the actual attack seemed to unravel in slow motion.

'Tears ... are souvenirs ... tears are not enough ...'

I responded immediately, jumped up, threw the tracksuited

troll off my back and sprinted fifty yards down the road, following the girls, only turning round to make sure he wasn't following, As I turned, I saw the razor dangling in his hand. He stood and stared at me, legs spread, chest pounding. Seconds later I was running towards King's Cross with Pascal and the others, the pumping blood in my head blocking out the ricocheting plastic soul of ABC.

We ran for what seemed like ages, and then stopped. There was a fuss, of course, because no one knew if I was badly cut. I still couldn't feel much, and I didn't think I was in serious danger, but as I couldn't see the wounds, I began to worry.

Hell, Hunter S. Thompson said it plain enough: 'It is one thing to get punched in the nose, and quite another to have your eyeball strung or your teeth shattered with a wrench.' Violence takes a great leap when it involves daggers, knives, barstools, or wrenches.

I haven't had my eyeball sprung (Thompson was summarising the violent outbursts of Californian Hell's Angels, circa 1966: 'You don't really jerk out the eyeball,' one explained, 'you just sort of spring it so it pops outta the socket. It hurts so much that most guys just faint'). I haven't had my teeth shattered with a wrench (though like most of us, I've met some particularly sadistic dentists). For me, being stabbed was enough.

I was inspected: I had been slashed on the back of the head and along my spine. Neither cut was deep, though the one in my back was bloody and long enough (six inches) to cause alarm. We eventually made it to the party, where I was inspected some more (it didn't seem so bad with half a dozen girls staring at my half-naked torso in a small kitchen), and where it was decided that I should be taken to hospital.

Although the stabbing had sobered me up somewhat, I was still drunk enough to be cavalier about the whole thing. I was wearing a brand new silver-grey zoot suit, and made a big deal of the fact that it was ruined, and how it had cost me over £100 and so on. Zoot-suited drama queen? Me?

And so we went to hospital. Pascal with his bruise, the girls with a Waitrose bag of Holsten Pils, and me with my torn suit, wounded ego and bleeding back.

As I sobered up in Casualty, it soon sunk in how potentially serious the situation had been. I should have been scared; if I had been sober I would have been petrified, and would have been worried if I hadn't been.

I can't remember whether or not I gave the police a statement; I probably did, but none of us was under the impression that anyone would ever be caught, let alone prosecuted. I do remember getting a tetanus jab in the backside (which was infinitely more painful than anything else that night), and over a dozen stitches. Waiting to be discharged. I tried getting drunk again, but by now my heart really wasn't in it.

When I thought about the attackers, it was in the abstract – I didn't know them, couldn't even remember what they looked like. They were out for blood, and ours just happened to be in the vicinity. The attack was territorial, and was in many ways predictable: we were walking through the wrong part of town at the wrong time wearing the wrong clothes. Shit, as they say, happens.

I made a point of going out the following night, knowing that I was unlikely to get stabbed again, or, come to that, have my eyeball sprung, or my teeth shattered with a wrench. Thankfully, I was right, though Islington, it must be said, remains one of my least favourite parts of London.

And as for ABC, whenever I hear the synthesized strings, over-produced drums and plaintive, heartbreaking lyrics of 'Tears Are Not Enough', 'Poison Arrow' or 'The Look Of Love', I think of running down a King's Cross backstreet in a silver suit, with blood pouring from my back.[1]

Now that's what I call a metaphor.

---

[1] Rather predictably, ABC's follow-up album was called *The Beauty Stab*.

10 The Virtual Megastore: Apple launches iTunes

How Steve Jobs resuscitated the music industry

January 2001 was a big month for Steve Jobs. It was exactly a year since his keynote address at the Macworld Expo, the big comeback speech, the speech where Jobs finally drew a line in the cybersand. 'I'm pleased to announce today that I'm dropping the "interim" title,' he somewhat flippantly stated, thus earning a standing ovation and confirming what many in the room had long thought: that since coming back to the company in 1997 Jobs would find it impossible to allow himself to leave again. After all, he had a job to do. Since the initial success of the iMac, the launch of the Power Mac G4 Cube had been greeted with a disinterested shrug by the industry, while Apple stock was taking a slow dive, along with most other companies associated with the dot.com bubble.

So the 2001 Macworld Expo was an important anniversary for Jobs, especially as he would be addressing his home crowd in San Francisco. It started well, however: not only did he unveil the super-cool titanium-clad PowerBook G4 as well as the Mac OS X operating system, he also announced the release – finally – of iTunes 1.0. At last, music software! Could this help the company move up through the gears? After twenty-five years, could music really be the answer to Apple's problems?

Ever since Jobs' return, Apple's 'big idea' had been the iMac.

But by the summer of 2000, just two years since the machine's debut, the company had sold 500,000 fewer iMacs than originally planned. The wine-gum-coloured PCs were fast losing their novelty, although not for the reason many supposed (which was that the market was apparently saturated). No, the problem was that Steve Jobs, a man not overly impressed by the dot.com craze, had missed one of the defining trends of the Internet generation: downloading. Many new computers had CD-RW ('read-write') drives that allowed users to burn CDs from the stuff they'd downloaded over the net, or fed in through their slot loaders. This was known in the trade as a 'killer application', and was one Jobs had successfully ignored. By the end of 2000, over 40 per cent of PCs had this function. But not one of them was built by Apple. Dell, yes; Hewlett-Packard, yes; even Compaq; but not the most innovative PC manufacturer of the age. As journalist and Apple critic Alan Deutschman said at the time, 'Nearly thirty million PCs with CD-RW drives were sold in the year 2000, and none of them carried the Apple logo. It was ironic that Apple slapped the letter *i* next to the Mac to imply that it was an Internet computer, when in reality Steve utterly ignored one of the Internet's hottest trends. Steve relied on his own instincts, but this was beyond his experience. Teenagers steal expensive things; billionaires don't have to.' iTunes 1.0 was a step in the right direction, as was the belated move of equipping Macs with CD-RW drives capable of burning audio discs, and updating Mac OS X to support this. But these steps merely put the Mac on equal footing with everyone else.

What could Jobs do to leapfrog his competitors? More importantly, did he realise he needed to?

Years ago, when I first began to experiment online, I found myself spending a small fortune on rare first editions from small independent booksellers in the wilds of Utah and Arizona. Having been a keen – some would say obsessive – collector of the works of Tom Wolfe since I was about thirteen, and having spent nearly thirty years pursuing his rarities through dealers and book-searchers, the Internet made it possible for me to buy rare editions of his books at a fraction of what they usually cost. And, predictably, I got the bug (which is an addiction, as opposed to the computer bug, which was so-called after a moth got trapped in one of the first mainframes). Soon, I was going online every afternoon, buying anything and everything I could get my fingers on – CDs I'd never find the time to play, books I'd owned and, having found them again, felt it would be churlish not to own again; videos and DVDs of impossible-to-get Japanese arthouse movies (porn); old magazines (lots of them); cushions; desk-tidies; the whole kit and caboodle.

I managed to find a copy of the first 'grown-up' book I ever read (*Redcap*), the 1000-piece jigsaw of Alan Aldridge's famous Beatles poster, half a dozen rare Beach Boys CDs, the lot. (In my wallet I carry an A4 piece of photocopy paper, folded in eight. It contains a list of records and CDs I'm looking for, and usually has about a hundred or so things on it. I've been keeping the list for about fifteen years, adding and deleting as I work my way through it. Some things I buy if I find them and they're cheap enough, some I just look at in record shops knowing they'll still be there when I really want them, and some things I know I'll never find. I went through a period a few years ago of replacing some of the punk singles I'd either lost or sold, and was buying them at such a rate that I had to keep a list on the sheet of everything I had, as I was starting to buy duplicates. It was such a long list, everything was typed in 9-point.[1]

---

[1] A few examples: the soundtracks to *Tenue de Soire*, *The Family Way*, *The Wrong Arm Of The Law*, *Butterflies Are Free*, *A Patch of Blue* and *Boom*, Fontella Bass's 'Our Day Will Come', a Nick Lowe boxed set, Apples In Stereo's *The Discovery of a World*, Pat Travers's *Don't Feed The Alligators* (for his version of Steely Dan's 'Black Friday'), Terry Randazzo's 'Going Out Of My Head', PFM's 'Celebration', Marlena Shaw's 'California Soul' (used in a KFC ad, bizarrely), Dory Previn's 'Coldwater Canyon', etc. One of the records I think I probably won't find is the one I want more than

And then two things happened: firstly, I started to spend more on things from the Internet than I was on my own family; and secondly, I got burned (or at least Barclaycard did). After the credit card company took my word for it – immediately, I'm happy to say – that I hadn't bought six internal flights in Belgium (are there six places worth visiting in Belgium?) or sixty-five secondhand luminescent phallic table lamps from a not entirely reputable wholesaler in Hamburg (why would anyone, etc.), I stopped buying online.

But then, something *else* happened. Something far, far more important. In a move that may well be remembered as a crucial turning point in the history of recorded music as well as the history of Apple, on 28 April 2003 Steve Jobs launched the iTunes Music Store, a revolutionary online venture that let customers quickly find, purchase, and then download music for 99 cents per song. And I wanted in. Other competitive online music services had been trying to 'suck coin' out of the MP3 music craze but had failed to gain widespread popularity because they required paying subscription fees, had incredibly unsophisticated user interfaces, were restrictive about what you could do with your downloads, and offered only a small number of songs (oh, and in most cases, were totally illegal). With its

---

any other. I can't remember why I bought it – I'd probably heard it on the radio – where I bought it, when I got rid of it, or indeed why. It wasn't a record I told my friends about, not a record I knew anything about, really (what was I, the mad boy in the attic, doing buying a single like this?). I can't have heard it since 1974 or '75, and obviously there's a slight worry that if I ever did, it wouldn't live up to expectations, but then that's to be expected. I can't even remember much about the record, only that the verse – I think – was one of the most haunting, nostalgic things I'd ever heard. It has a sort of staccato, plonky piano and deadpan, slightly off-kilter vocals, and I'm fairly sure I was let down at some point, possibly by the chorus. What is it? It was released in 1974, I think, on the old green Warner Brothers label: 'Girl On A Beach' by Spike Milligan. It wasn't a hit – at the time Milligan couldn't have hit a barn door with a banjo – I've never heard it on the radio since, and generally speaking it appears to have vanished.

seamless integration into iTunes 4.0 (Jobs had been updating like crazy), Apple's service was easy to use, and once you bought a 128 kbps AAC-encoded song, you were free to do almost anything you wanted with it: burn it to a CD, transfer it to your iPod or listen to it on a Mac. Since Apple was able to obtain the cooperation of 'The Big Five' music companies – BMG, EMI, Sony Music Entertainment, Universal and Warner – the iTunes Music Store featured over 200,000 songs at its introduction, all of which could be previewed at the. click of a button. Even though it was initially only accessible to Mac users, after just three months 'on air', iTunes had sold over six million songs. And by the end of October, the number of songs available had doubled; not only that, but the Windows version was released, causing sales of e-songs to surge. After paying royalties and transaction fees, Apple earned only pennies per song, so it was easy to believe that the real motivation for creating the iTunes Music Store had been to sell more iPods, which carry significantly higher gross profit margins. 'The iPod makes money. The iTunes Music Store doesn't,' admitted Apple senior VP Philip Schiller. But even though Apple's strategy of using digital music as a Trojan horse to sell iPods was clearly working – it had sold over 1.5 million units in less than three years – in the process Steve Jobs had initiated one of the most important changes in the music business since the dawn of pop. He had legitimised downloading culture.

The record industry was changed for ever in 1998, when Shawn Fanning, a teenage computer student from Massachusetts, launched a file-sharing network called Napster (his nickname). He was encouraged to start the site by his roommate, who complained incessantly about the slow-links and out-of-date music available on the Internet. Fanning's genius software allowed anyone with an Internet-connected computer to share MP3 files; he initially gave a test version to thirty of his friends and asked them to pass it on. Which they did, with impunity. By May the following year, encouraged and enlivened by the enormous response, Napster had over $2m of capital.

Six months later the US music industry's regulatory body, the RIAA (Recording Industry Association of America) sued the company for copyright infringement, alleging that 'Napster has created, and is operating, a haven for music piracy on an unprecedented scale ... a giant online pirate bazaar.' In June 2000 the RIAA got a temporary injunction to shut Napster down, although the court of appeal overturned the decision. Unsurprisingly, Fanning became something of a cult hero, and membership of the site shot through the roof, although it was finally closed down in July 2001, succumbing to the enormous legal onslaught. Then, in November 2003, after nearly two years in stasis, Napster was relaunched as a legal subscription service.

Of course, Napster wasn't the only company offering music online, and during the early Nineties there were hundreds of sites where you could find everything from old Pearl Jam tracks to Bob Dylan bootlegs – KaZaA, SoulSeek, Limewire, Gnutella, Morpheus, WinMX, dozens and dozens of the damn things. But not only did the recording industry begin clamping down on illegal users and lobbying for prosecution, artists got involved too: Metallica famously came out in favour of the record companies, and Madonna even made an MP3 of herself singing 'What the fuck do you think you're doing?', disguised it as a track on her new album and set it loose on the P2P world. Unsurprisingly, there were just as many artists who thought the industry was being too uptight about the whole thing. 'Imagine if book publishers decided they were against public libraries: Oh no, we don't like this because people can read books without paying for them and it's killing our sales,' said the Talking Heads' David Byrne. 'It's just not true. They might lose a tiny percentage, but they actually gain a lot more. When I was a kid you could check out LPs from the library, and that was file-sharing. I discovered all kinds of experimental classic music and electronic music I never would have stumbled on if I had to go out and buy it because you couldn't buy it in Baltimore. The local stores didn't have those records.'

Steve Jobs was bemused by the music industry's reluctance to satisfy the demand for Internet downloading that Napster had unleashed. After battering Napster to near-death in court, record companies had promised to launch paid services with the same limitless selection and ease of use. But they didn't, instead doing the polar opposite. Universal and Sony rolled out a joint venture called Pressplay. And AOL Time Warner (as it was, briefly, back then), Bertelsmann, EMI and RealNetworks, launched MusicNet. But instead of joining forces to attract customers, they competed to try and control the digital market, and refused to license songs to each other. Consequently neither service had enough songs to attract paying customers. Scared that downloading might cannibalise CD sales, these sites were subscription only, and – could you believe it? – not only could you only download MusicNet tunes onto only one computer, they disappeared if you didn't pay your bill. 'It was strictly the greed and arrogance of the majors that screwed things up,' said Irving Azoff, manager of the Eagles and Christina Aguilera. 'They wanted to control every step of the distribution process.' Both companies eventually improved their services, but neither was as imaginative or as simple as iTunes, one of Jobs' very finest epiphanies.

Jobs didn't set out to be the music industry's saviour, didn't intend to be its white knight, yet once he focused on music, he was consumed by it. How could it fail? He had the technology – he had the hardware, the software, and the distribution network – all he needed now was the content. And the world was full of content providers, full of them! Why couldn't it work? After all, as André Breton said, the man who can't visualise a horse galloping on a tomato is an idiot.

But when Jobs first approached record companies with a view to them getting on-board with iTunes, a lot of them were seriously sceptical.

'There's a lot of smart people at the music companies,' said Jobs. 'The problem is, they're not technology people. The good music companies do an amazing thing. They have people who can pick the person that's gonna be successful out of five thousand candidates. And there's not enough information to do that – it's an intuitive process. And the best music companies know how to do that with a reasonably high success rate.

'I think that's a good thing. The world needs more smart editorial these days. The problem is, that has nothing to do with technology. And so when the Internet came along, and Napster came along, they didn't know what to make of it. A lot of these folks didn't use computers – weren't on e-mail, didn't really know what Napster was for a few years. They were pretty doggone slow to react. Matter of fact, they still haven't, in many ways. And so they're fairly vulnerable to people telling them technical solutions will work, when they won't.

'When we first went to talk to these companies ... we said, none of this technology that you're talking about's gonna work. We have Ph.Ds here that know the stuff cold, and we don't believe it's possible to protect digital content. It only takes one stolen copy to be on the Internet. And the way we expressed it to them is: pick one lock – open every door. It only takes one person to pick a lock. Worst case: somebody just takes the analog outputs of their CD player and rerecords it – puts it on the Internet. You'll never stop that.

'At first they kicked us out. But we kept going back again and again. The first record company to really understand this stuff was Warner. They have some smart people there, and they said: we agree with you. And next was Universal. Then we started making headway. And the reason we did, I think, is because we made predictions.

'We said these [music subscriptions] services that are out there now are going to fail. MusicNet's gonna fail, Pressplay's gonna fail. Here's why: people don't want to buy their music as a subscription. They bought 45s, then they bought LPs, then they bought cassettes, then they bought 8-tracks, then they bought CDs. They're going to want to buy downloads. People want to own their music. You don't want to rent your music – and then, one day, if you stop paying, all your music goes away.

'Nobody ever went out and asked users, "Would you like to keep paying us every month for music that you thought you already bought?" The record companies got this crazy idea from some finance person looking at AOL, and then rubbing his hands together and saying, "I'd sure like to get some of that recurring subscription revenue."'

Even though Jobs was able to convince the Universals and the Warners of this world that iTunes was something to be embraced, they were not able to deliver all of their biggest artists, and so Jobs had to go to individual artists, one by one, and convince them to trust him. But he did it eventually, and succeeded in persuading the major record labels to stop fixating on their subscription models and take a radically different approach to selling music. iTunes not only commercialised online music sales, it clearly defined the previously hazy definition of what was legal and what wasn't. In 2003, the RIAA sued more than five thousand filesharers, and their tactics clearly worked: the number of people illegally downloading music files in the US plummeted from twenty million in May 2003 to eleven million four months later. During 2004, the BPI, RIAA's UK counterpart, initiated a clampdown on illegal downloading that had an immediate effect on filesharing. There was also a drop in the number of people using peer-to-peer sites such as WinMx and KaZaA, and a rise in the number of people using the legal download sites, iTunes and Napster included. In January 2004 there were only 15,000 legal downloads a week in the UK; by September this was up to 160,000. And while Internet piracy was still rampant, as was CD piracy, the number of music files freely available online fell in 2004 to about 800m from about 1.1 billion in 2003. By January 2005, over 6 per cent of industry revenues were coming from legal downloads.

'It's kind of extraordinary that it wasn't a music company that cracked the problem of piracy,' said Bono, adding that he thought it strange that music industry executives still refer to themselves as record industry executives when they 'don't even make records anymore'.

There is no clear idea yet of what a successful business model for online music sales will look like. The problem for record companies continues to be that more people are buying single tracks rather than whole albums. And because those companies make more money when people spend, say, $12 on a single artist rather than $2 on six different ones, either the quality of albums will be improved (there is too much filler on CDs these days, even ones by major artists – especially ones by major artists), or the album as we know it will die. Because the majors were slow to embrace downloading, treating it as their nemesis rather than an opportunity, sales of recorded music shrank by a fifth between 1999 and 2003.

Perhaps the whole process of making music will spin off into other areas completely. John Peel's last discovery before he died was a band called Steveless, who went through a period of releasing an album every week (they're called Steveless, by the way, because there's no one in the band called Steve).

When the record industry first discovered Napster, it was tantamount to discovering that your wife was sleeping around – with every man on Earth who happened to own a computer. But since the success of iTunes, the potential of downloading became suddenly apparent. No longer would we walk into record shops, flick through the sleeves in the aisles and make our selection; we would simply go on-line, browse, and then download like stink. And for the first time in two generations, the album was actually under threat as the primary means by which artists communicate with their audience.

Net-tune competitors pop up hourly, but with iTunes'

Windows rollout, Apple has 70 per cent of the US download market and four million songs sold worldwide a week. Even if some of that inevitably gets siphoned off, no one's likely to invent a product with more credibility than iTunes in Steve Jobs' (or Bill Gates') lifetime.

'Apple's in a pretty interesting position,' says Jobs. 'Because, as you know, almost every song and CD is made on a Mac – it's recorded on a Mac, it's mixed on a Mac, the artwork's done on a Mac. Almost every artist I've met has an iPod, and most of the music execs now have iPods. And one of the reasons Apple was able to do what we did was because we are perceived by the music industry as the most creative technology company.'

11 iPod a Spell on You

What *are* the best records ever made?

It's 1.30 in the morning and I've been at it for five hours. Having rushed home from work, I have been locked in the downstairs den since 8.30 p.m., gradually, methodically, pedantically working my way through my CD collection, uploading the chosen few onto iTunes, moving them into playlists as I go. For the past few days I've been working on *Ibiza*, which is basically all sorts of dance music, from 1960s soul to twenty-first century ready-mades; and *Sunland*, which is one I made for my wife to be played on the Altec Lansing portable speakers at the weekends: a fusion of West Coast early-1970s singer songwriters (Jackson Brown, David Wiffen, Jimmy Webb, Dory Previn); loungecore classics ('Girl In A Sportscar' by Alan Hawkshaw, 'Follow Your Bliss' by the B-52s and 'The Nearest Faraway Place' by the Beach Boys); lightweight supper jazz in the form of Grover Washington (a man I still think sounds like a hotel), Bobbi Humphries, Michael Franks, etc.; power pop; show tunes; ironic highway pop as produced by Phoenix, Air and Corduroy; plus the odd bit of sunny-side-up Van Morrison and Coldplay. (Oh, and currently my three favourite records: 'Everyone I Meet Is From California' by America, 'It Never Rains In Southern California' by Albert Hammond and '99 Miles From LA' by Art Garfunkel). There are 218 songs on this playlist and because of the Live Updating facility there will soon be many more. And so it goes on, ad nauseam, which is the point of the Pod.

I've just got into Smart Playlists, too. The joy of Smart

Playlists belies their ease of configuration. Just piece together a variety of criteria – artist, genre, rating, last played, etc. – and demand that iTunes create playlists based on songs that meet those conditions. So, for example, you might want a Smart Playlist that includes only reggae songs you've never played, all uploaded on the AIFF format and all lasting more than seven minutes (unlikely, I know, but you get my drift). Alternatively, you could configure the top row of your pop-up menus to read *Play Count is 0*, and enable the Live Updating option. Select this playlist on your iPod and you'll only hear songs you've never played before. I got one Prog-Rock tip from one of the many iPod-related magazines that began to swamp the market in 2004. This suggested I configure the top row of a pop-up menu to read *Time is greater than 15 minutes*. I was told to click the + button, and configure the next row to read *Genre is Rock*, and then to click the + button once again and configure this row to read Year is in the Range 1971 to 1979. And to guard against the collection degenerating into a Self-Indulgent Noodling Guitar/Bass/Drum Solo from Hell playlist, I was told to add the following: *Artist is not Grateful Dead*.

Tonight my plan is simple: I'm trying to create a playlist of the coolest records ever made. Not the best, but the coolest. Not the ones that make the critics cake the front of their pants, but the ones that look good lying around the house, the ones that look good piled up on the Habitat Daft Punk coffee table or the SCP glass shark ... the ones to impress your friends with. Personally speaking this is a lot more difficult than it would have been twenty or thirty years ago, when notions of hip were far more prosaic; then there was only a certain number of trendy people in the world but these days everybody's a trendy of one sort or another, and most people feel confident enough to offer an opinion on the subject.

Back in 1972, when I was eleven, I thought I was the only one who felt different, the only one who was obsessed with pop stars and what they wore, what they said ... what they didn't say. Sitting in French class, as odd-sounding adverbs swirled around my head, falling on deaf ears, my mind was full of David Bowie's hair, its colour, shape, construction. How did he get it that way? What made him think of it? I knew he had this whole space-age glitter thing going on, but honestly, he was so far removed from my life that he may as well have *been* from Mars. Perhaps all would be revealed when I borrowed Bruce's copy of *The Man Who Sold The World* on Friday. What I didn't know was that nearly 5 per cent of my generation felt exactly the same way ... but we were still in the minority.

I've bought some sort of recorded music every week for the last three decades, a third-year binge of glam rock, punk rock, disco and rap. Music has informed every part of my life since before I became a teenager, a life that has included, at various points, the Beatles, David Bowie, the Clash, Chic, Oasis, U2 and ten thousand more.

For three decades my life has been a world full of disparate pop stars and their disparate records. Some have changed the way I think, some have changed the way I act, and some of them have just been there when I've come home from work in the evening.

In its own way, every record I've bought since the age of eleven has informed my life, however randomly. And then suddenly, when I wasn't looking, Steve Jobs comes along and helps me put it all in one place.

What on earth was I going to do now?

The iPod has changed my life. The iPod has given me back the ability to obsess over records in the way I did when I was a teenager. But even though my obsession has been rekindled, I consume music in a totally different way than I did five, ten, thirty years ago – we all do. We now consume it laterally, and are just as likely to buy a Bob Dylan compilation or a repackaged Oasis album as we are the new CD from Kelis or Babyshambles. We also live in a world that defines itself by anniversaries, and modern pop has to fight for attention/publicity/airplay/ marketing budgets with the twenty-fifth anniversary re-release of The Clash's *London Calling*, the thirtieth anniversary re-release of *The Dark Side Of The Moon* or the tenth anniversary re-release of Oasis's *(What's The Story) Morning Glory*.

This has all been exacerbated by on-line music sales and the legalisation and legitimisation of buying music over the Internet. Instead of taking a lunch break, we can now sit behind our desks and download to our laptops to our heart's content. We can click onto iTunes and rip the new Rufus Wainwright album, a sampler from the new REM CD that you can't buy or hear anywhere else, or a Razorlight tune that has been specially commissioned by Apple and will only be available on-line. Alternatively, you could simply download *Never Mind The Bollocks, Here's The Sex Pistols* and be done with it.

These days, anything goes.

Taste, if we're being honest about it, is determined largely by cost and space. I can't afford a good original Warhol and my house only has enough room for one of those big Conran Shop sofas, the ones that make you feel like The Incredible Shrinking Man, they're so huge.

It used to be the same with music.

When I bought the Beatles' double *Blue Album* in 1973 (why was I spending over four pounds on a record, my mother demanded to know? What a terrible, unforgivable waste of money – four pounds, on a damn record, your father will be furious!), the first Beatles record I'd ever bought (although I seem to recall my parents had a few singles, 'Hey Jude' included), the track listing was the prism through which I appreciated them. Was 'Ob-La-Di, Ob-La-Da' really the crowning glory of the *White Album*? If I was told it was, then obviously I believed that. The *Blue Album* couldn't possibly house every classic Beatles song, so I got what they could fit onto four sides of vinyl, which was roughly eighty minutes of gear. When the Beatles's *1* appeared thirty years later, the criteria for inclusion was proscriptive, being singles that had actually got to number one (basically every single the band ever released), but with the *Blue Album* it was arbitrary in the extreme.

Which is kind of mad, isn't it? Even when I compiled cassette tapes in my teens, the maximum I could record was two hours (whether I was taping the Top 40 on a Sunday or a friend's James Brown collection), which, when you're talking about the Beatles, barely makes a dent in their oeuvre. I could take the good bits from *Abbey Road* ('You Never Give Me Your Money', the best Beatles song of them all), all of side two of *A Hard Day's Night* and the highlights from *Rubber Soul* and *Revolver* (there would have been nothing from *Sergeant Pepper*, which I still think is their worst album by some distance, a sort of psychedelic music-hall knees up), but not much else.

These days everything's available all the time, and we're surrounded by the past every minute of every day, hence the preponderance of lists like this.

So what are the coolest records in the world? Most lists of The Greatest Albums Ever Made are, by their very nature, repetitive, and invariably include the same old – and I stress 'old' – records. To wit: *Revolver, Astral Weeks, OK Computer, (What's The Story) Morning Glory?, Pet Sounds,*[1] *Blood On The Tracks, Let It Be* (the cake on the cover of which was baked, incidentally, by Delia Smith), *Automatic For The People, Sign*

---

[1] Although *Pet Sounds* obviously is one of the greatest records ever made – one of the greatest records that will ever be made – liking it doesn't make you particularly special (most people think it's pretty extraordinary). When I first heard it, at sixteen, the thing that shocked me wasn't the sophisticated arrangements, the minor key ballads or the Bacharach-like tunes, it was the unabashed honesty of the lyrics, expressing feelings that men just didn't admit to each other. When I first heard it, I was almost embarrassed by it. But of course, in the space of about three listens, I loved it. Which is more than this disgruntled customer did – the following was posted on Amazon.com: 'This is not the Beach Boys. It can't be. Why? No beach songs! I thought it was some kind of joke. All this offers is the opportunity to hear Brian Wilson whine for forty minutes, backed by elevator music.'

Of The Times, Led Zeppelin IV,[1] *Dark Side Of The Moon, The Queen Is Dead, Achtung Baby, London Calling, Nevermind* ... the list doesn't so much go on and on as go round in circles.

Whether the lists are compiled by the public or by critics, it's always a case of the usual suspects. These lists are as reliable as Volvos. Occasionally, the odd anomaly will creep in, purely due to current popularity (in one of these lists in *Q* in February 1998, their readers – in their finite wisdom – voted Ocean Colour Scene's *Moseley Shoals* as *the thirty-third greatest album ever made*, which is tantamount to claiming that T. Rex's 'I Love To Boogie' is the thirty-third greatest single of all time: objectivity doesn't come into it, as it simply isn't true).

Similarly, in 1987, when *Rolling Stone* marshalled together 'The 100 Best Albums Of The Last Twenty Five Years', in at No. 54 – with a bullet! – was Graham Parker's *Howlin' Wind*, a C+ record at the best of times, by a man who sits in the shadow of Bruce Springsteen the way the UK Subs sit in the shadow of the Clash. Bizarre. In the same magazine two years later, in a critics' poll of 'The 100 Greatest Albums Of The 80s', guess what was ranked No. 19? That's right, Lou Reed's *New York*, not just one of the worst records of his career, one of the worst records of anyone's career. Fifteen or twenty years ago there was still a large number of people – with IQs similar to that of broccoli, obviously – who thought of Lou Reed as a maverick, a cool, urban visionary ... whereas now we just think of him as, in the words of *GQ*'s Music Editor, Alexis Petridis, a 'grumpy old twat'.

These lists emphasise the transient and ephemeral nature of taste, and records which the country held to its collective bosom five years ago can, with the greatest of ease, be cast away like a cardboard coffee cup from Starbucks. If I want to recall what

---

[1] The album's cornerstone, the irritatingly ubiquitous 'Stairway To Heaven', was recorded partly as a response to George Harrison's comment that Zeppelin never did ballads. Jimmy Page even included a few bars of the Beatles' 'Something' in the finished track.

my life was like before the advent of punk, all I really need to do is look at John Peel's Festive 50 of 1976,[1] which was not only a fair representation of what his listeners (Me! You!) liked, it was a pretty fair representation of what we all liked. The counter-culture was easily defined in those days, even if, at the time, we thought it was nigh invisible to other people. John Peel's death in 2004 affected me in much the same way it affected anyone who had had cause to listen to his Radio 1 programme in the last thirty-odd years, causing me to look back at my own life and remember the particular records that

---

[1] 1. 'Stairway To Heaven' by Led Zeppelin. 2. 'Layla' by Derek & the Dominoes. 3. 'Desolation Row' by Bob Dylan. 4. 'Echoes' by Pink Floyd. 5. 'All Along The Watchtower' by Jimi Hendrix. 6. 'All Right Now' by Free. 7. 'They Shoot Horses Don't They?' by Racing Cars. 8. 'Shine On You Crazy Diamond' by Pink Floyd. 9. 'A Day In The Life' by the Beatles. 10. 'Like A Rolling Stone' by Bob Dylan. 11. 'Rose Of Cimarron' by Poco. 12. 'Cortez The Killer' by Neil Young. 13. 'Brown Sugar' by the Rolling Stones. 14. 'Hey Jude' by the Beatles. 15. 'Paralysed' by the Legendary Stardust Cowboy. 16. 'Voodoo Chile' by Jimi Hendrix. 17. 'Strawberry Fields Forever' by the Beatles. 18. 'Big Eyed Beans From Venus' by Captain Beefheart. 19. 'Whole Lotta Love' by Led Zeppelin. 20. 'Freebird' by Lynyrd Skynyrd. 21. 'Madame George' by Van Morrison. 22. 'Riders On The Storm' by the Doors. 23. 'Visions Of Johanna' by Bob Dylan. 24. 'White Rabbit' by Jefferson Airplane. 25. 'Child In Time' by Deep Purple. 26. 'Long Distance Love' by Little Feat. 27. 'Pickin' The Blues' by Grinderswitch. 28. 'Rocky Mountain Way' by Joe Walsh. 29. 'Won't Get Fooled Again' by the Who. 30. 'I Can Take You To The Sun' by the Misunderstood. 31. 'Supper's Ready' by Genesis. 32. 'No Woman, No Cry' by Bob Marley & the Wailers. 33. 'Roadrunner' by Jonathan Richman. 34. 'Maggie May' by Rod Stewart. 35. 'Late For The Sky' by Jackson Browne. 36. 'Kashmir' by Led Zeppelin. 37. 'Hey Joe' by Jimi Hendrix. 38. 'Jessica' by the Allman Brothers Band. 39. 'Jumping Jack Flash' by the Rolling Stones. 40. 'Dark Star' by the Grateful Dead. 41. 'I Wanna See The Bright Lights' by Richard Thompson. 42. 'The Weaver's Answer' by Family. 43. 'Fountain Of Sorrow' by Jackson Browne. 44. 'Hurricane' by Bob Dylan. 45. 'Light My Fire' by the Doors. 46. 'O Caroline' by Matching Mole. 47. 'When An Old Cricketer Leaves The Crease' by Roy Harper. 48. 'Go To Rhino Records' by Wild Man Fischer. 49. 'Willin'' by Little Feat. 50. 'And You And I' by Yes.

had punctuated it. As a Peel listener, one moment sticks in my mind more than any other: I am sitting in my mother's cottage in the wilds of Suffolk in the spring of 1977, having come up to visit for a few days. After they separated in 1976, my father had stayed in High Wycombe while my mother moved back to East Anglia, which is where she pretty much stayed (to be rejoined by my father a few years later). It is around 10.15 p.m., and I am listening to the Peel show on giant black headphones, the sort that are so large and so synthetic they leave a cool damp patch covering your ears when you take them off. I am waiting for something in particular, and soon enough it comes, preceded by Peel simply saying, 'Here's Sheena'. What follows is one of the greatest intros ever heard on vinyl: 'Sheena Is A Punk Rocker', two and a half minutes of Spector-esque power punk, with a hook and a bass line sent straight from God (via Queens, Coney Island and Rockaway Beach).

The Ramones would eventually recede from my thoughts, although they would reappear, as all records eventually do, in a fashion show – Versace's spring/summer show in July 1999, accompanying Naomi Campbell and a small army of muscle-bound male models as they sashayed down the catwalk, acting out the balletic courtship techniques of streetwise Montagues and Capulets. Since becoming a journalist I have probably been to around two thousand fashion shows (London, Paris, New York, Milan, Barcelona, LA, Toronto, etc.), and I have to say that the things that remain with me from a lot of them is the music. The music you hear at fashion shows is never incidental, and can often be the most important aspect of the entire exercise. More than any other social barometers, fashion designers live in the moment, and their choice of music – particularly the way in which it is juxtaposed – can make or break their season. The indiscriminate blips and squeaks that accompany a designer's clothes as they sashay down the catwalk in front of the world's press can be zeitgeist-determining.

It also helps if the designers tap into the correct, fetishistic record of the moment. Each season there will be a song you'll hear two dozen times in the space of six weeks; one season all you heard was 'I'm Too Sexy' by Right Said Fred, another season's soundtrack was the first four songs on the Scissor Sisters CD. Fashion show DJs were as important in the development of modern pop as the Bronx House Party DJs of the late Seventies. Grandmaster Flash and Afrika Bambaataa may have mixed hip-hop beats with the likes of Queen and Kraftwerk, but at the same time, fashion show DJs in Paris and London were mixing Dvorak with Dollar, Pinky and Perky with Irish jigs, heavy metal with Beethoven, Gregorian chants jumbled up with deafening hi-energy. Models would career down the runway accompanied only by bird noises or the sound of a typewriter, by machine-gun fire and orchestral explosions, by Shostakovich and the Sex Pistols. I even tried my hand at it once (albeit unsuccessfully) when I played DJ at the Alternative Fashion Show at St Martins in 1980, sending Blitz Kids out onto the stage to the strains of ABBA, Mott The Hoople, George Clinton and Gary Glitter.

So just what is cool these days? Stuart, my tennis buddy, whom I graciously allow to thrash me every Saturday morning in Paddington Recreation Ground, has a penchant for Chris Rea, a man hitherto unburdened by cool; yet even he (Rea, not Stuart, obviously) has recently been anointed. My brother Daniel (you may have heard of him; Elton John wrote a song about him) has, for his sins, been the world's No. 1 ELO fan since God was a boy, and while this may not seem like the coolest thing in the world, is there anyone out there who doesn't harbour a grudging respect for 'Mr Blue Sky' (even though it sounds like 'A Day In The Life' as interpreted by Morecambe and Wise)?[1]

---

[1] My brother is resolute in his convictions, and although it would take some sort of universal seismic volte face to make Genesis fashionable, maintains that 'Entangled', from *A Trick Of The Tail* (their first post-Peter Gabriel LP, from 1976) is his favourite song. Good luck to him, I say.

What is cool? Well, what was considered hip six months ago is probably a lot different from what was meant to be hip a year ago, and compared to what was hip five years ago ... ? Well, you only have to guess. Cool changes with the wind, and often simply because of it. Hip, by its very nature, is fleeting and fickle, and that's as it should be.

There have always been those records that people always said they liked, always said they listened to in the privacy of their matt-black garrets, but which in all honesty lay untroubled and virgin-like in their cardboard sleeves and jewel cases, gathering dust and disdain in equal measure. This sort of blind appreciation usually starts with adolescent intellectual one-upmanship, which surely has to be the explanation for the 'popularity' of albums such as Jane's Addiction's *Ritual De Lo Habitual*, the Blue Nile's *Hats* or anything by Billy Bragg. The same goes for Patti Smith's *Radio Ethiopia*. I've lost count of the number of flats, houses and parties I went to in my youth where I saw this lying around nonchalantly, daring someone to play it, having been put there purposefully by some proud but insecure owner. And no one ever played it. Ever. We had all loved *Horses*, and would quite like *Easter* when it came out a year or so later, but *Radio Ethiopia* (a *succes d'estime* if ever there was one) gave us all a headache. The same goes for Siouxsie & The Banshees' *The Scream*. I liked the idea of Siouxsie a lot, and the pinboard in my room at Ralph West was covered with her photographs, but while her concerts were amazing, the record stank. When a friend of mine said the only thing Jacques Derrida had in common with Marx was a huge fan club and a great lagoon of unreadness, I knew what he meant.

My subjectivity has produced blind spots, too: there are – count them – no songs on my machine by the Doors (I adored them until I spent a year researching and writing a book about them); almost no country (Lucinda Williams and Johnny Cash, but not much else; country music is often called the music of the Republican Party, whereas I always thought it was music for the after party – i.e. the after everyone has gone home party);[1] almost no 'world' music (I ran an African club in Soho for a year and that put me off it for life, and there are only so many times a person can listen to a Gasper Lawal record and that number is 0); no Elvis and only 34 reggae songs (I sold most of the stuff I had when I was poor and have never bothered to replace it; well, apart from 'Ob-La-Di Ob-La-Da').

Scarcity has proved extremely important when considering what is and what isn't cool, and it's a sad but honest fact that both Neil Young's *On The Beach* and the Beach Boys' *Smile* have both been somewhat diminished by, in the former's case, finally being released on CD, and in the latter's, being rerecorded, valiantly but in karaoke fashion by Brian Wilson.

And so here I am, late on a Friday night, lost in thought, lost in music, building the perfect music library, a library that contains every significant piece of music ever recorded, from Strauss and Schubert through Gilbert and Sullivan to Simon and Garfunkel. As I move through the architecture of iTunes, like a digitised motorbike in a computer game, I hit Buddy Holly, the Beatles, the Clash, Dr Dre, the Monkees, Joy Division and Franz Ferdinand (the Joy Division Monkees). This box contains all my memories, four decades of the things: friends, lovers, family, they're all in here somewhere. And what is the greatest of them all, the greatest record ever made? With a digital library you are faced with an endless multiplicity of truths, a string of infinite possibilities. Which causes endless, infinite problems: if you've got all this stuff at your fingertips it makes it very difficult to edit it all down to a small, finite

---

[1] Q: 'How many country and western singers does it take to change a lightbulb?' A: 'Four. One to put the new one in, and three to sing about the old one.' Note: this joke was told to me by a bartender in Texas. Behind him on the bar was a sign which read, 'We have both kinds of music here, country and western.'

list. In fact the point of the machine is that this small finite list is one of many thousands of such lists, and one way to make sure you have the best is by having everything; then you can't lose.[1]

Capacity is paramount in the world of the 'Pod. When I decided to get involved, I didn't muck about with any of the smaller capacity machines – 15 GB? Are you mad? 20 GB? What do you take me for, eh? No, when I went in, I went in big, and opted for the Big Daddy, the 40 GB. Anything less would have been an embarrassment. Friends of mine have invested in the iPod mini, but even with the silver finish I'm not convinced; after all, when you can squeeze a lifetime into a machine, why settle for just a decade or two?

A few weeks after getting my machine, I began slipping into a predictable pattern of conversations, trying to force everyone I met into having some sort of opinion on this latest technological manifestation of the future. Did they have one, and if not, why not? If they did, what was on it? And why? And after a few polite minutes where I would nod and smile a lot and pretend I was impressed by their esoteric taste ('Oh, you've uploaded all the Police albums, have you? Interesting …'), I'd drop the Big Question.

'So, which version do you have? How big is it?'

And if they pretended not to know, or were vague in their response, I'd push some more.

'So, how many songs can you get on it? You know, HOW BIG IS IT? Your iPod?'

And then I'd get the downcast eyes, the furrowed brow and the shifting from foot to foot.

'I've, er, got the middle one, you know, the twenty.'

'The what?' I'd reply, pretending not to have heard. 'The forty?'

---

[1] Hemingway loved having this problem: 'I am trying to make, before I get through, a picture of the whole world – or as much of it as I have seen. Boiling it down always, rather than spreading it out thin.'

'No, the twenty. The twenty gigabyte. The middle one ... but I can get loads of songs on it and how many can you really listen to at any one time I mean I think it's ridiculous the way people go on about how many songs they can get on their iPod I mean it's babyish isn't it and anyway I haven't got time to listen to my old records let alone new ones so actually I'm not sure if it's such a great invention anyway the papers are always full of the things and I think I'm going to start going back to CDs I really only got it for my girlfriend and she only likes what's in the charts anyway so anyway ...'

So anyway, I would let them blabber on for a while, then mutter 'amateur' under my breath and move on to my next victim.

'So, what's on your iPod then?' I'd say, as though I were asking, in a nasally suburban whine, 'So, what you driving at the moment then, eh?'

Towards the end of 2004 there developed something of a pissing contest in our office, and water-cooler conversations began to veer away from Reality TV, football, the fluctuating fortunes of Sky News, or the latest BlackBerry, towards the number of songs on our iPods. And while you may have thought it was perfectly acceptable to casually admit you only have, say, 1200 songs on your memory box, for a few weeks it was very easy to become an object of derision for not taking this seriously enough. For a while there was definitely a quantity over quality issue, a sort of digital penis envy ...

And although this was a very male thing, I had always thought the iPod was asexual, like a Walkman or a mobile phone. It is, of course, highly sexual, and has an innate, tactile sexuality, but I'd never thought of it as gender-specific. It is such a thing of beauty, such an abstract object of desire, yet it is somehow *above all that*. Until I heard someone refer to it as feminine, that is. He – this ... man! – was describing the JBL On Stage speaker system, a disc-shaped port in which your beloved 'Pod nestles, while ... 'unleashing a respectable six watts per channel and charges her up for the day.' Her? *Her?* When did the 'Pod suddenly become feminine? How did that happen? Was I away that day, toying with Microsoft or Sony? Had I been lying in a darkened room, mobile turned off, surrounded by the impenetrable wash of Yes' *Tales From Topographic Oceans?* I think it was fairly obvious that the iPod minis, in all their metallic (adonised aluminium) pastel glory were aimed at the female market, but was this chap really saying my chrome 40GB 3G monster wasn't masculine, that he was somehow 'not as other hardware'?

And so overnight my iPod became male, just because someone had said it was feminine. Pathetic of me, I know. But very male all the same. And if the iPod is gender specific, then its sexuality is predicated, I think, on capacity. On *oomph.* So I think my machine is an Ivan rather than an Irene (hairless though it may be). And anyway, in France it's *le iPod*, not *la.* So there.

Jonathan Ive, who is an industrial designer first and a soothsayer second, is adamant that it's neither. An unaffected man, in his eyes the iPod isn't sexual at all. 'The iPod is not masculine or feminine, and if the appeal was just about about the look then it wouldn't be compelling for very long. It's a small, white, plastic and chrome music player. The object was always to make the nicest music player possible.' (My friend Stuart, who is a diplomat by profession as well as at play, complicated matters by calling it metrosexual, which I didn't think was helpful at all.)

Yet anthropomorphising my iPod wasn't going to help it orchestrate a list of the coolest records in the world (right now). I'd have to do that.

But as soon as I started I got sidetracked. As I began poring over my Steely Dan playlist (which contains everything they'd ever released, including 'Dallas' and 'Sail The Waterway' from a mid-Seventies EP, as well as a bootleg copy of 'The Second Arrangement', the great lost song from *Gaucho*), I started doing due diligence on *Aja*, trying to work out exactly why it's the best record ever made (not the coolest, you understand, just the best). I felt like one of those early computer programmers, those educated young men of dishevelled appearance, with glowering sunken eyes and megalomaniacal fantasies of omnipotence.

Then I wandered off into the Beach Boys, then Van Morrison, then Coldplay ... oh, it was becoming oh so predictable and oh so boring. And so I thought back to when I was seventeen, when being 'cool' probably occupied my thoughts more than at any time before or since, and wondered what I'd feel like if I were like that today, and every consumer decision was based on how other people would interpret it. What (twenty, say) records would I leave lying around the house? What CDs would I have sitting in the car? What would I keep open on my iTunes in case anyone wandered past my PowerBook?

Well, right now, as I'm writing this, they are as follows, in no particular order: 1) *Back in The USA* by the MC5 (a classic proto-punk record that still sounds like it can't believe it's so excited). 2) *Sign O' The Times* by Prince (a veritable smorgasbord, and the best album of the Eighties). 3) *Kind Of Blue* by Miles Davis (a record impervious to criticism or fashion). 4) *London Calling* by the Clash (ditto). 5) *Isaac Hayes Live At The Sahara Tahoe* (the best soul album ever recorded). 6) *The College Dropout* by Kayne West (2004's nomination for the best hip-hop album ever made). 7) Any obscure Johnny Cash album (the worse the better). 8) *Grace* by Jeff Buckley (a hardy perennial). 9) *Two Sevens Clash* by Culture (the best punk reggae album). 10) *Solid Air* by John Martyn (*One World* is better but this is cooler). 11) Any Kraftwerk album (literally any; they all do what they're supposed to). 12) *The Koln Concert* by Keith Jarrett (the best piano album ever made). 13) *Waltz For Koop* by Koop (good, but obscure – so great). 14) *Physical Graffiti* by Led Zeppelin (once banished, they're now back for ever). 15) *The Bends* by Radiohead (works in every country in the world). 16) *Everest* by the Beatles (it doesn't exist so you'll have to make it up). 17) *The Libertines* by the Libertines (it's better than the first record and don't let anyone tell you otherwise). 18) *World Without Tears* by Lucinda Williams (a sexy Tom Waits). 19) *The Crickets* by Marcos Valle (you'll never find it). 20) *Aftermath* by the Rolling Stones (the epitome of Swinging London).

But then I realise I've forgotten to include *Goodbye Yellow Brick Road* (Elton's coolest record, even though it doesn't include 'Tiny Dancer'; and he was originally going to call it *Vodka and Tonic*), *Elephant Mountain* by the Youngbloods, ('Sunrise' is officially a better ballad than 'Yesterday'), *Dusty In Memphis* and a thousand more ...[1]

---

[1] Alternatively, and if I had written this list after one too many cappuccinos, you could use the following: 1) *Horses* by Patti Smith (an old favourite that comes back into fashion every few years or so). 2) *Electric* by the Cult (still big in the *GQ* office). 3) *Future Days* by Can (probably not as cool as it once was but still a contender). 4) *The Thom Bell Sessions* by Elton John ('Are You Ready For Love', *et al*). 5) *Blonde On Blonde* by Bob Dylan (impossible to disregard). 6) *The First Songs* by Laura Nyro ('Wedding Bell Blues', 'Stoney End', etc.). 7) *Taking Tiger Mountain (By Strategy)* by Eno (unbelievable foresight). 8) *The Thorns* by the Thorns (roll over Roger McGuinn and tell Gram Parsons the news). 9) *Wish You Were Here* by Pink Floyd (*Dark Side Of The Moon?* Well, yes, but actually this is better ... as they say). 10) *Too Late To Stop Now* by Van Morrison (most live albums are rubbish; this isn't). 11) *Blood & Chocolate* by Elvis Costello & the Attractions (with the amazing Lennonfest, 'I Want You'). 12) *The Lexicon Of Love* by ABC (a designer concept album!). 13) *Kill City* by Iggy Pop & James Williamson (punk ballads!). 14) *Pink Flag* by Wire (play it on a beach). 15) *Slaughter On 10th Avenue* by Mick Ronson (inc. Bowie's 'Growing Up And I'm Fine'). 16) *Always Be Clothing* by Hesitation Wound (so scarce it's frightening). 17) *Scott 2* by Scott Walker (the Scott Walker record you're allowed to like). 18) *Bridge Over Troubled Water* by Simon and Garfunkel (adored by my friend Oliver and about twenty million other people). 19) *Warm And Beautiful*, a collection of Paul McCartney cover versions produced in Japan featuring Matthew Sweet, Robyn Hitchcock, Semisonic and more. 20) *Life For Rent* by Dido (just kidding).

12 The Beatles: With a Little Help from My iPod

The best Beatles records are not the ones you think . . .

The den where I Pod is a converted garage on the ground floor of our house in Paddington. It is windowless, with one door, and floor-to-ceiling bookshelves on three sides. It's a very modern room, and looks not unlike a library might look in one of those Case Study houses, the ones that overlook Los Angeles. There is a grey utilitarian carpet, a 40" plasma TV, and pop paraphernalia all over the place.

On my desk there is an enormous Kenwood amp, an auto reverse double cassette player built by Sony, an Audio-Technica turntable, a Sony CD player, a pair of KEF C series speakers, two PowerBooks, an iMic (for recording onto iTunes directly from vinyl), and one very full, very proud, and very sexy iPod. And right now it is connected to my laptop, updating like crazy, the Apple logo winking at me as it goes. My laptop has told me my iPod has just eaten *A Grand Don't Come For Free*, Brian Wilson's *Smile* and the Libertines' *Up The Bracket*, wolfed them down in the time it takes you to lick your lips.

On the wall by the door there is a huge framed photographic print of the cover of David Bowie's *Pin-Ups* signed by the photographer Justin DeVilleneuve ('Ziggy and Twiggy, for Dylan'), and an equally large framed screenprint of Guy Peellaert's cover of the Rolling Stones' *It's Only Rock'n'Roll* given to me by the fashion designer and fellow iPod obsessive Paul

Smith. One wall is covered with CDs, the other two with books and magazines (thousands and thousands of magazines, many of which I have at some time either worked for or edited). At the last count I had 63 Beatles books, 40 of which are proper book size and are grouped together on three shelves, the rest of which are large-format illustrated coffee-table books that lie horizontally on a shelf behind my desk.

I have more than eighty Tom Wolfe books, mainly first editions (including an Italian imprint of *Ambush At Fort Bragg*, the short story he published in *Rolling Stone* in the mid-1990s), although it's the Beatles' books I keep coming back to: books about the records they didn't release and the women they didn't marry, books about the drugs they took and the books they read, about the holidays they took and the clothes they wore. You want Beatles books, you come to me (or rather you don't, because I don't lend).

Like millions of other people, I have never stopped being fascinated by the Beatles, by the idea of the Beatles, by the music of the Beatles. Unlike any other group or cultural event since the 1960s, interest in the Beatles is exponential, never ending, and, for some all-consuming. And each new generation brings with it its own mirror, its own way of looking at them, its own idea of what it means to be a fan. And being a fan always brings you back to the records. I've been making Beatles compilations since the age of twelve, on cassette, mini-disc, CD, even recently with specially designed covers ... of albums that didn't exist, albums that will never exist. I *always* go back to the records, always try and reconfigure them in some way, always try and imagine What Would Have Happened If ... if the *White Album* had been a single instead of a double, if 'Penny Lane' and 'Strawberry Fields Forever' had been on *Sergeant Pepper* (allowing them to be siphoned off, according to George Martin, was 'the biggest mistake of my professional life'), if they hadn't broken up until 1973, if George Martin had stopped producing their records in 1966 instead of 1969.

Sir George Martin is one of those men who, when you first meet them, has the ability not only to make you feel as though you've known him for ages, but also to make you feel as though everything you say is laden with staggering significance. He is an affable, charming man, someone who has rarely – publicly, anyway – had a bad word to say about anyone. These days, though, he may be loosening up a little.

Although he doesn't like being asked about it, if pressed Martin will admit that the reason he didn't produce the last two Beatles singles, 'Free As A Bird' and 'Real Love' (the ones bashed together by the three remaining Beatles in 1995), is because George Harrison didn't want him to (the gig went to Jeff Lynne, archduke of the moptop knockoff). When 'Free As A Bird' was released on the first Beatles *Anthology*, Martin used his partial deafness as an excuse, and said he didn't have the time. Considering that he could hear well enough to produce every other song on *Anthology I*, *II* and *III*, and that he had spent years doing so, the excuses rang hollow. Now, he says different.

'I wasn't asked. I heard the quality of what they had to deal with, and it was quite a problem. If I had been asked to do it then I probably would have done it, but I wasn't asked. I didn't have any great regrets, so it was no skin off my nose. I think if l had produced it, it would have been a different sound.' And then some.

'Free As A Bird' is a potentially anthemic record that was ruined in part by two bewilderingly obvious factors: Paul McCartney's apparent reluctance to substitute a decent middle eight (which has been publicly criticised for sounding a little too similar to the bridge in the Shangri-Las' 'Remember (Walkin in the Sand)'), and Jeff Lynne's trademark 'fat' drum sound. While it now must be acknowledged that Ringo was a better singer than he was a drummer, his talents, such as they are, aren't shown here in their best light. In the hands of Martin (producer of nearly every Beatles song, apart from those helmed by Phil Spector on *Let It Be*), it could have been turned into a classic, but in Lynne's clammy, eager little mitts it sounds like an ELO B-side. (John Lennon once said that the reason Lynne's ELO stopped having hits was because they'd run out of Beatles records to copy.)

The reunion record was never going to sound any different. When McCartney came up with the idea of recording a 'new' Beatles record to supplement the outtakes, demos and forgotten songs which constitute the *Anthology* albums, Harrison took the chance to get his own back on Martin. The Beatles producer had never been enamoured by Harrison's writing, and, with help from Lennon and McCartney, had kept him at arm's length from benediction by making sure he only got one or two songs on each album. So when McCartney suggested the record, Harrison insisted they get Jeff Lynne, his fellow Traveling Wilbury, to produce it.

When they came to record the song, a John Lennon fragment he'd recorded as a demo in the mid-1970s, and which had been given to them by Yoko Ono, McCartney suggested they imagine that Lennon had simply recorded his part before going off on holiday, and that the remaining Threetles were going into the studio to polish it off.

When you finally heard it on the radio, after months and months of hype, the best thing one could say about 'Free As A Bird' was that at least it was better than the Traveling Wilburys. Just.

A few months later came a second Jeff Lynne travesty, 'Real Love', another dusted-down Lennon song bowdlerised by Lynne's shuffle-drum sheen, used to hype up *Anthology II*. Paul, George and Ringo were reluctant to record it as they felt the song wasn't up to scratch, and apparently only agreed to do so at Yoko's request. You can tell their hearts are not in it; it sounds lacklustre and hasty, the arrangement appearing to encourage the song to end as quickly as possible.

What most people don't know is that there was meant to be a third reclaimed song, to be included on *Anthology III*. This is the Beatles record that never was. Third time around, the Beatles tried three old Lennon songs – 'Now and Then', 'I Don't Want To Lose You', and 'Grow Old With Me' (all of which were simple home demos, recorded on a cassette machine on top of Lennon's famous white piano, the one used in the 'Imagine' promo) – and a new song written by McCartney and Harrison. But nothing worked, and they decided to let things be. 'Now and Then' had quite a lot of work done on it, but 'Grow Old With Me' was discarded almost from the start. Which was a huge mistake.

'Grow Old With Me' originally appeared on Lennon's *Milk and Honey* in 1984, a collection of twelve songs by John and Yoko intended to follow up their 1980 *Double Fantasy* album, until Lennon was murdered by Mark Chapman at the year's end. 'For John, "Grow Old With Me" was one that would be a standard,' says Yoko Ono, 'the kind that they would play in church every time a couple gets married. It was horns and symphony time.' Like 'Hey Jude', Lennon imagined it as the sort of song people would sing around campfires. '[It] was a song John made several cassettes of, as we discussed the arrangements for it,' says Yoko. 'Everybody knew how important those cassettes were. They were in safekeeping ... all of them disappeared except the one on the end of the record. It may be that it was meant to be this way, since the version that was left was John's last recording ... recorded together in our bedroom with a piano and a rhythm box.'

The Lennons identified closely with Elizabeth Barrett and Robert Browning, and 'Grow Old With Me' is a response to Ono's own song 'Let Me Count The Ways' (based on Barrett and Browning's *Sonnets From The Portuguese*), reflecting Browning's 'Rabbi Ben Ezra' ('Grow old along with me, the best is yet to be'). Although unfinished and unpolished, the songs on *Milk and Honey*, in the words of Lennon expert Paul du Noyer. 'diarise his hopes and fears with compelling honesty'. 'Grow Old With Me' was no different, an emotive plea that sounds not dissimilar to the bootleg demo of 'Free As A Bird' – over-reaching vocals and faltering keyboards. It would be ten years before the song was turned into Lennon's last mini-classic.

Having had it rejected by the remaining Beatles for the third *Anthology* single, in 1996 Yoko asked Martin to overhaul the song for inclusion on the four-CD *Lennon Anthology*, and he did it with ease. Martin liked the song more than any other Lennon demo he had heard since his death, and used his considerable skills to give it the gravitas it needed. Its arrangement is unassuming, even businesslike: the strings swell and the flutes trill in all the right places, leaving Lennon's plaintive, occasionally maudlin voice to carry the song to its inevitable conclusion. Martin's judgement is perfect, letting the song sing for itself. With its stately 'Imagine' feel and the same vamping piano, 'Grow Old With Me' is one of Lennon's less flinty songs (when he chose to, Lennon was capable of mining even deeper seams of sentimentality than McCartney), almost a hymn.

If you feel the need to wallow, play this; a cathartic lump in the throat will appear. You can also hear it on the single CD of his *Anthology* highlights, *Wonsaponatime*, along with similarly moving versions of 'Imagine', 'I'm Losing You' and 'How Do You Sleep'. (Try placing it right at the end of the *White Album*, right after – or instead of – 'Good Night' and see how well it fits.)

The Beatles should have persevered with 'Grow Old With Me'. As a last hurrah it would have been a more than fitting denouement. And it wouldn't have sounded anything like ELO.

I was only a baby when JFK died, yet I can still remember where I was when I heard that John Lennon had been shot, lying in bed in my room in the eaves of a freezing cold flat above a pebbledash and anaglypta greengrocers in Stamford Hill, north London (birthplace of both Marc Bolan and Malcolm McLaren). The mantelpiece was covered with a grand parade of empty (and cheap) whiskey bottles and one wall was covered with a gargantuan poster advertising Joy Division at The Lyceum (personally ripped off a shopfront round the corner from St Martins). I heard the news on Capital Radio at 8 a.m., and although I was not exactly enamoured of Lennon's recent record (to me *Double Fantasy* sounded limp, over-produced and sentimental – still does, actually), I was shocked that someone so famous *to me* had been killed. I shared the flat with a bunch of St Martins students and I was equally shocked by their total lack of interest in the murder. To them Lennon was already a hasbeen, a fogey who had exhausted his finite talent. I felt the same disappointment that John Peel felt three years earlier when the announcement of Elvis' death at the Vortex, the punk club in Wardour Street, resulted in an exultant roar.

I thought about my old flat as I walked into the Dakota building seventeen years later. The first thing you notice as you enter Yoko Ono's seventh-floor apartment in the Dakota, the huge gothic block on New York's Central Park West, is John Lennon's white baby grand, the celestial piano on which he wrote 'Imagine' and many of his other classic songs from the early Seventies. Though it has been home to Ono since the couple bought it in 1973, to a visitor the gigantic nine-room apartment feels somewhat like a private chapel. I was asked to remove my shoes, and the sensation was intensified as the afternoon sun caught the piano's white keys and the silver picture frames on top of it.

Lennon is everywhere: staring down at you from the Warhol painting in the 'black' room, in the photographs on the walls in the kitchen, and in those silver picture frames on top of his piano (John with Yoko, John with Sean, John with Julian, John with Paul ... but mainly John with Yoko). Apartment 72 is something of a museum, too, since apart from the acres of Egyptian antiques and dozens of Ono's own installation pieces, it is littered with paintings, lithographs and famous silkscreens: a de Lempicka here, a de Chirico there. It was here on 72nd Street that John and Yoko spent their five years of role reversal, until Lennon's death at the hands of Mark Chapman in 1980. While Yoko spent her days in their office on the ground floor,

John would be upstairs, attending to their son Sean and 'watching the trees change colour' in Central Park.

'This is where John used to bake bread,' said Yoko, as she showed me into the kitchen, with its spice jars, chopping boards and the unremarkable detritus of domesticity. 'Every day he'd get up and make Sean's breakfast while Sean played on the floor. Then he'd get up and make bread while I went to work downstairs. Often I'd work at the kitchen table just to be near them. We were a family and this was our home, Sean's home, and because of that I'll never leave.'

Ono has had more than her fair share of bad press in the years since she first met Lennon. Since his death, her press seems to have actually been worse, as if we somehow can't bear the thought that she's still alive while he isn't. (One of her American publicists even asked if I had any deep-rooted animosity towards Yoko, as though it were a given.) This vilification is a cross she'll probably have to bear until she dies, much like Linda McCartney who, until her death, was also, rather disgustingly, considered to be Paul's undoing, at least creatively.

I'd separately spent time with Paul McCartney, Ringo and Julian Lennon, and have built up considerable first-hand Beatles experience of my own. I've come away from each encounter with fairly customary evaluations – I'd found McCartney to be genial, pleasantly cocky, and strangely insecure; Ringo was the rather resentful ex-clown whom people expect these days; and Lennon was a fascinating if not altogether successful example of the first generation of celebrity offspring (and who had only recently stopped abusing himself). The only Beatle person to confound expectations was Yoko.

In person, Ono certainly didn't seem like a business barracuda at all, but then it's obvious from the way in which her underlings scattered from the apartment with the wave of her hand that she is a formidable boss. Tiny, dressed entirely in black, she is extremely birdlike, and talks in short, staccato sentences. It's easy to forget how old she is – she was born in 1934 – and, in conversation, seemed endearingly dotty rather than demon-strative, often repeating herself or misunderstanding questions. I'm sure she's acutely responsive when studying the bottom line, but then, as the custodian of John Lennon's estate, she ought to be.

The office on the ground floor of the Dakota is crammed with all sorts of valuable Beatles memorabilia and Yoko sits there every day with her assistants, approving advertising artwork, CD releases and plotting the administration of the estate. In her private office next door, fluffy white clouds float across the sky-blue ceiling. There is a bronze sculpture of an apple with two bites out of it, and, on her desk, a framed blank cheque, made out to Yoko and signed by John; I'm sure to some it would be an apposite approximation of their relationship.

'There are those who will never forgive me,' she said, as I was leaving that day. 'They called me a professional widow, called me a dragon lady, called me lots of things, but you have to take strength from that. I can't change the way people feel, I just have to deal with it in my own way.'

Because the Beatles have been so objectified, because every tiny aspect of their lives has been examined time and time again, and because the records have been analysed to the point of absurdity, increasingly they've become the subject of conjecture. Should George Harrison have been allowed more songs on the albums? Did Lennon really get his fair share of A-Sides? Who really wrote the middle eight to 'Birthday'? This is the sort of thing I've been doing for years, and the iPod has only made it easier. Just imagine ... I mean, just imagine ... anything ...

Just imagine. In January 1970 the Beatles are in a state of flux. Just three months previously, *Abbey Road* has been released to universal acclaim, although the album's success belies the band's interpersonal relationships. At various times during the previous year, all four members have threatened to leave, and it is only Paul McCartney's diligence that has kept them together. In short, they are finding it very easy to hate each other.

They have money problems, too. Unable to secure any kind of deal for themselves, both Allen Klein (John Lennon's choice as financial advisor) and Lee Eastman (McCartney's) have fled back to New York to lick their wounds, leaving the band's financial affairs seriously in limbo. Also, Apple continue to haemorrhage cash, and the band have to dissuade Ringo Starr from his plan to tour the country with a sixteen-man brass band, recording any half-decent pub singer he comes across. But even though they dislike each other, they can still get on when they have to. And so in February 1970 they decide to get together to record one last album, *Everest*.

While the tensions created by the ill-tempered and eventually aborted *Get Back* sessions at the beginning of 1969 are still in evidence, the *Abbey Road* sessions have been more enjoyable than any of them had anticipated. Far more enjoyable. A lot of this is down to McCartney. Having led them through *Abbey Road* and the debacle that would become *Get Back*, during the sessions for *Everest* McCartney seems to have tired of being in charge, and gradually steps aside as the de facto leader, allowing Lennon, and particularly George Harrison, to have more of a say in the record's construction.

Consequently, George and Ringo are no longer quite so sullen, and John is pulling his weight, something he hasn't done since 1966. Plus – important, this – the tension caused by Yoko Ono's presence in the studio during the *Get Back* sessions has eased; she has been seconded to China by a group calling themselves the Zurich Peace Police, where she has been asked to produce a conceptual installation that will echo the Great Wall. (Many assume the Zurich Peace Police are none other than Paul, George and Ringo.)

The atmosphere in the studio is also helped by the presence of several guest musicians; *Everest* contains fleeting appearances from Billy Preston and Eric Clapton, as well as Crosby, Stills and Nash and – on a couple of George Harrison's tracks – even Bob Dylan, who comes out of retirement especially for this record.

Harrison is instrumental in making *Everest* happen, convincing Lennon and McCartney that they should put off the split for at least one more record. 'You owe it to me,' he tells John during the recording, 'I deserve my own shout.' Harrison also leads the way creatively, inflicting dozens of stored-up songs on his pals. The album is even going to be called *All Things Must Pass* – after one of Harrison's more prescient songs – until George Martin suggests *Everest*, one of the original names for *Abbey Road*. The name comes from engineer Geoff Emerick's cigarettes, and the band intend to fly to the Himalayas and have their picture taken with the peak. 'That's a good name, it's big and expansive,' says McCartney, before wavering. 'We said, "Nah, come on! You can't name an album after a ciggie packet!"'

Released on Apple in June 1970, *Everest* becomes the last proper Beatles album. The band know this while they are recording it, and though they want it to acknowledge their differences, they are also determined to make it sound like a Beatles record. That they achieve this is a remarkable feat. Knowing *Everest* is to be their last hurrah, the band try out dozens and dozens of songs, both old and new, including Lennon's 'Gimme Some Truth', 'Mother' and 'Child of Nature' – later to turn into 'Jealous Guy' – and McCartney's 'Great Day', which won't see daylight until 1997, when it appears on his *Flaming Pie* album. There are a few old songs which make the grade – 'Let It Be', 'Across The Universe', 'Junk', 'The Long And Winding Road' etc., though the rock'n'roll run-throughs that will later be excavated for the inconsequential and rootsy, post-split *Get Back* album (eventually released in 1972, having been remixed by Dave Edmunds – both John and Paul were big fans of Edmunds's version of 'I Hear You Knocking'), are left locked in the Abbey Road vaults. The only track to make it is McCartney's 'Teddy Boy'.

One song that receives more than its fair share of attention is 'You Know My Name (Look Up My Number)', which they first started recording in May 1967, and which is eventually composed of five different parts, each recorded separately. In April 1969 John and Paul had added some extra sound effects, including hand-clapping, coughing, spluttering and slipping in the odd vocal pastiche reminiscent of Bluebottle in *The Goon Show*, but they won't finish it until the *Everest* sessions. They both love this song, and Lennon is so desperate for it to be released that he says he'll issue it under the name of the Plastic Ono Band if the Beatles don't want it. Even though Paul has deep affection for it – 'It's probably my favourite Beatles track' – it is only released on the B-side of 'My Sweet Lord', *Everest*'s only single. Bizarre.

Everest is George Martin's album as much as anyone else's, and he excels himself both with his technical wizardry (i.e., making the Beatles sound like a band when they aren't really one at all) and more importantly, with his diplomacy.

The album has a sharper, crisper sound than any previous Beatles record, and is not unlike the demos recorded by Lennon's pet project, the Plastic Ono Band. Essentially, Martin takes the edges off some of Lennon's more abrasive material and forces McCartney to embellish his slapdash demo tapes. He does away with excessive multi-tracking and over-dubbing, preferring instead to clean up the live takes the band perform in Abbey Road's Studio One. *Everest* has the same disparate influences which made the *White Album* such a chocolate box – with Lennon tending towards aggressive and intense introspection and McCartney celebrating the joys of domesticity – but it has such strong production one can be forgiven for thinking that the band has experienced a rebirth. If the Beatles can still write and record songs like this, then they can surely write and record them for ever.

More than this, Martin is particularly proactive with Harrison, sensing that in his creative birthing lay the Beatles' future. Martin steers Harrison through dozens of songs, and the two build up such a bond that it was Lennon and McCartney's most public confidante whom Harrison asks to produce his 1971 solo debut, *Not Guilty.*

All in all, *Everest* is an inspired record, or at least a cleverly orchestrated, hard-working and laborious experiment that is manipulated to sound like an inspired record. John, Paul, George and Ringo will soon come to despise the Beatles and will try to tarnish the myth, but for now they are intent on producing their last great wheeze, the behemoth that becomes *Everest.* *Rolling Stone* calls it 'a fitting end to a decade of unexpected transcendence', and, unable to shower enough praise on the album, the *NME* asks four different critics to review it. Predictably, they all love it.

As for the record's format, having briefly discussed another double album, or even a triple this time – to accommodate more of the songs recorded during the *Get Back* sessions as well as half a dozen more Harrison tunes – common sense prevails and the group decides on a normal length album, along with a free EP. Having produced a double album, and then – with *Magical Mystery Tour* – a double EP, this was to be another first. For the very last time ...[1]

Everest is just one example of how an entire oeuvre can be reconfigured using iTunes, how a whole career can be re-examined, re-edited and born again. In the case of the Beatles, the software enables you to easily break the component parts down into individual songwriting blocks, and of the 175 Beatles songs on my iPod I would say that 85 of them are largely the work of Paul McCartney. Does this mean that Paul wrote more Beatles songs than John? Definitely. Does it mean that Paul's songs were the best Beatles songs? Probably. Of my 175 songs,

---

[1] A full track listing of *Everest* appears on page 259.

the ones which are unquestionably the best, which obviously makes them the best Beatles songs of all time are probably, in order: 1) 'You Never Give Me Your Money', the enormously well-considered snippet from the lengthy song-cycle on *Abbey Road*, which manages to portray both extreme frustration and a giddy sense of freedom; 2) 'Hey Jude', the epic 1968 singalong single which for ever defined the band as masters of the global gesture; 3) 'I'll Be Back', the bitter, minor-chord masterpiece that closes the second side of *A Hard Day's Night*; 4) 'Goodbye', a Paul McCartney demo of a song he wrote for Mary Hopkin and which outstrips both 'Blackbird' and 'Yesterday' in its eerie simplicity.

Of these, you'll notice that only one is written by John Lennon ('I'll Be Back'), which, I think, proves that Paul McCartney is unquestionably the better Beatle.

There have always been more John people than Paul people. At least since 1970, when the Beatles split, and especially since 1980, when John Lennon was shot.

Lennon is untouchable now, immortal. His myth can be flattered in perpetuity because he is no longer with us. Lennon the rebel. Lennon the sage. Lennon the mystic enabler. Voice of the people. Blah blah blah. The labels will stick for decades, centuries. But while Lennon is part of the cavalcade of the tragically slain, McCartney has had to be content with growing old, happy and saggy around the middle, not least metaphorically.

It is always Lennon we are encouraged to revere, Lennon whose visage fills the shelves in the book departments of HMV or Virgin, Lennon whose face can still be seen walking down Carnaby Street on the T-shirts of Scandinavian students and Japanese tourists. McCartney, meanwhile, has suffered at the hands of critics, an increasingly apathetic public, and – how could it not be so? – fate. Paul McCartney: the Beatle who should have been shot. Macca the slacker: a man who was once Picasso but who turned into L. S. Lowry.

While it would be silly and pointless to say that Lennon was the weaker half of the Lennon/McCartney partnership, at his worst he was certainly the more excessive sentimentalist. Yet it's his former partner we like to dismiss; McCartney who tends to come off worse in comparisons.

At first sight there is certainly enough to criticise him for. He is, after all, the man who was blamed for splitting up the most important group in the world; the man who put his family before ambition, and who rested on his laurels for longer than most artists have careers; the man responsible for some of the most fatuous pop songs of the last thirty years, songs that could easily accompany TV advertisements for deodorant, soft cheese or sanitary towels.

McCartney has released a sufficiency of unpalatable material in the last thirty years, displaying a surprising gaucheness rarely seen in pop: he wrote 'Ebony And Ivory', 'Mull Of Kintyre', and plenty more nursery rhymes loitering on the outskirts of awful. He can pen a classic too – 'Maybe I'm Amazed', 'Distractions', 'Heaven On A Sunday' – but his quality control is erratic to say the least.

Like his 1960s contemporary, the Beach Boys' Brian Wilson, in his thirties – he's over sixty now – McCartney seemed to rush screaming into the kindergarten, hastened by a belief that the key to his success lay, simply enough, in simplicity. And whereas Wilson's twee meanderings were the result of deadening medication and a wandering mind, McCartney's seemed willed by an arrant desire to turn his domestic life into his career. What else can explain the lurid nonsense of 'Mary Had A Little Lamb', 'Wonderful Christmas Time', 'We All Stand Together' or 'The Girl Is Mine' (recorded as a duet with terrible infant, Michael Jackson)? In the space of just a few years, McCartney went from being the coolest man on the planet to being everyone's embarrassing uncle.

If in the early days of their partnership Lennon and Mc-Cartney were sparks and petrol threatening to mix (McCartney jealous of Lennon's cynicism, Lennon mindful of McCartney's commercial sense of purpose), by the time they had been unleashed from the Beatles both were eager to wallow in the joys of domesticity. With Lennon this decision was almost militant – John and Yoko against the Man! In Bags! In Bed! In The Amsterdam Hilton! – but in McCartney's case it was exactly the opposite. If Yoko Ono was Lennon's way of shouting at the world, Linda Eastman, the photographer whom McCartney married at Marylebone Registry Office in London in March 1969, was the ex-Beatle's means of settling down. Both men flaunted their women on their record covers and in their PR pictures, recording with them, performing with them. They showed enormous arrogance in thinking the world would be interested in their respective spouses, but the truth is that it was. Commonplace now, three decades ago this type of personal publicity was a novelty and, as Beatle Paul and Beatle John brandished their women on their arms, we sat up and listened. Was Linda the new John? Was Yoko the new Paul?

Linda McCartney became not only one of the world's most famous consorts, but eventually her husband's muse. Every song seemed to be about her in one way or another. And while his fans were initially fascinated by McCartney's eagerness to sport his badge of love, the fascination didn't last long; when his records started to celebrate the banal, his public became restless and his critics impatient. Linda couldn't sing. Didn't play an instrument (like it mattered). She was dragging him down. Stopping him from being a genius. Stuff like that. ('What do you call a dog with Wings?' The gags were endless ...)

Beatle Paul didn't care. In McCartney's world his family *became* his career, while his obsession with domesticity became his calling card. Other musicians have quietly eulogised the joys of home and hearth, but few have done it with such unabashed devotion. With McCartney his home life became a celebration rather than a catharsis. His priorities, right up to his wife's death in 1998, were stubbornly defended. 'I still get wounded, but I've come to the point where I tell myself, "Give yourself a break. No one else will,"' he said just before she died. 'I *like* ballads. I *like* babies. I *like* happy endings. They say domesticity is the enemy of art, but I don't think it is. I had to make a decision: am I going to be just a family guy or should I go up to London three nights a week, hit the nightclubs, occasionally drop my trousers and swear in public? I made my decision and I feel OK with it. Ballads and babies. That's what happened to me.' And you had to be emotionally inert not to be happy for him.

McCartney's first records after leaving the Beatles were slight affairs, brimming with melody if not meaning. After years of wanting more and more and more and more, McCartney suddenly wanted less – the one thing celebrities are never meant to do. Furious that Lennon and Harrison had allowed legendary producer Phil Spector to remix his beloved 'The Long And Winding Road' on *Let It Be* (layering it with a wash of James Last-style strings), McCartney released his first solo album – *McCartney* – three weeks before it in the spring of 1970, hoping to steal its thunder. At the time, the album was considered a disappointment – the makeshift quality and conspicuously handmade nature of his early work annoyed those who were acclimatised to sophisticated Beatles product – though, in hindsight, its almost scatter-shot celebration of 'home, family, love', as McCartney called it, seems remarkably tender and unequivocally sincere. The imagery on the cover included cloying snapshots of Linda, the kids, the dog and the cat, as though he was abdicating from the counterculture. Predictably, the critics hated it and the music it contained, calling it 'suburban pop'n'roll', the kind that 'positively reeks of cosy domestica ... the kind of environment that stifles all creativity'.

Critics like to say that McCartney's career is analogous to Orson Welles', who started out with *Citizen Kane* and ended up doing sherry commercials. (The same could be said of Francis Ford Coppola. I overheard him in the Carlyle Hotel in New York a few years ago telling an admirer: 'I've had my brushes with creativity. I used to make films to make art; now I make films to make wine.')

But McCartney carried on regardless, releasing album after single after album of home-grown, humdrum paeans to love and marriage. He had had years of holding his funhouse mirror up to the pandemonium around him, and was now content to sink into the bosom of his family.

If the most evocative pop music resembles westerns – epic, grandiose, an assault on the senses – think Bruce Springsteen at his best, the Clash at their worst – then McCartney's early records were more like home movies, with the same bad editing, half-hearted ideas and 'little moments' that often mean little to those uninvolved with the subject. They did, however, overflow with charm. His songs are often little more than doodles, but as the late, great *New Yorker* cartoonist Saul Steinberg once said: 'The doodle is the brooding of the human hand.' And, in McCartney's case, the human heart.

McCartney was forever experimenting with words that had a pleasing and convenient sound, seemingly forgetting the fact these homespun bleeps and blurts would eventually be released to the public. He has been guilty of committing appalling crimes against the lyric (to wit: 'Wo, wo, wo, wo, only my love does it good,' from 1973's 'My Love'), though whether this was out of laziness or arrogance, it's difficult to tell (it's probably a mixture of both).

Today he admits he has been somewhat slack about his records. 'There's some rubbish,' he says. 'I'm not saying everything I've done is great. Some of them are a bit ... "that'll be a nice song when it's finished".'

Fundamentally, McCartney's horizons shrank. He had a penchant for whimsy even in the Beatles – 'When I'm 64', 'Your Mother Should Know', 'Honey Pie', 'Ob-La-Di, Ob-La-Da', etc. – but he went gaga when he went solo. The critics shouldn't have been surprised by his fascination for the ordinary, for the Vera, Chuck and Daves of this world, as there was always an

Edwardian tradition about the songs he wrote. It soon became prosaic, though; by the time the 1960s slipped into the 1970s, McCartney's unique way of capturing and captioning the lower middle classes had been hijacked by everyone from the Kinks to the Small Faces (something that continued with the Jam, Squeeze, Madness and Blur).

McCartney saw himself as a variety artist, a music-hall tinker able to knock off a ballad as well as a sweaty R&B workout; an all-round entertainer firmly rooted in the tradition of the music hall and early American rock'n'roll. Always a staunch traditionalist, the man responsible for some of the most far-reaching and influential music ever recorded has, in following years, often seemed tyrannically nostalgic for the early days of pop – his neon-garlanded world little but a giant replica of a jukebox.

In much the same way as Bob Dylan decided to shatter his own myth with the release of various out-of-character albums at the end of the 1960s, so McCartney's initial solo career can be seen as an image-burning volte face. Those early records were a reaction to the giddy production values of the Beatles' final work; exhausted from acting as both the band's musical director and stand-in manager during their final three years, McCartney was determined to move down a gear or two. But to paint him as pop's first real slacker is a mistake, as his garrulous sequence of solo albums proves. When he formed the lamentable Wings with his wife at the end of 1971, he again put his head above the parapet, and so risked constant comparison with his 'previous group'. McCartney wanted success. Badly. And during the 1970s he turned Wings into a stadium-filling supergroup. Releasing seven albums, from the sublime (*Band On The Run*, 1973) to the ridiculous (*Back To The Egg*, 1979) via the merely ordinary (*Venus And Mars*, 1975). And though this was almost beyond the call of duty, for some it was never going to be enough.

Having said that, many of McCartney's post-Beatles songs have been criminally undervalued, and it's possible to imagine lots of them sitting quite happily next to Lennon's abrasive psychedelia or Harrison's partially composed complaints on any number of Beatles LPs. Try replacing 'Good Day Sunshine' with 'Let 'Em In' (*Wings At The Speed Of Sound*, 1976), say, or 'Martha My Dear' with 'Girlfriend' (from the largely mediocre 1978 album, *London Town*). Imagine 'Monkberry Moon Delight' (*Ram*, 1971) on the *White Album* or 'Letting Go' (the 1975 single) on *Abbey Road*. With iTunes you can do just that. Some of the things McCartney's written in the last thirty years are easily as good as anything he wrote in the previous ten. Is there really so much wrong with 'Bluebird' (from *Band On The Run*, the album with which McCartney initially redeemed himself), 'Dear Boy' (*Ram*), 'My Brave Face' (*Flowers In The Dirt*, 1989), 'Every Night' (*McCartney*, 1970), 'Young Boy' (1997's *Flaming Pie*) or 'Some People Never Know' (*Wild Life*, 1971)? What about 'Jet', a whole open-topped summer in four minutes, or 'Dear Friend', about which the *Independent* journalist Richard Williams said: 'If "Dear Friend" had been the first track on the *White Album* instead of the last track on his least successful post-Beatles effort [*Wild Life*], it would be as well known as "Yesterday". It starts with a piano part that's like Thelonius Monk playing a Chopin nocturne and finishes with the horn section from a Sicilian wedding band.' Personally, I think he can be forgiven anything for writing the exultant brass coda at the end of his 1982 hit 'Take It Away', one of the most glorious, epiphanic forty-two seconds you'll find on a record anywhere.

For many, McCartney's crime has surely been the fact that he is no longer a Beatle and for some thirty-five years hasn't wanted to be. For others, his greatest failing has been his reluctance to enthusiastically work with an editor. In 1989, after another decade of wildly varying solo albums, he briefly allowed Elvis Costello to collaborate with him on an equal footing; a partnership which resulted in nearly a dozen decent songs, including 'My Brave Face', 'You Want Her Too' and 'Veronica' (recorded by Costello, for his 1989 album *Spike*).

McCartney soon ran scared when he realised the relationship reminded him too much of the one he had shared with Lennon. He has occasionally worked with George Martin, though again this has proved somewhat attritional. McCartney's been his own boss for over thirty years; he's too long in the tooth to go back to being a Beatle.

If McCartney has been guilty of anything, it's his hapless attempts at always wanting more. His autobiography, *Many Years From Now*, written with the help of Barry Miles and published in 1997, was a bizarre exercise in revisionism in which he broke down various Lennon and McCartney songs in percentages, including 'In My Life' and 'You've Got To Hide Your Love Away' as well as dozens of other Beatles songs that have always been closely associated with Lennon. Listen to McCartney and he'll tell you he wrote 40 per cent of 'Ticket To Ride', 30 per cent of 'Help', 50 per cent of 'Lucy In The Sky With Diamonds' and 40 per cent of 'A Day In The Life'. The book is a fascinating portrait of Swinging London – in parts better even than Jonathan Green's remarkable *Days In The Life* – yet it seems preposterously egotistical. This self-aggrandisement also led to rumours that he tried to reverse some of the compositional credits to McCartney-Lennon on the *Anthology* series. Carl Davis, with whom McCartney worked on the project that ended up as *Paul McCartney's Liverpool Oratorio* in 1991, also hinted the ex-Beatle was reluctant to share credits, showing a ruthless streak which jars with his image as a wacky, thumbs-aloft good ol' boy.

Rolling it back to the beginning, McCartney was always an ambitious soul; a keen, if quiet, little boy with a perpetual bob-a-job yearning in his eyes. His ambitions have proved to be limitless, almost as if being in the Beatles wasn't quite enough. He sought out Michael Jackson and Stevie Wonder and recorded with them both. He made uncredited dance records as The Fireman in 1994, and wrote a full-length symphony with the London Symphony Orchestra And Chorus – *Standing Stone* –

to mark EMI's 100th anniversary in 1997. He has even started to exhibit his paintings, and appears to want to excel at everything and anything at all, even the things he doesn't seem to be particularly good at.

Still, his career has been well irrigated with money, and Sir Paul is rich now. Each year he jumps a few places in the *Sunday Times'* Rich List, with a fortune well on its way to £1b. In 1997 Apple Corp, the Beatles' master company, of which he owns 25 per cent, produced record sales of £41.8m, while McCartney's own company, MPL Communications, saw turnover of some £9m. He has an art collection worth over £50m, and properties in Sussex, New York, London and Arizona, as well as farmland in Campbeltown and the Mull of Kintyre. Since marrying Heather Mills in 2002, he has bought another property, a relatively modest house in Brighton. He is a pop overlord now, part of the rock aristocracy.

Yet above all this, after all the myths have been put away, Paul McCartney has a dignity it's hard not to love. He is someone to admire almost in spite of himself. As the columnist Auberon Waugh once wrote of the much-maligned Princess Anne, 'To be as awful as that, and prepared to show it off without the slightest awareness of what you were showing suddenly became distinctly lovable.' How could you not love a man who recorded nursery rhymes as though they were standards; a man who determinedly put his family before his career; who has spent the best part of the last thirty years singing about Moses baskets and moonbeams? Heroes are to be applauded for what they do, not what they say, as they so often change their minds (just look at Lennon).

Now north of sixty, a member of a generation still trying to find its place in the world, Paul McCartney is a star and a half. Perhaps he hasn't harnessed his talents as well as he might, but then how many have strived for so much more while being equipped with so much less? Those stubborn neophiliacs, those afflicted by a morbid love of the new, have long since consigned

Paul McCartney to the fringes of history. Although he helped create the social meltdown of the 1960s, waltzing around Swinging London in his maroon silk brocade ties and fawn Chelsea boots, looking like a bejewelled demigod, the velvet rope is now up. He is not trendy, not cool anymore – no longer an icon of style. But in a way he has surpassed all of that. He is, after all, a Beatle, whose fabness remains undiminished. He is, for ever and ever, Paul McCartney. Always has been, always will be.

As Prefab Sprout's Paddy McAloon said not so long ago, 'Because it's impossible to write about the power of melody without sounding vague or soft (which was the ultimate crime in the brittle-hip world of 1960s pop criticism), most Beatles commentary has focused on their social impact, Lennon's more obviously autobiographical lyrics, or plain old gossip.' Author Blake Morrison agrees: 'I know it's deeply shaming to admit to a preference for bland Paul over subversive John. But McCartney was always the melodic one, and when I think of, say, ten of the more haunting and elegiac of the Beatles' songs, it turns out that Paul wrote nearly all of them. I'd put "Fixing A Hole" first, with "Eleanor Rigby", "Things We Said Today", "She's Leaving Home", "Blackbird", "Back In The USSR", "Hey Jude". "Let It Be", "Getting Better" and "Penny Lane" close behind.'

When Linda McCartney died of cancer in 1998, the tragedy seemed somehow compounded by her husband's enormous and very public devotion to her. The love of his life, his muse, the reason he had seemed to exist for over thirty years, a love that had been expressed in ballad after ballad after gorgeous ballad. Gone. Rather selfishly, we hoped that his tragedy would result in another 'Hey Jude', another 'Yesterday' or another 'Here, There And Everywhere', some huge cathartic masterpiece that would bring a little salvation to us all. Seeing as he has written some of the century's most enduring standards, and created one of the most important bodies of music of our lifetime – the man responsible for 100 per cent of 'Let It Be', 'All My Loving',

'Blackbird', 'Paperback Writer', 'You Never Give Me Your Money', and nearly a hundred other Beatles songs – this may have seemed greedy ... but then he *is* the only person who can write a Paul McCartney song. And there are only so many left to be made. So far, his new wife has yet to inspire him in the same way, but the show's not over yet.

As the T-shirt worn by his daughter (fashion designer Stella McCartney) so eloquently proclaimed when Paul was inducted into America's Rock 'n' Roll Hall of Fame a few years ago: 'About Fucking Time'. Her father should take heed.

13 112 Van Morrison Songs

Did the Belfast Cowboy make the best
album ever?

Like any true fanatic, I came to this thing rather late. I had
bought Van Morrison's *Veedon Fleece* back in 1974, when I was
barely a teenager, and, although I liked it, at that time it
was just another weird record by another weird, long-haired
visionary. In those days they were ten a penny. No, this Van
thing came to me in my thirties, when I had all but exhausted
any fascination I might have had for short, balding, irascible
visionaries. But when it finally hit, it stung. Obsessions tend to
be things you grow out of, but Van Morrison was definitely one
I grew into.

Why? I don't know. In my teens I tended to like stuff that
was short and sharp, and Van just seemed too intense, too
bound-up in himself, and frankly, that was my job. In my
troubled youth I wanted the world to come to me, to understand
my own personal burdens, not worship at the altar of someone
else's. At the time – fourteen, fifteen – I couldn't imagine that
anyone wouldn't be interested in the cross I had to bear, couldn't
imagine anyone not being transfixed by my monosyllabic
grudge against the world. I could understand people like David
Bowie and Bryan Ferry because they painted an especially vivid
picture of the world, one where ennui and introspection were
indulged and treated with respect. Why did I need Van Morrison
to complicate matters? I had my own problems.

But as I say, I eventually learnt. I can't remember where I
first heard of him, certainly can't remember where I was when

I first heard one of his records, but eventually I came to realise that he was far more important than I had originally thought.

Over the years he has been called everything from Van the Man, to Van the Mystic, to the Belfast Cowboy, but in reality he is the scowling sage, a difficult old goat with a belligerent streak in him as wide as the Irish Sea. To say that Van Morrison is terse would be like calling Alan Clarke promiscuous or Wayne Rooney prolific. 'I never ever said I was a nice guy,' he once told the journalist and DJ BP Fallon. 'OK? Never. I'm not a nice guy ... If somebody says I'm grumpy, I'm a cunt or whatever, that's OK, because I don't profess to be an angel.'

As he once said of himself, 'I'll be great when I'm finished.'

A typical example of his irascibility (true or not) was told to me some years ago by a friend who was producing a short film about Van for a television arts programme. Having communicated to the presenter his customary distaste for talking about himself, the producers wisely took him through a dry run on the morning the programme was due to be recorded. Afterwards the presenter appeared satisfied, if not a little relieved.

An hour later, when recording began, Van was asked his carefully rehearsed question, only to reply, 'You must be fucking mad if you think I'm going to answer that ...'

Stories attach themselves to Van Morrison like lint: he was apparently so alarmed by an unofficial biography in 1993 that his management team offered to buy up all 25,000 copies from the publisher Bloomsbury. And he allegedly instigated legal proceedings against the Belfast Blues Society in 1991 for attempting to place a commemorative plaque by the door of the house where he was born (prompting a cartoon in a local newspaper showing a Belfast City Council plaque inscribed with the words 'Van Morrison Was Miserable Here, 1960'). Stories of his ill temper are so legion, and so often repeated, that it's difficult to doubt their veracity or their provenance. A musician who once played with Van remembers an all-night barstool argument with the portly, obstinate Ulsterman. Morrison apparently argued the case, an arcane philosophical point, with such force and gusto that the musician eventually caved in, conceding defeat and siding with Van.

'I agree with you, Van,' he said.

'You what?' asked Morrison, somewhat perplexed.

'What you said. I agree with it.'

'Well, in that case,' the singer shot back, 'in that case, you're wrong.' Not only is this typical Van Morrison, but as anyone who has ever spent time in a Dublin pub will tell you, typically Irish.

He reserves much of his wrath, predictably, for the fourth estate. Marianne Faithfull, who occasionally lives in Dublin and bumps into Morrison all the time, once said, 'Van can be difficult, I'm sure, but belligerent? No. Anyone who says otherwise is probably a journalist – I'm sure he gives them a hard time. He's a creative artist; what the fuck do journalists expect them to be? Van is really a very good friend, almost like a counsellor, or a priest. With Van it's a bit like having a hotline to God.'

My iPod is my hotline to God, with Van being the celestial being himself. There are 112 of Van's songs on my machine, stuck incongruously between Van McCoy's 'The Shuffle' and the Velvet Underground's 'Who Loves The Sun'. This area is my church, a sanctuary away from the chainsaw guitars of the Clash or the Strokes or the madcap looning of Robbie Williams or Rod Stewart. In here, crouched over my knees in the Power-Book's virtual pew, I am at peace, even if the bloke making the music is constantly at war with himself.

For Van Morrison, success has rarely been more important than achievement. His is not the world of *OK!*, *Hello!* or *Heat*, but then their world isn't his either. He regards music as a vocation, not a step towards celebrity. 'I believe that an artist does not belong to the public but to himself,' he'll say. 'I don't want anyone to know about my personal life.' His aversion to the press is legendary – particularly to those who try to stifle him by definition. 'Nobody asks a bricklayer about laying bricks,' he said once. 'Why ask me about writing songs? There's no difference. I just do what I do.' 'It ain't why,' he once sang, 'it just is.' As Gerald Corbett of Railtrack used to say, 'We are where we are.'

But can you blame him for being so difficult, so shy, so definite in his desire to remain private? Not me. I've still got a few heroes left, and past experience has taught me that meeting them can be terribly anticlimactic. Although it might be fascinating to sit and talk to him and find out more about this tortured soul of his, I would be quite happy to know no more about him than I do today. As long as I could still listen to his records, that is.

And the work, as Van would be keen to point out himself, is the important thing.

Successful musical miscegenation is rare, yet Morrison is one of the few people who has convincingly fused rock, soul, blues, R&B, jazz and traditional pop styles (including doo-wop), with the result always being more than the sum of its parts. His music has always bypassed current trends; it hasn't just co-existed in some quasi-spiritual parallel world – one filled with haunting keyboards, onomatopoeic vocals, brushed drums, acoustic bass and barely perceptible wind instruments – it's always been the canon to curl up with after a night on the tiles. And it doesn't matter how ingrained your musical allegiances might be, whether you like garage, alt country or nu-metal, in the privacy of your own home, particularly in the privacy of my own home – the Man conquers all. After all, Van Morrison was chill out before there *was* chill out. His records have even occasionally replaced those of Marvin Gaye as the most popular tools of seduction. Even celebrities use them: to help Glenn Close relax for the sex scene in *Jagged Edge*, co-star Jeff Bridges played her Van's 'A Sense Of Wonder'; to do the same for Rachel Ward in *Against All Odds* he used 'Inarticulate Speech Of The

Heart' (well, you wouldn't use Phil Collins, now would you?).

If you believe the music press, and the bold type pop critics of the last thirty years, you'll believe that *Astral Weeks* is Van's defining statement, an album recorded in New York in just forty-eight hours in 1968 when he was just twenty-two. With a sense of self that was suddenly unassailable, and displaying a sense of abandonment seldom heard in rock music, with *Astral Weeks* Van Morrison somehow managed to define the unimaginable. It was 'nostalgic', had an 'eerie mood', was 'full of impressionist strings and woodwinds', had a 'virtuoso sense of drama', was 'rich with cryptic suggestion'. And all the rest.

Some critics believe Morrison has spent the last forty years trying to better this LP, and that his frustration at being unable to do so has led to a rather jaundiced world view. I wouldn't believe it. Nostalgia is usually little more than a stick with which to beat the present, and in fact Van's very best work came five years later. *Astral Weeks* was certainly a milestone in terms of broadening the parameters of rock, but it is not Van's finest work, not by a long shot. No, Morrison's masterpiece is 1974's *Veedon Fleece*, a record of such pastoral beauty it puts Albinoni, Chopin and Mendelssohn to shame. One critic described part of the record as the sound that grass makes when it's growing, and if there was ever a musical equivalent of Walt Whitman, then this is it. As Liam Neeson once said, 'The guy can take a walk through a meadow and go home and write an album about it.' *Veedon Fleece* sits in its own little corner of the church in my library, oblivious to everything around it. Magisterial. Calm. Sublime.[1]

---

[1] Nick Cave is a huge fan of *Veedon Fleece* too: 'Of all the records I've had, this is by far the one I play the most. To me, it's better than *Astral Weeks*, in that I can get sick of *Astral Weeks*, but I can never get sick of *Veedon Fleece*. I've been in the same room as Van Morrison. I've seen him toddling around with a drink in each hand, but it didn't look like he wanted to be disturbed. He's a hero of mine, and it often pays to steer clear of your heroes.'

In between these two records came *Moondance*, *His Band And The Street Choir* (both 1970), *Tupelo Honey* (1971), *Saint Dominic's Preview* (1972) and *Hard Nose The Highway* (1973), a remarkable body of work that would have lasted other artists a lifetime, and loads of which are on my 'Pod. Since then there have been dozens of records (he has made more than thirty albums), which range from the prosaic to the bewildering – every one exploring Morrison's obsessive quest for personal enlightenment. Along the way he has written the occasional pop classic too: 'Jackie Wilson Said', 'Bulbs', 'Bright Side Of The Road', 'Have I Told You Lately That I Love You'. Lyrically, he has been obsessed with the lost, legendary dreamland of Avalon and the rain-soaked Irish countryside. As befits an Irishman, he worships the rain, and it's rare to find a Morrison record that doesn't mention something about 'gardens wet with rain after a summer shower'. In Morrison's world, every day is a grand, soft day.

It is too easy to dismiss the effect that music can have on you. For some it is the Buzzcocks, for others it is Hank Williams, for me it is Van. I am obsessive about everyone from the Ramones to Marvin Gaye to U2 to Del Shannon and beyond, but Van strikes chords in me I didn't know I had. Of course, it is possible, while listening to some of his work, to feel consumed by peace and completeness – Morrison 'concentrates on capturing the evanescent quality of the moment through impressionism', writes one of his biographers, Johnny Rogan – but it can also be most disconcerting. Listen to 'Across The Bridge Where Angels Dwell', 'Into The Mystic', 'Hymns To The Silence' or 'Flamingoes Fly' (one of Van's lost tracks from *The Philosopher's Stone*, recorded in 1974 but only released in 1998), and it can all well up – euphoria, melancholy and all points in between. For me, listening to Van Morrison is sometimes like life squared.

Like any maverick, Van Morrison has done some odd things. As well as being overwrought and pompous, he has embraced scientology, dabbled with gestalt therapy, recorded a duet with Cliff Richard and covered a song made famous by Kermit the Frog ('It's Not Easy Being Green'). But hell, you expect this kind of nonsense from your heroes. After all, he is a soul of torment, isn't he? Isn't that what it says on the tin? Like his good friend Bob Dylan, Morrison seems to hate the way he looks, determined to contort his face and body, no matter how ludicrous he appears. His suits are usually too pinched (at least two sizes too small), his body constricted, and when he does dress well, even then he tries to disguise himself, slipping onto stage in his dark, velvet-collared John Rocha jacket, pork-pie hat (he loves a hat, does our Van) and sunglasses, looking not unlike a West Brit Blues Brother.

The very idea of being a pop star is just anathema to him. He is genuinely enigmatic, and goes to great lengths to distance himself from the world of pop. Some years ago, he wrote a letter to the Irish *Sunday Independent* complaining about their constant references to Van Morrison the Rock Star. 'To call me a rock star is absurd,' he wrote, 'as anyone who has listened to my music will observe. On the one hand I am flattered by the sudden attention, having spent most of my life living the role of anti-hero and getting on with my job.' On the other hand ... in Morrison's eyes, being a troubadour is a noble vocation, like being a craftsman or a poet – someone who works with their hands, if only to lift a pen.

Morrison's influence has never been in doubt, and he's been an inspiration to Bruce Springsteen, Mike Scott, Ryan Adams, Tim and Jeff Buckley, Kevin Rowland – the list just goes on. (Incidentally, Morrison's 1972 single 'Jackie Wilson Said (I'm In Heaven When You Smile)' failed to chart until ten years later when it was revived by Rowland's Dexy's Midnight Runners. The song confused the *Top of the Pops* production staff so much that they screened a backdrop of darts player Jocky Wilson during Dexy's performance.) Morrison has become something of an established figure too. His song 'Days Like This' became the unofficial anthem of the Irish peace process after being licensed by the Northern Ireland Office in 1995, and his face has even graced a stamp issued by the Republic. Morrison's Irishness is something he wears like a badge; it's not just manifested in his music but in everything he does. Steven Pillster, one of Morrison's tour managers, witnessed the beginnings of his search for his heritage when he knew him in Dublin years ago. 'I always thought Van had a tough time finding his centre,' he says. 'It really came to me in Dublin that he's really a mad Irish poet. That's his genetic make-up.'

I realise it's a cliché – and not just an ordinary cliché but a motherfucking enormodome of a cliché – but I fell in love with Van at the same time as I fell in love with Ireland. In 1991 I met a Dublin girl called Jackie, and in the process of our affair she took me there, a city that had yet to benefit from the injection of European investment or suffer the indignity of becoming first choice for British stag weekends. What a beautiful and wondrous place. Could I live here? Having spent a decade building a career, I began to consider what it might be like to bow out, to leave everything I had worked so hard to achieve. And while Dublin was only 40 minutes away from London, it felt more in keeping with Vienna or Prague, a northern European chocolate box of a city (dark chocolate, of course).

Some of Jackie's friends were, however, circumspect about her London style-magazine editor – one of them, when introduced to me, said, 'Aha, another fuckin' Brit, cold as frozen snot'; and *The Crying Game* director Neil Jordan accused me of pretty much the same malaise: 'Why is it with you Brits we have to go through the whole bollix again when we meet you a second time? Meet an Irish person once and you're friends for life. You have to meet a Brit six times before he'll fuckin' say hello to you.' Which I thought was fair enough, really.

But I fell in love with the place anyway, hook, line and tinker. Over the course of the next eighteen months I spent over eight weeks there, and was quietly beginning to wonder if I could live there. In the end the relationship faltered (my fault, obviously); however, it did prove to me that I was probably looking to fall in love – not with a country, but with a girl. And bizarrely enough, just a short while later it happened.

As for Morrison, his 'job' doesn't seem as important now as it once did, and Van hasn't really surfed the zeitgeist for some time now. He still makes records, and some of them are very good, yet he seems to have drifted off the cultural radar a little. His last truly great record was *Hymns To The Silence* in 1991, a double CD characterised by nostalgia gospel. The blues seem to be his current obsession, and, again like Bob Dylan, he feels obliged to embrace it in a bid to dignify his old age. As Keith Richards always liked to say, if the bluesman is still allowed to perform in his sixties, then why can't the white man? Van Morrison is one of those 1960s musicians who once saw them-selves as menaces to society but who now look upon themselves as endangered species. 'I don't think I will ever mellow out,' he says. 'If you mellow out you get eaten up.'

I've bumped into Van Morrison a few times, most recently at a private benefit concert in aid of Tibet he gave at London's Grosvenor House (where Morrison. in typically contrary fashion, turned a twenty-minute showcase into a glorious two-hour set that belied the anodyne location and weathered the interruptions of Richard Gere, who insisted on jamming with Morrison and his band), but I've never particularly wanted to approach him as I figure he deserves his privacy. I've never really seen the point of just hurling yourself at a celebrity. If you're introduced, fine, but otherwise it's just embarrassing. Plus, you also run the risk of being blanked, like the journalist who approached Russell Crowe at a party in London. 'How are you?' the journo asked. 'I'm not doing interviews,' Crowe allegedly replied. Cheers. In Van's case, who needs another starfucker asking you to explain the lyrics to 'Linden Arden Stole The Highlights' or 'Caravan'? (It's music of love and devotion, what else do you need to know?) Lord knows, I've had my chances; I'd often see him in the Nisa supermarket in Notting Hill Gate (he had a house near there in Holland Park for a while). I'd be sifting through the microwave pizzas and Super Tuscans only to turn around and see Van's taciturn face staring back at me; dressed in a baby-shit-brown leather jacket, voluminous dirty jeans, a pair of battered cowboy boots and a scowl, looking rather like a cab driver who has just been poorly tipped.

Which brings me to my favourite, though surely apocryphal, Van Morrison story. A few years ago, to celebrate the end of another successful Womad festival, a famous rock star threw a party in a barn near the festival site in the West Country, inviting all the stars who had performed at the festival, plus any celebrity who happened to be passing through. Said rock star invited Van, telling him that it would be a fairly low-key affair, and that his presence would be most welcome. Van, who at times can be pathologically antisocial, said that he'd try to come. Secretly both the rock star and Van knew that he would be unlikely to turn up.

Anyway, the party was a raging success, full of the great and the good, and all those in the smiling and nodding racket. But, unsurprisingly, no Van. At two in the morning, with only a handful of punters remaining, there was a quiet knock on the big barn door. The security guard opened it slowly, took a look at our badly dressed hero, a more taciturn than usual Van Morrison, and turned to face the stragglers. 'Anyone order a minicab?' he said.

It would be heart-warming to think that Van Morrison would have seen the funny side of this, but as the man knows himself, things are rarely that easy.

14 It's Still Sinatra's World: We Still Just Live In It

In which I get my hands on a Sinatra demo tape

It has just gone ten in the evening and I am deep, knee-deep, in shag-pile. I have disappeared under a blanket of piping horns, tortured vocals and lush string arrangements. I am deep in loungecore, wallowing in a bed of Burt Bacharach, John Barry and Frank Sinatra. I am in my den, my lounge, uploading Sinatra's *Songs For Swinging Lovers* as well as a recently compiled Rat Pack CD and wishing I were wearing a snap-brim hat. I am in playlist No. 3, rather pretentiously called Deep Lounge, and I intend to stay there for a while (*The Sopranos* doesn't start for another hour). Three hundred and eighty-eight songs, 22.4 hours of music taking up 1.89 GB (one song from Air, eight from America, one from Andrew Gold, nine from Andy Williams, etc.). Three hundred and eighty eight songs including everything from the obvious (Burt, Barry, etc.), to Thomas Leer (weird post-punk electronica) and the Swingle Singers (the tremendously unfashionable 1960s vocal group) via Sergio Mendes (Brazilian MOR), Brian Eno and some pretty twee 1970s pop (Alessi, Chicago, the Guess Who, etc.).

And when I say an hour, I don't mean an hour listening to my iPod, I mean an hour (OK, it will soon turn into two – *The Sopranos* I can catch on DVD) ploughing through iTunes, editing, uploading, moving (prefixing artist names in order to create a playlist-within-a-playlist), and generally pootling about. I am consumed. Obsessed. Podded. If I find myself with five minutes to spare, I'm down in the den, Podding – editing, uploading, moving. The other night, while my wife and I were watching Johnny Depp trying to pass himself off as Keith Richards in *Pirates of the Caribbean*, I nipped downstairs during the boring bits – and there are enough of them, let me tell you – to fillet the first Jamie Cullum CD (three songs initially chosen, although many more would follow: 'Twentysomething', 'I Could Have Danced All Night', 'Wind Cries Mary'). I Pod before I go to work, Pod as soon as I get home. I have yet to get up in the middle of the night to Pod, but in principle I have nothing against the idea.

Lounge has been something of a particular obsession for me. And where once it was simply a rather large part of my record collection, now it is a playlist. I have loved lounge since before I was ten, not that it was called lounge then, more like records my parents had lying around the house (which, let's be honest, isn't much of a name for a marketable genre of pop, or a playlist, come to that). And not just the sound of it, but the look of it too. I suppose it stems from growing up in a house where Dean Martin and Frank Sinatra were rarely off the turntable. From England's 1966 World Cup victory through to the moon landing, my earliest memories revolve around listening to 'Return To Me', 'Volare', 'Fly Me To The Moon', 'Under The Bridges of Paris' and 'I've Got You Under My Skin'. I also remember riding a chopper, reading *Goal!* and eating butterscotch Angel Delight, but for me my pre-adolescence was defined by smarmy Italianate men who never seemed to take their hats off. For me, those songs have always defined a certain kind of nostalgic sophistication, however ersatz it may have been. These guys were the business – cool, savvy, with the sort of dark brown voices which put you safely to sleep at night.

The Dean Martin and Sergio Mendes records were not only the ones that meant the most to me, they were always the ones I kept. Whenever I went through a period of reinvention –

pretty much every year from the age of thirteen to twenty-one – and parted company with a bunch of records which I thought had become embarrassing – in 1974 this would have been the Gary Glitter singles (bought in 1972), in 1976 it was the likes of Genesis' *Trick Of The Tail* (bought six months previously) and Jethro Tull's *Aqualung* (1974-ish), etc. – the soundtracks and the John Barry compilations were always the albums that made the cut, the ones sitting stoically at the back of the record box, under the bed or under the stairs, quietly minding their own business.[1]

It wasn't just the music, of course – it never was. Whether it was Frank Sinatra or Alice Cooper I was fawning over, the way they looked was always as important as the way they sounded. And there was one man in particular who pricked my interest. The man pictured on the LP sleeves I found under my parents' record player was like no man I had ever seen; you didn't get many Italian-Americans swanning around East Anglia dressed in herringbone sports jackets, open-neck shirts, pin V-neck cardigans, white slacks, white silk socks, and black suede loafers. Not even on the air-force bases where I grew up. But then that was the point, I guess. Dean Martin inhabited a world that wasn't easily accessible to an eight-year-old who had yet to buy his own trousers, let alone visit the Sahara Tahoe.

The image sank deep and took hold. I would never forget the louche, debonair gadabout who sang like an angel and dressed like a gangster on his day off. Soon enough, I realized that Dino

---

[1] A.A. Gill is, rather unbelievably, still a big fan of 'the Tull', and one day when we spoke on the phone, as I was in the middle of the book, he had their album *Stand Up* playing on his iMac as he was finishing his restaurant review for the *Sunday Times*. Far from being embarrassed, he seemed enormously proud of the fact he'd been caught, and proceeded to give me snippets from his iTunes collection. 'Go on, listen to this, you'll never guess what it is! I bet you haven't heard this for years!' Adrian's enthusiasm for Mott The Hoople and Stealer's Wheel was unlikely, but incredibly charming. His hatred of rap is more predictable and far more understandable ...

wasn't alone in his sartorial elegance, and after discovering Frank Sinatra – with his club bow tie and straw hat – and the rest of the Rat Pack (Sammy Davis, Jr, Peter Lawford, Joey Bishop), I became quietly besotted with the surface smarts of 1950s America. At the age of ten it wasn't just Marc Bolan who was rocking my world, it was a weedy big band singer from Hoboken and his genuinely Italian pal. Tragically, I was a style obsessive before I was a teenager.

And as for the music, it was my parents' copies of *Sinatra's Songs For Swingin' Lovers* and *A Swingin' Affair* that really made my heart leap. Even at that young age I could tell that when Sinatra sang 'Stars fractured 'bama last night' he was being as irreverent and as playful as Alice Cooper or David Bowie. This, along with the legend that is 'I've Got You Under My Skin' – unnegotiably Sinatra's best-ever performance on record – and 'It Happened In Monterey' – the sort of glamorous travelogue that really kicks in with an adolescent – convinced me that Sinatra was the coolest man ever to walk the earth.

He liked the ladies too, though at the time this was merely an assumption on my part. I later found out that Sinatra had an almost hourly need for sex, and when he wanted a girl, it didn't really matter who she was. It was like a food chain: when he was 'dialing for pussy' as he called it, he'd start with the film stars, then work his way down through the ingénues and finally the hookers. The only time he wasn't chasing the ladies was when he was 'in training' for an album; then, he was a monk.[1] Seriously, how could you not love this man?

For years this was a fairly one-sided love affair, although

---

[1] When the legendary director John Ford asked the equally legendary Ava Gardner what she saw in her 'one hundred and twenty pound runt' of a husband, she shocked the veteran Ford by retorting, 'Well, there's only ten pounds of Frank, but there's one hundred and ten pounds of cock.'

eventually I got the chance to live my own particular Sinatra anecdote.

Some years ago in our office there worked a lovely (if slightly high-maintenance) girl called Anthea Anka, a young Los Angelina whose father is Paul Anka, the hugely successful teen idol of the post-Elvis era who went on to write the English lyrics to 'My Way'. I was in Los Angeles in 2001 on business with some friends from work and Anthea arranged for us to see Paul one night. We booked his favourite table at The Ivy, dressed up in our finest Savile Row threads and turned up a respectable twenty minutes early ('Sir, you might be more comfortable in this seat, as Mr Anka likes to sit there,' our server pointed out).

Anthea had briefed us to not *at any point* mention Frank Sinatra, or 'My Way', or anything to do with the song. She was vaguely aware that there had been some sort of bust-up between them (singer and composer) and that we shouldn't tempt fate by reminding him of this.

And so when Mr Anka arrived (even we were beginning to get reverential by now), we dutifully asked him how his Vegas residency was going, how his publishing was doing, and what life was like on the road ('Great', 'Great', and 'Great', I seem to remember the answers being). At no point did we mention Big Frank, the 'song', or indeed anything of the sort. I think Alex at one point half-mentioned the fact that the Rat Pack were becoming quite popular again in London, although I'm not sure our guest heard (and Alex's observations were curtailed somewhat sharply by both Bill and I kicking him sharply in the shins).

But after only about ten minutes or so, the Ankatola floors us all by asking, completely unprompted, 'So, are you boys Sinatra fans?'

Well, you have never seen three grown men try and ingratiate themselves so much: 'Yes, Paul, I've got every original Capital album before he left to set up Reprise.' 'Yes, Paul, I actually saw him on his last trip to London.' 'Yes, Paul. I especially like the bossa nova albums he made in the 1960s ...' etc., etc. We were nauseating, but I think Paul was pleased. We'd loosened up, stopped acting like British stuffed shirts, and were still blowing smoke up his ass an hour later ('So, Paul, what was he really like?' 'Was he a shit in the studio?' 'Were there, you know, always women around?').

I'm sure he could tell that we really were massive Sinatra fans because after a while he began telling us about ... the 'song'. He told us that Sinatra had called him up and asked him to work on it, told us how he'd sweated for days to get the lyrics right, how Sinatra had asked him to tweak it, and, finally, how Sinatra had invited him to the session.

We were ploughing our way through the Pinot Grigio by this time, and we were all getting worked up, as was Paul, in the retelling of the story. Finally, he turned to me – maybe realising that, out of the three of us, I was the saddest, most obsessive Sinatraphile – and said, safe in the knowledge that he had the answer on hand, 'Guess how many takes it took Sinatra to nail it?' I can't quite remember what we volunteered, but I think the responses were in the low numbers. But none of the guesses was right.

'You know how many takes it took Sinatra to nail "My Way"?' asked the composer. 'One, just one damn take. Now that man was a professional. That man was *the* man.'

The night dragged on, and ended in the small hours in a cigar club somewhere in deepest Hollywood, where we all sat around smoking Silk Cut and Cohibas. As the three of us got up to leave Paul to his Lah-Di (...-Dah=cigar), he asked if I'd like to hear Frank's first take of 'My Way'. As rhetorical questions go, this was one of the best I'd ever had, and I obviously said yes. 'Yes,' I said, 'I'd love that Paul, that would be great.'

'Well, I'll send it then,' he said, as a curl of blue smoke coiled its way from his mouth to the ceiling.

Thirty seconds later, in the lift going down to the car park,

Bill turned and said, 'That, I guarantee, is not going to happen.'

But it did. Ten days later a package arrived by FedEx from LA, inside of which was a freshly cut CD in a blank jewel case, and a little note from Paul: 'Enjoy', it said.

And when I played it – on my Mac, about five seconds later, that's exactly what I did. The CD contained Frank Sinatra's very first take of 'My Way', the one you hear on the record; although, unlike the record, all you can hear is Frank. You can vaguely make out the backing track seeping from Sinatra's headphones, but for the purposes of the argument it is only Frank's vocals that you can hear. The first time I played it was like some sort of quasi-religious experience, like listening to Paul McCartney first play 'Let It Be' for the Beatles (*Anthology III*), or watching the Clash perform 'Complete Control' in front of a captive audience (Victoria Park, East London, 1978). Considering how good studio jiggery-pokery is these days, it would be easy to assume that Paul had simply edited out the instruments, leaving Frank to sing to his heart's content, but this was an actual take – the first take, for fuck's sake! – of Frank Sinatra singing not only one of his trademark songs but one of the defining popular songs of the twentieth century – live, by himself, unaccompanied!

Paul's CD has since become one of my most treasured possessions, which is ironic seeing that 'My Way' was never one of my favourite Sinatra songs, not at all. For me 'My Way' was always a prime example of Pub Frank, one of those obvious karaoke Sinatra songs such as 'Strangers In The Night' or 'Chicago' that over-refreshed Sinatra fans think they can get away with come closing time, one of the broader, more populist tracks from the Reprise years, rather than the Classic Capital years. But without the strings, the embellishment, the heavy-handed production, 'My Way' becomes a plaintive letter from the check-out lounge, a poetic summation of a life lived large.

There are 131 other Sinatra songs on my iPod, and all of

them subscribe, in one way or another, to the man's particular way of looking at things (enthusiastic till proven otherwise). They have kept me going for years, although for most of those years I felt pretty much alone. Liking Sinatra, liking lounge, was always a fairly guilty pleasure, until about 1994 when it all became trendy again. Suddenly, record shops were full of yards and yards of hastily compiled CDs featuring dodgy Jose Feliciano b-sides and rare Free Design cover versions previously only found in Japan. All the stuff I'd spent twenty years collecting was suddenly nestling next to Oasis records in HMV. Why? Because the rave generation woke up with a headache and needed something to calm it down I suppose. Overnight, this stuff was everywhere. And it wasn't just the sound that people loved, it was the record covers, the clothes, the very idea of it. Lounge was a world of possibilities, life in the fast lane set to xylophone and flute. And in the departure lounge of, er, lounge (a place clothed – naturally – in leopard and sharkskin), there was room for the furious ultra nova of Marcus Valle, the idiosyncratic supperclub doo-wop of Tommy Edwards and the dessert-wine-wafer-thin-mint-and-raging-gas-fire-soul of Dusty Springfield; room for torch singers, crooners, swingers and lounge lizards. Here there was room for brunch baroque, space-age bachelor pad music and elevator noir.

And, of course, room for Sinatra too (there was always room for Sinatra).

By my early thirties, easy had become the music I felt defined by. Like Steve Martin in *The Jerk*, I had found a music that spoke to me! This was my music, music that made me feel clean, unsullied, satisfied and complete. It was also the music I inadvertently used to seduce my wife, Sarah. These were the records I played when I dragged her back to my Shepherds Bush flat, the records the tapes played as we darted along the A303 on country weekends, the records I sang to her as we strolled through Notting Hill on Saturday mornings. On our third date I took her to the Atlantic Bar & Grill, which had just opened off Piccadilly Circus, a venue I had seen for the first time a few weeks previously.

Criticising a friend's entrepreneurial forays is tantamount to criticising his intelligence. It's almost as bad as criticising his woman, or, God forbid, his clothes. So when Oliver Peyton gave me a guided tour of a dilapidated sunken ballroom in the depths of Piccadilly, telling me he was going to turn it into the biggest bar in London, I bit my lip and nodded enthusiastically. Even with his seat-of-the-pants success – being the first man to import Sapporo beer and Absolut vodka into the UK, running a dozen or so successful nightclubs, managing implausibly popular pop groups – there was no way he was going to turn this Titanic-style wine lodge, with its brocade furnishings and vaulted ceiling, into a must-visit venue.

What did I know? It soon became the hottest bar in the world, and is still going over a decade later. It took me six years to summon up the courage to tell Oliver I didn't think the Atlantic was going to work. We were, quite naturally, in the Spearmint Rhino in Las Vegas. 'You didn't think it would work?' he said to me, as the libidinous strains of lapdancing disco wafted around our ears. 'Fuck me, neither did I. But I thought, if I'm going to go tits-up, then I may as well do it properly.'

Back in 1994, as Sarah and I made our way along Regent Street, en route to Oliver's new post-modern gin palace (my wife wearing an eau-de-nil mini kaftan and a pair of black Robert Clergerie mules, and myself wearing a crinkly antici-patory smile), I swung round a lamp post and burst into song, croaking out the first two verses of Sinatra's 'Learnin' The Blues' – 'The tables are empty, the dance floor's deserted', etc. My wife says it was this public display of emotion more than anything else that convinced her she should allow herself to be proposed to.

'Music was obviously Dylan's thing,' she says, 'especially all the Frank Sinatra, Burt Bacharach stuff. When I'd been taken back to boys' flats in the past they'd just stuck a record on, but

Dylan stood over his stereo like it was his desk, a man totally in charge of his domain. His stereo was the only thing in his flat that wasn't covered with dust. He'd play one song and then whip it off seconds later saying, "You just *have* to listen to this." He even whipped off the songs I liked. He was in a trance, like a DJ, always thinking of the next record. It was a form of seduction but it was also a way of editing his life by using particular soundtracks. There'd be a soundtrack for waking up, going to work, coming home, everything.

'He was incredibly territorial, and whenever we were in a situation where music was required, Dylan would immediately take charge. He just assumed he had greater knowledge and better taste than everyone else. And he usually had.' (OK, those last four words shouldn't have been in direct quotes.)

It was only when I asked my wife about this particular period that I realised how monomaniacal (or, perhaps more appropriately, boring) I had been. A decade before the iPod would become my own equivalent of Marcel's Petit Madeleine, I was already an obsessive fantasist.

'Every dinner party would have a series of tapes specially recorded for it, anticipating the changes of mood, and guests' own particular tastes. He used to force-feed people the Swingle Sisters, too, although not that many wanted seconds.'

In 2002, I had an affair with hubris when I agreed to record a song for *Anything But Summertime*, a charity CD organised by pianist and former Blockhead Rod Melvin on behalf of the Groucho Club. Ignoring one of the cardinal rules governing cover versions – you don't mess with Frank – I decided to try my hand at 'Learnin' The Blues' (from wannabe to gonnabe in one misguided fell swoop). I've sung it enough times to my wife and children, I thought I'd let the world know how good a crooner I was (or if not the world then at least the thousand or so odd souls who might be coerced into buying a copy in the Groucho). Sade's Andrew Hale produced it, recording my voice and Roddy's piano up in Andrew's Queens Park studio. Encased in a cylindrical recording booth, with my cans on and a Sure-esque microphone brushing my lips, I felt like I was deep in the Capital Building in LA in 1956; all I needed was a snap-brim hat, two fingers of scotch and an unbelievable singing voice. As you may have already gathered, I didn't have any of these things, and my version of 'Learnin' The Blues' proved I was the one thing worse than a pub singer – a theme pub singer (and, remarkably, a worse singer than Frank Sinatra Jr, something I thought was technically impossible). I was, however, in good company, as the album also contained Nigel Planer ruining 'You Do Something To Me' and Simon Kelner (editor of the *Independent*) and Tristan Davies (editor of the *Independent on Sunday*) performing major surgery on Glen Campbell's 'Wichita Lineman' (without, I should add, an anaesthetic).[1]

If I think about it, I've been singing for as long as I can remember, right back to the days when I used to clap along to Disney songs. I didn't stammer when I sang; on the contrary, singing helped me fly. I used to sing so much I started doing it involuntarily, launching into Rod Stewart, Frank Sinatra or the Who at the drop of a trilby. We can often be caught absent-mindedly singing along to the most recent song we've heard, but what do you find yourself singing when you don't even know you're doing it? For years, when I was in the shower, the bath, or just walking to work, I would sing 'Synchronicity II' by the Police, a song I neither like nor admire, but obviously one that had some cruel, subconscious hold over me. This would come out at the most inappropriate moments, suggesting perhaps that I suffered from an incurable case of Bad Pop Tourettes (I remember one such incident when I was bringing a

---

[1] Simon, Tristan and I once sang this song around a piano in a bar in Paris, after a rather protracted lunch at Alain Ducassé's famous restaurant. As we took breath to launch into the second verse, one of the barmen tapped me on the shoulder and said, with as much benevolence as one would expect from a French waiter confronted with a gaggle of drunk Englishmen, 'Can your friends actually hear the music?'

girl a cup of tea in bed after a night of designer debauchery, only to find myself singing Sting's appalling lyrics as I paraded naked around the bedroom; the thought still unnerves me fifteen years later). I also went through a phase of singing Paul Weller's 'Bull-rush' and the theme tune to *Friends* (the shame, the shame), and throughout the process of writing this book have been afflicted with an ability to launch into the Buzzcocks' 'I Believe' at any time of the day or night. Weird.

Air guitar was never really my bag, only appealing to me around the age of twelve, when I did what every male proto-teenager did at the time, and pose in front of my bedroom mirror with my invisible starburst finish Les Paul, emulating the power chords of Pete Townshend and the homoerotic electro rockabilly of Mick Ronson on Bowie's 'Hang Onto Yourself'. But even at that age I thought it looked a bit daft; singing just seemed to be more sophisticated, more appropriate.

However, I have learned that the trick when playing air guitar is to look enthusiastic. Every year *GQ* has a Christmas lunch in the boardroom at Vogue House, our offices in Hanover Square. It's a staff event to which we invite a selection of friends and contributors – Tony Parsons, Boris Johnson, Peter Mandelson,[1] Piers Morgan, Rod Liddle, Abi Titmuss, Simon Kelner, Peter York, etc. In 2001 we invited the disgraced Tory MP Neil Hamilton and his bubbly wife Christine, largely because we'd

---

[1] I was always trying to get Peter Mandelson to write about music instead of politics in his *GQ* column, yet he was stubbornly resistant, as he was with most things. He didn't much like writing about the press either, even though he was particularly good at it. Once, over lunch at The Ivy, as his two security guards looked on from a nearby table, I tried to get him to write about his relationship with the papers, as it was one of the few subjects he rarely pulled any punches on. 'You should really think about this, Peter, as you're always good at kicking up dust,' I said. 'You're always being hounded by the press and it's good to get your own back every now and again. I mean, just imagine what it would be like if you were a celebrity instead of a politician.' At which he stopped eating, looked at me plaintively, and said, 'But I *am* a celebrity.' Fifteen-love.

just photographed them naked for the magazine, posing as Adam and Eve (a joy, let me tell you), and thought it would be a wheeze to ask them along. We couldn't have wished for better sports, and while Neil stripped down to his boxers in order for one of our girls to shave his chest hair, Christine, emboldened by seven or eight glasses of champagne, leapt onto the board-room table and played the most enthusiastic air guitar I've ever seen, belting out Townshend-esque windmill chords to Rod Stewart's 'Maggie May' without a care.

Good scenery deserves a decent soundtrack, music which can add more than pathos to the vista in front of us – music that can complement the feeling of careering around the Amalfi coast in an open-top sports car, conjure up images of sharp-suited secret agents cavorting about in Portmeirion, Monaco or the Florida Keys, or simply evoke the languor of a moonlit tropical beach. Easy/lounge, call it what you will, is that music, a passport to international listening pleasure, a soundtrack for life; the loungecore fan can drive to the shops like anybody else, but with the right Sinatra track on the iTrip – and I would suggest 'Around The World', 'Summer Wind', 'Come Fly With Me', 'It's Nice To Go Trav'ling' and 'Night And Day' for starters – he does it in split-screen Technicolour, in a Maserati, accompanied by glockenspiel, clave and marimba. 'I always tried to make songs that were mini-movies,' said Burt Bacharach, as though aural picturesque travelogues were the most natural thing on earth.

Critics would say that Bacharach's music offered a respite from reality, but his stuff was anything but easy, and while his and Hal David's songs might have seemed like snapshots of sunny prosperity, there was often a cruel subtext hovering just behind the sundeck; David's words full of heartbreak, Bacharach's convoluted music never less than maudlin (a song like 'Promises, Promises' changes time signature in almost every bar, and was one of the many Bacharach songs that Sinatra found it impossible to sing). Lyricist David often wrote against the mood, too. If you had been presented with a tune as bright and as rhythmic as 'Do You Know The Way To San Jose', you might have thought it warranted an instinctively happy lyric, although in David's hands it became an ode to foiled aspirations and tarnished dreams.

But easy or not, it was the stuff of personal obsession (*my* personal obsession) and, in the Nineties, global attention. If, in 1990, someone had offered to pay you a substantial amount of money to predict how pop culture would develop over the next ten years, what would you have suggested? Internet sex? Morphed movie stars? The iPod? Surely a re-appreciation of Burt Bacharach couldn't have been further from your mind. Easy listening was largely ignored by consumers and critics alike, always considered rock music's poor relation. And when it was appreciated, it tended to be from a camp perspective (how many 'serious' music consumers express an ironic penchant for ABBA or 'the greatest guitar solo committed to vinyl', the one buried in the Carpenters' 'Goodbye To Love'?). The buzzwords were always pejorative: quasi, ersatz, kitsch, mock, Music Lite. For years lounge was so maligned you could have been forgiven for assuming it had been responsible for some form of cultural genocide. When Elvis first flicked his five inches of buttered yak wool in the mid-1950s, rock'n'roll pushed mainstream pop, the diet of the previous generation, into the margins, a world where it soon became known as MOR, or Middle of the Road. And that's where it pretty much stayed for forty years, with the likes of the Sandpipers, Nat 'King' Cole and Tony Christie destined to languish in the charity shops of this world, nestling between the bad career moves of REO Speedwagon and Westlife.

Twenty years ago the death of MOR was considered a forgone conclusion, but these days, not a day goes by when something is not revived; it might be a crime writer, a fashion statement, an architectural movement, even a decade. Today it's impossible to let bygones be bygones. Look through any newspaper supplement and you'll be told that – bloody hell, *already?* –

minimalism is back, or the platform shoe, or the 1940s, or the 1960s, or – with increasing regularity – even the 1980s. Popular culture, by its very nature, is blessed with built-in obsolescence, but today it comes complete with its own revival button, too. Press once to consign it to oblivion, press twice to bring it back. In the world of fashion – where lasting statements are scarce – revivals and homages are commonplace. The fashion industry used to do one decade at a time, but now they're all playing simultaneously. You can be Frank Sinatra on Monday, Brian Jones on Tuesday, Elliott Gould Wednesday, Burt Bacharach Thursday – and, if you're particularly unlucky – Tony Hadley on Friday.

Bacharach is hardly a surprising choice. Sergio Mendes and Herb Alpert might have been masters of the aural sunset, yet for many their Latino style was a little too phony; while exotica stars Esquivel and Martin Denny were not exactly fashion pin-ups. It was Bacharach who had the jet-set cool – the looks, the urbane sophistication, the cars and the girls. Like Sinatra personified the 1950s, Bacharach personified the 1960s bachelor, a man whose life actually mirrored those of the characters you saw in the movies. If Brian Wilson and Phil Spector were the kings of the dashboard radio, then Bacharach was the ruler of the open-plan hi-fi, a man who pushed 1950s mood music into tomorrow. If Kennedy was your president, then Bacharach was your composer.

And on top of all this – and the reason that Bacharach was noticed in the first place – was the fact that he wrote like an eiderdown dream, creating dozens of modern-day standards that are up there with anything by Porter, Gershwin or Berlin. If Hal David used the iconography of the Sixties like his own private alphabet, then Bacharach painted a world that allowed it all to happen, producing songs and records that eclipsed the work of many soundtrack composers. Speeding along the great suburban highways of sunshine superland, a Bacharach symphony was all you needed.

And if Frank Sinatra was the only singer who could sing a semi-colon, Bacharach was the only composer who could make a minor chord sound like a breaking heart.

When lounge bounced back in the 1990s, suddenly, no hip-hop tenement opera or paean to mail-order youth culture was complete without a knowing glance towards the eccentric orchestration of Bacharach, Nelson Riddle or Billy May (remember the Bacharach-inspired syncopated trumpet break in Blur's 'The Universal'?). The sophisticated schmaltz and beguiling soundscapes designed by Esquivel and Les Baxter not only created a credible lineage for the perpetrators of modern ambient and trance music – from Stereolab to Stock, Hausen & Walkman – but newcomers to the lost genre also developed their own musical language, one employed by British bands as diverse as the Divine Comedy (pretentious art school muzak) and Corduroy (breathless Sergio Mendes pastiches). Eclecticism became the key, which is why loungecore is perfect for the iPod.

One of the weirdest things about its new-found popularity was that everyone looked suspiciously like they were jumping on the lounge bandwagon because it was the only one left, and Bacharach, Jackie Trent and Andy Williams seemed only to have been resurrected from the cultural grave because everything else had already been dug up. Since the rules were rewritten in 1976, blue beat, country, punk, heavy metal, glam and futurism had all been recalled from the pop-cultural skip, so why not MOR?

There was a period just after punk broke in Britain when young bands fell over themselves to pick their way through pop's past, reinventing themselves using everything from Sixties power pop and plastic dresses to industrial metal and constructivist graphics; groups became lab-coated technicians, *Thunderbird* puppets, urban loners and blue-collar academics (if you were Wire, Pere Ubu or ABC, you either had to have a good story to tell or a funny hat: the music was nothing if it wasn't contextualised). Ska, soul, rockabilly – everything came back in all-too regular four-month cycles. And so having exhumed most of the immediate past, the public turned to lounge, another victim of the post-modern blender, the post-modern loop.

It is a loop that contains more than music. Pop critic Albert Goldman – who savaged Elvis' legacy with his 1981 biography – used to say that pop music was a way of staying young, a refusal to grow up, a way of keeping your world around you as you push on in life. Extreme, perhaps, though his views wouldn't be out of place amongst those put forward by *Vanity Fair* journalist Gail Sheehy, who in 1996 identified a trend towards 'half-adulthood'. 'Adolescence is now prolonged for the middle classes until the end of the twenties,' she wrote. 'True adulthood does not begin until thirty.' Or indeed forty, or even fifty. By some weird process of post-modern metrication, the seven ages of man have been squashed into three.

This reluctance to grow up could explain why so much in modern easy-listening concerns itself with travel – arrival, departure, perpetual motion: never being around means never having to say you're sorry. But pop anthropology is a growth industry, clouding what is often just a combination of circumstance and time. It also tends to deny the remarkable life-affirming power of music, and its ability to make both happiness and sadness seem almost confrontational. The underbelly of lounge achieves an irresistible blend of melancholy and optimism. Someone once said that the Walker Brothers made the statement 'My ship is coming in' seem ineffably sad and the assertion that 'The sun ain't gonna shine anymore' supremely uplifting. Which is, after all, why I'm here, right now, deep in Pod, bouncing around between the light and the dark. Scott Walker understood – along with Frank Sinatra, Burt Bacharach, John Barry, Brian Wilson and all the rest – that music is not only too important to be treated lightly, but also, when the occasion demands it, too important not to be.

At the cocktail party of my dreams, Burt, Barry and Brian

will all be there, along with Frank Sinatra, Julie London, Dean Martin and the entire Nelson Riddle orchestra. In my own exotic ranch-style space-place – reachable only by a two-door supersonic Skyway jet – *Songs For Swingin' Lovers* is rarely off the turntable, Donald Fagen rarely off the piano; Paul Anka holds court by the pool as Quincy Jones and Kim Novak attempt the perfect martini.

Here in my Polynesian Populuxe dreamworld high above the city, prosperity and convenience surrounds me ('Jeez, this chaise longue has tail-fin arms!'), as do the stabbing saxophones, angular banjos, swirling Moogs, giddy basslines and gorgeous intrusions of massed violins. Here, in my *faux*-frontier fantasyland, night closes in, the moon casts extravagant shadows on the street below, and the robotic fizz of canned laughter crawls from the TV.

Walking slowly towards the kitchen, I pick up *The Very Best Of Martin Denny*. 'Listen,' it commands on the sleeve, 'if you hold the album cover up to your ear you can hear the sea.' So I do. And indeed I can.

15 What a Long, Strange iTrip it's Been: Big American Car Music

How Bruce Springstein and Route 66 reinvented the rock epic

There are few greater joys than being in an open-top car, speeding across one of those American states with big skies (Texas, Arizona, New Mexico, Nevada, California etc) and stumbling on the perfect radio station, the one that plays the best driving records known to mankind, a combination of the rock records you know and love, the classics you've always been a bit too cool to buy, and the slightly corny stuff that you would never dream of buying but actually sounds great as you're speeding through the desert with the wind blowing through your hair. This is that radio station ... 'More Than A Feeling' by Boston, 'She Sells Sanctuary' by the Cult, 'Can't Get Enough' by Bad Company, 'Layla' by Derek & The Dominoes, 'The Boys Of Summer' by Don Henley, 'Yellow' by Coldplay, 'Sweet Child O' Mine' by Guns N' Roses, 'Like A Hurricane' by Neil Young, 'Wide Open Space' by Mansun, etc.

Most of the essential stuff, the stuff that works in a mono-lithic, epic way – constantly reminding you how important it is because of how old and revered it is – was made in the 1970s, when rock music was the standard, the benchmark, the order of the day. It wasn't ironic, wasn't post-anything, didn't have to be self-referential or cute, didn't need to reference the past ... it was just rock music, the sort that just sort of ... rocked, actually. And while a lot of it was British – Free, Zeppelin, Eric Clapton, the Who – most of the truly iconic stuff, the stuff that conjured up visions of dark, desert highways, palm trees, Cinemascope skies and hitch-hiking honeys in cut-off jeans and too-tight T-shirts, was American. The Big American Car Music of the time – the Eagles, Doobie Brothers, Steely Dan, Meat Loaf, Van Halen – still sounds like it was built for the journey (i.e., built for comfort rather than speed), and sounds even better now than it did then. American cars don't have gears, and rarely does the best Big American Car Music – it's either all in fifth, or it slides between them without you noticing, moving effortlessly from verse to bridge to chorus to coda as the highway cuts through the landscape.

Previously, when I made tapes for the car, or racked up CDs in the boot, it was Big American Car Music that I'd always come back to. I'd make these spur-of-the-moment tapes that included the best of the new releases – Suede, the Auteurs, the Boo Radleys at one point – mixed up with rare blue-eyed soul, Bowie (always some Bowie), U2, some weird electronica, trenchant disco, even a bit of Carpenters – but I learned to drive in my late twenties, when I was finally ready to re-evaluate the Led Zeppelins, Neil Youngs and Steve Millers of this world. Also, having passed my driving test, the first place I drove was in America (I was doing a piece on the big Jewish resort hotels in the Catskills), so immediately associated car music with Big roads, Big skies and Big saloons.

The same was true when I got an iPod. The memory box hasn't just been successful because it can house your entire record collection. It's been successful because it's portable. And while I've rarely considered running or jogging with mine (it seems too much like multi-tasking to me), the fact that you can hook it up to any number of third-party mini speakers means that you can take it anywhere. But using the iPod in the car had been problematic, for me anyway. I'd tried the iTrip (tuning the Pod into a radio frequency and playing it back through the car's speakers), but the reception had never been impressive. And I'd tried the cassette version – attaching the iPod to a cassette which was then used to amplify the Pod – but the sound quality was poor in the extreme (and how many cars have a cassette facility these days?). So I had a proper dock fitted, a Blaupunkt Bremen MP 74 that turned out to be the perfect solution. Did it work? Only completely. It didn't just sound fantastic (even with compressed files), it was as easy to use as a radio. Not only that, but the cradle was suitably reverential, treating its charge with majesterial deference, holding the iPod aloft like a stag's head or a particularly well-made cappuccino.

But as well as being able to make ad-hoc playlists featuring everything new and different – the Thievery Corporation, Marjorie Fair, Mooney Suzuki – my in-car iPod has also allowed me to indulge myself and make my Seventies compilations even bigger, even more pompous, even more full of excruciating guitar solos and histrionic caterwauling – my Drive Time playlist has 122 songs on it, and, properly edited, could easily be up to 300 in a matter of hours. And my Bruce Springsteen playlist has nearly everything he's ever recorded, or at least the best of it, some 90 songs.

What is it with Springsteen? I shouldn't like him, but I do. A lot. In America his fame has always been presidential, where in Britain we've always been slightly embarrassed about allowing ourselves to enjoy something so unambiguous, so prosaic, so old-fashioned. In the Seventies, when he was ostensibly still in his larval stage, he used to throw his woolly hat in the air, turn towards the audience, put his hands behind his back and catch it as it fell, just as the band cut the final chord. It was corny but it was fabulous. He was worse in the Eighties, as the industrial-strength muscle-bound MTV hero of the Eighties – 'Ah-one-two-*thray*!' – revelling in sweat-stained bandannas and air-punching aerobics (a man who could reasonably be blamed for both Bono and Bryan Adams). But with his dustbowlthin cheekbones and blue-collar brute force he's made some of the most mesmerising music of the last thirty years.

Few people would call Springsteen a grabby man, especially when compared with other icons of Eighties US pop, such as Prince, Madonna or Michael Jackson. Sure, he has the same career aspirations as any 'artist' (i.e., immortality), but he's always known when to curb his excesses. Perhaps this is why he's had so much success: trying to capture the nature of Everyman is a daunting task, and Springsteen has endeavoured to do it time and time again.

For the best part of thirty years he has imbued the aspirations of smalltown blue-collar America with a mystic glow. With a much-lampooned repertoire of songs extolling the virtues of pink Cadillacs, Jersey girls and gimcrack homesteads, Springsteen has affected the American psyche in a way that Woody Guthrie could only dream of. Take *Born To Run*, that glorious statement of intent from 1975: it's *West Side Story* on wheels, a ruthless pursuit of sensation that sounds like Bob Dylan produced by Phil Spector, only much, much better. You only had to hear it once to know that no one believed in the redemptive power of rock music quite as much as blue-collar Bruce.

Automobile imagery was crucial to those early romantic notions of sex and freedom, and the heroes of his mini-parables were poets-cum-car mechanics – dreamers and schemers who linger aimlessly on the low-rise industrial park fringes of society, down in 'Jungleland', 'Thunder Road', 'Spirit In The Night's' Greasy Lake or the infamous 'rattlesnake speedway in the Utah desert' (from 'The Promised Land'). Most of the time, though, was spent on the Jersey Shore, drinking warm beer beneath rotary fans in dilapidated diners as their fuel-injected suicide machines sat patiently outside, gently humming after a 200-mile journey across a dozen county lines. Jesus, it was hard work being this disenfranchised.

Bruce would claim that he'd never had an image, though it

would be hard to find another rock star so easily objectified, and it's as easy to distil the Springsteen myth from the way he looks as it is from listening to his music. In the early days – the long days and dark nights of *Greetings From Asbury Park NJ* and *The Wild, The Innocent And The E Street Shuffle* – Bruce's beard and pimp cap gave him the air of any East Coast troubadour trying to draw attention to himself; but by the mid-Seventies he was starting to look generic: lumberjack shirt, faded blue jeans, leather jacket and motorcycle boots. He perhaps looked his best towards the end of the decade – the time of *Darkness On The Edge Of Town*, which probably remains his defining statement – along with four-fifths of *The River* it's his best album – with his drawn, gaunt face, V-neck T-shirt and windcheater making him seem more like Jimmy Dean than Bobby Zimmerman.

Five years later it was Annie Leibovitz's iconic cover of 1984's *Born In The USA* which rubber-stamped his image: a white capped-sleeve T-shirt, a studded cowboy belt, and Levi's 501s with the red baseball cap hanging out of his right back pocket. Looking at it two decades later, it doesn't just look ironic, it looks stereotypically gay. Who knew?

During this period Bruce was briefly co-opted by the Right, who not only misinterpreted the beleaguered irony of *Born In The USA* itself, but thought that Springsteen's onstage persona was comparable to Sylvester Stallone's jingoistic stooges, Rocky and Rambo (when Ronald Reagan tried to appropriate the song Springsteen immediately snatched it back again). For some this was an easy mistake to make, as Springsteen had been working overtime in the gym, pumping up his body to beefcake proportions with the help of a personal trainer. But Bruce never exploited his maleness, and although his classic songs tend to celebrate the male experience, he has spent equal amounts of time pondering his own masculinity.

In this way Springsteen has never been an especially libidinous performer, and you'd never exactly call him a sexy star, not compared to, say, Steven Tyler, Marvin Gaye or Kid Rock.

Although he has found happiness with backing singer Patti Scialfa, his modus operandi in the world of love always makes me think of Enzo Ferrari when he said: 'The conviction has never left me that when a man says to a woman, "I love you," what he means is, "I desire you," and that the only real love possible in this world is that of a father for his son.' Springsteen was always a family man – even before he became one – and his downhome values were Norman Rockwell through and through.

His fanbase has always been more male orientated as he's always appealed to boys who desperately want to be older, as well as men who wish they were younger. Like the boys in Camus' *The Outsider* (another male adolescent passion) who leave the cinema with affected gaits after watching cowboy films, songs like 'Thunder Road' made men in Golf GTis think they were driving souped-up Thunderbirds, made men working in photocopy shops dream of cruising down Route 66.

Personally I didn't 'get' Springsteen for years. Having been brought up on a diet of glam rock, punk and Frank Sinatra, Springsteen's overblown pomp just seemed silly (how could a Home Counties schoolboy identify with a lovelorn steelworker or a Vietnam vet?). But then I went to America and it all made perfect sense. The space. The sky. The open roads. A big country demands big music, and that's exactly the sort of music Bruce Springsteen made. Epic. Cinematic. Unashamedly unironic. Never an inadequate like so many British pop stars – Ray Davies, David Bowie, Pete Shelley, Morrissey, etc. – Springsteen was a man whose internal workings were all on the outside.

Whereas punk celebrated the mundanity of urban, lower-middle-class life, Bruce helped me escape it. Springsteen sang about 'highways jammed with broken heroes on a last-chance power ride', while all I was doing was driving to the off-licence.

In 1987 Springsteen made an effort to escape his own

environment and deflate the myth he had taken so long to build by releasing the decidedly low-key *Tunnel Of Love*, managing to distance himself from his enormous fanbase in the process (if Bob Dylan could dismantle his image then surely Springsteen could too). The cover shot compounded the effect, Bruce's sombre black suit and faintly ridiculous bootlace tie making him appear more like the manager of some upwardly mobile cocktail and enchilada joint in the Midwest than an out-and-out rock god (he looked like he'd walked out of *Paris Texas* straight into *Miami Vice*). Literally and metaphorically, the shirtsleeves were back, the revisionism taking him from superstar Everyman to self-doubting thirtysomething (intensely intimate, it's his most personal memoir, a 'divorce' record about his failed marriage to Julianne Phillips).

These days a lot of rock stars seem to use up the bulk of their inspiration by the time of their second CD, but with Bruce it took twenty years, when he moved to the West Coast after a lifetime based in New Jersey. He famously benched the E Street Band, got married again, had a bunch of kids and started writing songs about watching TV ('57 Channels [And Nothin' On']). He swapped the gauche pink Cadillac for a $14m Beverley Hills mansion, parked the battered '69 Chevy in his double-fronted garage, hung up his cowboy boots and settled down for a night with his wife and a couple of bottles of Californian Chardonnay. He indulged in self-parody, too: cavorting about the stage looking like a Rodeo Drive vagabond in neatly pressed jeans, gypsy shirt and dagger-pointed boots; a rich man in a poor man's shirt. The idea of 'Bruce Springsteen' became rather naff, and for men over a certain age he became a guilty pleasure, like jumping up and down at a Sham 69 reunion gig. It was just so adolescent.

Throughout the 1990s he made the long, slow walk back from the wilderness. First came 'Streets of Philadelphia' (bagging him an Oscar), then the critically well-received but most difficult album of his career, *The Ghost Of Tom Joad*, in 1995. A dour acoustic record full of John Steinbeck and Woody Guthrie tidbits, unsugared and devoid of artificial colouring, it sold around 120,000 in the UK, roughly a tenth of *Born In The USA* (I hated most of it, and still do). Middle age brought a fully fledged reunion tour with the E Street Band four years later, along with the release of *Tracks*, a celebratory four-CD boxed set of mostly rejected material, followed by the release of *18 Tracks*, an edited version including a reworking of 'The Promise', a song he wrote and recorded for *Darkness On The Edge Of Town*, but which lay around for twenty years while he decided what to do with it. It is considered by some to be the best song he's ever written, and its mournful romanticism – 'two-bit bars', 'broken spirits' and 'broken cars' (any more clichés up your chambray shirtsleeve, Springsteen?) – was a reminder to fans that what he did best was synthesise the pulp American experience. (It may be hearsay to say so, but I still maintain that the best Springsteen song was actually written by Tom Waits, 'Jersey Girl', to be found on *Live/1975–85*; not forgetting that Waits was also responsible for the best Eagles song, '01'55', from *On the Border*.)

When it was announced in 2002 that Springsteen was to make his first record with E Street Band since *Born In The USA*, the anticipation was 'mixed' (i.e., negative). Some used to say that all Springsteen really needed to rediscover his muse was a car crash, but in the end it was the attack on the Twin Towers and everything that came in its wake. Apart from a rhinestone-covered fistful of appalling country songs, until *The Rising* US pop culture had struggled to respond to the terrorist attacks, as though the event itself were somehow sacrosanct. So perhaps it was only natural that rock's most foremost chronicler of the 'grandiose' common experience should find himself carrying the baton. For what it's worth, *The Rising* is a great record, probably his best since *Tunnel Of Love* and certainly a lot more spirited (it's got more energy and passion than a dozen Starsailor albums). Ironically, it's also got two of the best holiday records you're ever likely to hear, 'Waiting On A Sunny Day' and 'Let's Be Friends'.

The twenty-first-century Bruce Springsteen is a lot more mature than he could have been, and far more circumspect about the validity of the rock myth (just listen to the Dylan-like introspection on his most recent record, the occasionally brilliant *Devils & Dust*). The Annie Leibovitz portraits and the Messiah-like poses may have gone but his belief in the re-demptive power of pop remains absolute. Especially if that redemption somehow involves a Big American Car.

In 1994, having imagined myself doing it for over two decades, I finally drove down the Free Love Freeway, all the way from New York to LA via Philadelphia, Washington, Nashville, Memphis, Oklahoma City, Amarillo, Albuquerque and Las Vegas, a two-week crash course in monolithic scenery and downhome hospitality. The idea was to drive down to Texas and then pick up Route 66 and take it all the way to California, all the way to the beach. I went with my friend Robin and, while we may have kidded ourselves that we wanted to explore the great beyond, what we really wanted to do was experience the joys of listening to loud rock music in big American cars, with the windows down, our feet on the dashboard and the radio on (as Jonathan Richman sang, incessantly, back in 1977). I had spent months planning the itinerary, and, ever the anal musicologist, spent even longer making the tapes to go with it. I'd planned the Leaving New York Tape (as prescience would have it, a decade before the REM song), the Alt-Country Tape for the long drive through the Blue Ridge Mountains (Gram Parsons, Rockingbirds, Byrds, Stan Ridgeway), the Doo-Wop Tape for the truck-stop diners and cheap motels of Tennessee, and a Hard-Drivin' C120 of pure, prime 1970s California-style cock rock. There were songs for every step of the journey: 'Phila-delphia Freedom' by Elton John, 'Leaving Las Vegas' by Sheryl Crow, 'Hoover Dam' by Sugar, 'Is This The Way To Amarillo' by Tony Christie, 'Cars & Girls' by Prefab Sprout ('Albuquerque!'), and a large chunk, or trunk, of *The Joshua Tree*. But because I was so obsessed with driving Route 66, I failed to realise that Wichita (which I didn't visit) was only about 150 miles north of Oklahoma City (which unfortunately I did). Thus I was unable to drive through town listening to Glen Campbell's definitive version of Jimmy Webb's 'Wichita Lineman', which, for the record, is one of the ten best records ever made. (Once, while driving through California in 1990, I stopped and asked for directions not far from San Francisco so I could actually ask, 'Do you know the way to San José?')

Robin and I had been getting up to no good for over a decade (to try and compensate for this he agreed to be the best man at my wedding three years later). He had just become the art director of *Vogue*, while I had been at the *Sunday Times* magazine for about six months. This was to be our very own Two Lane Blacktop, our slapstick Thunderbolt & Lightfoot, *The Odd Couple Go West*. Robin is the only man I know who is grumpier than I am, and as we sat, one April morning in the Time Café in New York, just hours before the start of our drive, he tapped me on the arm and said, 'I'd like to finish this trip knowing as many people as I did when I started. When in doubt, don't introduce me.' To anyone. As I embraced the whole 'Have a nice day' culture at the heart of America, Robin was very much of the opposite persuasion: 'Is service included? Well, can I have some then?'

We argued about much on the trip, mainly music. I'd known Robin since we both worked at i-*D* together, since the days of warehouse parties and club culture, when belonging to a style magazine was a passport to peripheral fame and an invitation to behave badly all over the world (such was the nature of our relationship I'd once called Robin from my hotel room in Toronto at four in the morning simply to a) Wake him up, and b) Tell him I was drunk – which I was, uproariously); and in that time we'd never agreed about music: he thought I was too easily impressed, I always thought he was far too pedestrian (he still liked Deep Purple, for chrissakes, and still owned a copy of *Made In Japan*).

And as we reached our thirties, he told me that he'd heard enough music and didn't really want to hear any more. 'Great, and enough,' he said, a phrase he often used to describe his relationship with mutual acquaintances. And so whenever I banged on about the joys of Suede, Oasis or Pulp, he'd just look at me dismissively and suggest I was refusing to grow up. Of course I had a professional interest in new music, but I had an intensely personal one too (plus I was fairly obsessed with not becoming overly cynical; cynicism is a trait that envelopes us as we get older whether we like it or not, and I'd never seen the point of embracing it before time, like so many journalists I knew). And so my enthusiasms with Robin tended to fall on deaf ears; when I started explaining just why Sugar, say, were so refreshing, he'd look at me with the resigned bewilderment of an indulgent parent whose five-year-old had just stuck their fingers down the waste disposal.

In truth I'm not sure he was even that keen on music per se, and although he had a few requisite teenage obsessions – he is the only man I'd ever met with every Sensational Alex Harvey Band LP, and he can recite the opening monologue of David Bowie's 'Diamond Dogs' in its entirety – I think he finds it all a bit silly. Once, when I took him, in the formerly fashionable spirit of irony, to a Rod Stewart concert at Wembley Arena in 1991, he turned to me after four numbers and said, without a hint of embarrassment, 'Can we go now? Rod's leather trousers are beginning to chaff.'

The one thing we did wholeheartedly agree on was Bruce, because with Bruce there was no ambiguity. Bruce was pure, unadulterated 12-bar machismo, and it was Bruce we mostly listened to as we sped along Route 66, imagining ourselves in brushed suede Stetsons and cap-sleeved T-shirts.[1]

---

[1] Robin has since widened his musical landscape, and having forced himself

And Route 66? Well, as ineffably joyful journeys go, it is one of the best, as well as one of the longest. As road journeys go, there is nothing to touch it. US Route 66 was stamped on the American public's consciousness in 1962, when the highway was christened. It soon became known as America's Main Street, a road that stretched all the way from Chicago in the North East, to Santa Monica Beach on the West Coast. Snaking its way across eight states (Illinois, Missouri, Arkansas, Oklahoma, Texas, New Mexico, Arizona and California), this concrete and asphalt ribbon was once America's favourite thoroughfare, down which millions of tourists pushed their Detroit steel, looking for the new world, or simply the definitive road experience.

What it did best was move people in large numbers. During World War II it was used to shift millions of US troops, while a decade earlier it became an escape route for dust bowl pilgrims, fleeing in packs for the balmy palms and optimism of California. Sixty-six came to encapsulate the Great Depression, most famously in John Steinbeck's *The Grapes of Wrath* (he re-christened it The Mother Road) as well as in the songs of Woody Guthrie.

But Mother is not what she was, and since the route was disenfranchised, both traffic and people have slowed to a trickle. The most renowned stretch – from Oklahoma to Los Angeles – is now serviced by Interstate 40, which runs along much of old 66, making a mockery of its maverick status. Here cars are few and far between, driven by people who aren't in too much of a hurry. As Michael Wall writes in *Route 66: The Mother Road*, 'Sixty six is for people who find time holy.' It still is.

The road cuts a swathe through three of the continent's eight bioregions, through the Great Plains and the Colorado Plateau. It also passes the Mississippi River, the Grand Canyon, the Hoover Dam, and the Joshua Tree forest, crossing mountains,

---

to 're-engage with popular culture', now enjoys Lucinda Williams, Johnny Cash's Rick Rubin years and Ryan Adams. Get him!

deserts, plains and canyons. If it's American history you want, then The Mother Road has it in abundance.

It has made history, too, and during the 1960s even got its own TV series; in 120 episodes of *Route 66* two teenagers called Buz and Tod travelled the strip in their souped-up Corvette.

It also got a song: Bobby Troupe's '(Get Your Kicks On) Route 66' was never an adolescent rite of passage; not a late-1950s teen-dream soap opera, nor an early 1960s cruisin' classic like the Beach Boys' '409'. Written in 1946, and made famous by Nat King Cole, Troupe's singing road-map helped create the highway as much as Route 66 helped him write the song. Since then it has been recorded by everyone from Chuck Berry and the Rolling Stones to Mel Tormé and Depeche Mode.

Once, the only way to negotiate the road was by buying a copy of Jack Rittenhouse's *Route 66 Guidebook*, written, like Bobby Troupe's song, in 1946. This was the first guide to cover a transcontinental highway. Combining historical data, road information, and accommodation in one volume. Three thousand copies were sold at a dollar a piece, to the bookshops, news stands, cafés, and 'tourist courts' (no one called them motels in those days) along 66. Rittenhouse made several reconnaissance trips . . . 'On my final trip I had to inspect the scenery,' he wrote in the preface to the 1988 facsimile edition, 'So I drove from dawn to dusk at thirty-five miles an hour. There were no tape recorders then, so I scrawled notes on a big yellow pad on the seat beside me. Each night I dug out my portable manual typewriter and typed my notes.'

To drive Route 66 is to step back in time, to relive an age when travel was still an adventure, not a necessity; an age when the car was still king. My own personal road movie began in Oklahoma and took me all the way to Santa Monica, and Palisades Park. Driving the empty, lonely Roman-like blacktop towards the Pacific is like no other experience in America, and one that is to be treasured.

It is the long stretch of the road through New Mexico, Arizona and California which conveys the strongest sense of what it must have been like to make the great crossing in the Thirties; towns out here finish before they begin, fading away into scrub. Arizona is a moonscape of monstrous proportions, Route 66's tow-lane blacktop cuffing through it like a charcoal arrow. Towards Winslow there is a raggedy little section of the old route that is still flanked by telegraph poles that stagger over the horizon like old men looking for the sea.

Winslow itself has been immortalised in The Eagles' soporific classic 'Take It Easy' ('I'm standing on the corner in Winslow, Arizona/It's such a fine sight to see . . .'). In fact, driving through the Arizona heartland, the superannuated sound of Seventies FM rock really comes into its own – Steely Dan, Lynyrd Skynyrd, the Edgar Winter Group, the James Gang, and the rest. This, coupled with the woebegone strains of primetime doo-wop, is the soundtrack the scenery commands – the music of perpetual motion. Hip-hop doesn't make much sense out here, nor the arch role-playing of post-punk indie-darlings. And as for Britpop, forget it. As you're driving through the barren, tumbleweed plains of Arizona, you want the exponential sonic architecture of Pink Floyd or Crazy Horse, not the Beastie Boys, Scritti Politti or Muse.

Arizona also contains the longest remaining uninterrupted stretch of road, between Seligman and the Colorado River at Topock, some 158 miles. This section is also one of the most beautiful, as well as one of the most haunting. The country here can make you light-hearted with solitude – creviced arroyos, harsh desert and wild bush scrub. 'Sometimes, toward either end of a long driving day,' writes Tom Snyder in *The Route 66 Traveller's Guide and Roadside Companion*, 'a run through this country brings up an ancient German word, *Sehnsucht*. It has no equivalent in English, but it represents a longing for, a need to return to, a place you've never been.' Which, fundamentally, is exactly what the best sort of pop music conjures up.

American highways are always changing, being redirected,

realigned and rebuilt. Some just disappear. Route 66 went out of official existence on 27 June, 1985, when the national organisation of highway authorities decertified it. Sixty years after it was born, the highway was stripped of its identifying markings and signs, superseded by various six-lane Interstates. Not all of the road remains – some of it is closed, some of it is destroyed, while other parts have fallen into terrible disrepair – but it is still possible to find patches of the old road using new guidebooks and old maps.

In Seligman we came across a barbershop-cum-record-shop-cum-Route 66 junk shop, run by a Mr Angel Delgadillo, an ebullient old-timer who kept interrupting our conversation to tend to his customers ('You still cuttin' hair, Angel, or what?'). There are dozens of such places scattered along 66's two-thousand-mile stretch, and the road is littered with cafés, bars and diners straight out of the past – hundreds of little grocery stores and gas stations displaying the generic Historic Route 66 signs in their windows. The road has not been allowed to die, nor is it crassly exploited; it is being fondly remembered by people who actually care about its legacy.

It was just outside Winslow that we found our own Holy Grail. The sun was falling in the sky, promising a rich, dark sunset as we sped along the highway towards Two Guns. In the distance the Juniper mountains cut across the horizon like tears of pale blue tissue paper. As we gunned towards them we looked to our left and saw a deserted Drive-In, standing forlornly in the dirt, casting shadows that stretched all the way back to town. Suddenly I felt like an extra in *American Graffiti*, sitting in the custom-built benchseat of a Hot Rod, my cap-sleeved right arm around my girl, my ducktail brushing the rear-view mirror, and Del Shannon's 'Runaway' pouring through the dashboard speaker.

Here was the true spirit of Route 66 in all its faded glory. Like the highway itself, the Tonto Drive-In was a totem of America's glorious past, a testament to the new frontier, the freedom to travel, and the democratised automotive dream of the Fifties, when a car was still every American's birthright. This deserted cathedral, standing stoic and proud in the burnt sienna sunset, was, quite literally, the end of the road. Suddenly, California – with all its promises of eternal youth, and 'two girls for every boy' – seemed a long, long way away.

When I finally arrived in LA, I spent four days in the Sunset Marquis before moving up to the Chateau Marmont, where I wasted ten days lolling around the lobby, with the likes of Spike Lee, Julia Roberts and Helmut Newton, waiting to interview Shirley Maclaine. A short while later my friend and future *GQ* colleague John Naughton was in LA to interview Hugh Grant, to publicise the forthcoming release of *Four Weddings and a Funeral*. After the interview, which was far more cordial than most of these affairs, Grant, a relative stranger to Los Angeles, asked John if he fancied going for a beer. John declined, saying he had to haul himself back to his room in order to file his piece back to London. It would be easy to assume that John turned down a drink with Hugh Grant because a drink with Hugh Grant would perhaps be the thing that John would enjoy least in the world, but the truth is that he wanted to make a protracted visit to Tower Records and drop a couple of hundred dollars on painfully obscure Badfinger CDs. So it was that Hugh Grant had to fend for himself that night; which is why, a few hours later, he was caught with his dick in Divine Brown's mouth.

16 How 'i' Learned to Stop Worrying and Love Jazz

It's big, it's clever, it's grown up

So there I am, in the large HMV near Selfridges on London's Oxford Street, some time in April, around 4.30 on a Friday afternoon. I've just dropped about £80 – on *Elephant* by the White Stripes, Blur's *Think Tank*, a second copy of the Strokes' first album, a new Marmalade compilation (their 'I See The Rain' has recently been used in a Gap ad), plus *The Last Waltz* and *The Wicker Man* on DVD. On top of all this I have, uncharacteristically, also spent another £40 on three jazz CDs: one fairly useless acid jazz compilation that I'll never play again, and two of the greatest records I've heard for over a year: John Coltrane's *Giant Steps* and Duke Ellington's *Far East Suite*. I bought them on a whim, at the suggestion of friends, two suggestions that have changed my life in considerable ways.

Every week since then I've been going back for more, building up a jazz library that threatens to dwarf everything else in my collection. Having kept jazz pretty much at arm's length for the best part of my life, I've found myself embracing it as an estranged father might embrace his long-lost kin. Getting into jazz is like suddenly discovering you have an extended family you knew nothing about, although the family in question runs to thousands of members. Like turning the world upside down and finding another one underneath, a world where they only ever listen to jazz.

I even have a playlist – of course I have a playlist! – devoted to jazz. I haven't called it anything cute yet, it's just called jazz, rather weedily (no inverted commas, nothing), as though I couldn't really be bothered to call it anything else, as though I'm somehow embarrassed about it, but I'm not. It's probably just because it's a work in progress, which it most obviously is. With every other playlist I think I'm pretty much there, you know what I mean? Of course I'm going to add the next Coldplay album in its entirety – and probably the one after that and the one after that – and I occasionally get converted to things I used to hate (Jeff Buckley, Led Zeppelin, ELO – I now have more ELO in iTunes than Oasis), but I don't feel I have to wade through all of Jimi Hendrix's back catalogue – I've done that, thanks, and don't much care for it. Is there much rock music I didn't really know I liked? Are there many Spooky Tooth or Fairport Convention albums out there I don't know but will fall in love with at some point over the next ten years? Maybe, maybe even probably, but I've spent thirty years covering the waterfront, so I think I know what I'm talking about (Van Morrison and Nick Drake are good; Simple Minds and Uriah Heep are crap – you get the gist). But with jazz, I'm still pretty much at a loss. My current playlist has 653 songs on it, enough for a good bank holiday weekend – 2.1 days, 3.67 GB. There's a lot of Miles Davis, a lot of classic Blue Note, and tons of bossa nova, but nothing too difficult. I don't like difficult jazz; I find it too ... well, difficult. And annoying and self-serving and unnecessarily complicated and pretentious and unwieldy ... but mostly just difficult.

My newfound fascination started during a boys' trip to Japan, for the World Cup in 2002. Oliver, Andrew and I (Peyton, Hale & Jones, solicitors to the glitterati) had all got pink slips from our wives to go to Japan for the two weeks of group games, where we would watch the three England and three Ireland matches. I'd been to Japan twice before, and had always been blown away by the place – technologically, architecturally, culturally

... Ironically – really ironically – one of the country's most significant cultural characteristics was its carpetbagging of Western pop culture, eating it up with Pacman-like zeal. The Japanese were very good at appropriating the methods and styles of fashion and pop, without ever having to experience the catharsis of original birth, that is. When I first went, in 1983 (to model in a fashion show for the Men's Bigi label, of all things, having been approached by some scouts in a Soho nightclub called, rather appropriately, White Trash), the record shops were full of knock-off pop, and you could tell what they sounded like just by looking at the covers. When I went again in 1996, to catalogue Paul Smith's ascendancy as Britain's greatest cultural export (at every public appearance he was mobbed like no Brit had been mobbed since the Beatles, thirty years previously), the music had improved considerably, although it was still derivative. But when I walked into the Beams record store in Shinjuku-Ku in Tokyo in May 2002 (a sort of shining twenty-first century Xanadu of Pop), I was presented with thousands of cool-looking CDs, none of which had covers that gave any indication as to what they contained. In between the low garble of generic US hip-hop and weirder-than-weird Japanese pop, the in-house stereo began pumping out this mad, disjointed, almost insane jazz arrangement. The assistant told me it was Electric Bath by the Don Ellis Orchestra, and it was simply the maddest thing I'd ever heard, and the sort of thing you tend only to hear in Tokyo record shops. So I bought it, and vowed to properly delve into the jazz labyrinth as soon as I got back to London.

When I told my friends about my new quest, Andrew was both indulgent and helpful, suggesting dozens of records, including a whole bunch of rare Herbie Hancock LPs. Oliver, meanwhile, was typically dismissive: 'Jazz? What do you want to listen to that for? It's all fuckin' shite' (which, to be honest, is what Oliver tends to say about everything unless he discovers it first).

While I was compiling my playlist, jazz started to replace

every other form of music in my life. If I were on *Desert Island Discs*, I thought to myself rather conceitedly at one point, what would I bring? Would any of them be jazz records? What about if I made them all jazz records? After all, what would be the point of bringing your eight favourite records with you to a desert island? Wouldn't it be better to take eight things you didn't know, eight records you could grow to love just by dint of listening to them *ad infinitum*? What would be the point of taking your favourite Aphex Twin, U2 and Earth Wind & Fire records if you're going to hear them day in, day out, for the rest of your life? It's something of a pointless exercise, I know, but how many times can you listen to the first side of *Moondance* before it begins to pall? Why not just take a shit-load of jazz, eight of the maddest, longest, most out-there jazz records in the shop? But then I remembered I didn't like the difficult stuff and calmed down a bit.

After my dual-carriageway-to-Damascus experience, I became a man possessed. I only had to meet someone for five minutes before I asked them what their favourite jazz record was. Experts were eager to please, friends couldn't stop suggesting things. One introduced me to lots of (very good) jazz guitarists, not knowing that I have a natural aversion to anyone sporting a mullet; so that ruled out Pat Metheny, Mike Stern, Frank Gambale, and a lot of decidedly odd Germans. I also developed an aversion to 'soft jazz', and foreswore the likes of Spyro Gyra, David Sanborn and the kind of soporific stuff l always seem to hear whenever I accidentally turn on Jazz FM.

Not a week went by without me adding to my iTunes library. In my obsession I even resorted to buying some of those '100 Greatest Jazz Hits' CD compilations you find in petrol stations, the kind compiled by people who think Al Jarreau and Glenn Miller are cut from the same cloth (people who might even think that Al Jarreau and Glenn Miller are the same person).

I began compiling an imaginary list of the best jazz records of all time, a list that started to occupy my every waking thought. I'd be in a meeting at work, trying to figure out a way to squeeze a piece about the Angolan civil war into six pages (difficult, but not impossible), and I'd begin comparing the respective voices of Sarah Vaughan and Ella Fitzgerald. (Was 'Lullaby Of Birdland' better than 'Ev'ry Time We Say Goodbye'? Who knew?) I'd be half way through a client pitch and begin wondering if Dexter Gordon's 'Getting Around' was more impressive than his 'Our Man In Paris' (I'm still undecided on this one). If you've ever made lists of your favourite rock songs about California, your favourite punk singles, disco 12"s, songs with the name of your girlfriend or wife in them; if you read *High Fidelity* and immediately rushed off to make your own list of Top Ten Break-Up Records; if you're still reluctant to give up the clandestine obsessions of your youth, by which I mean being unable to stop yourself from trawling through record shop racks mentally totting up the CDs you've already got ... if you've ever done any of these things, then you'll know what I'm talking about.

So how do you build a collection? How do you compile the perfect jazz iPod playlist? (Could you fill up an iPod just with jazz?) What do you do once you've summoned up the courage to wander off into the jazz section, what do you buy? What do you do when you get there? Not only is there just so much ... *stuff*, but there's more stuff every day. It's an ever-expanding world, the jazz world. I mean, even if you knew everything there was to know about jazz, how could you possibly own it all? There are nearly as many jazz albums as there are women in the world, and how could you sleep with all of *them*? As with any other type of music, there are some classic records you'd be mad to ignore, but with jazz you really have to plough your own furrow. The jazz police are a proscriptive lot – look to them for recommendations and they'll tell you that Norah Jones and Stan Getz aren't jazz, that Blue Note shouldn't have signed St Germain, and that Dave Brubeck's 'Take Five' is only ever good for paint commercials. However, these are probably the same people who, twenty-five years ago, would have told you that ABBA don't make good pop music, or that punk was a flash in the pan.

But there were certainly things I just didn't get. Ornette Coleman was one. At the same time as Miles Davis was breaking through with modal jazz forms, Ornette Coleman invented free jazz with *The Shape Of Jazz To Come*. Nearly fifty years after the event it is difficult to recapture the shock that greeted the arrival of this record, but it just gave me a headache. Coleman played a white plastic saxophone that looked like a toy, he dressed like a spiv, and was a master of the one-liner, the 'Zen zinger' (stuff like, 'When the band is playing with the drummer, it's rock'n'roll, but when the drummer is playing with the band, it's jazz'), so I really, really wanted to like his music. But I couldn't, no matter how much I tried. As far as I was concerned, he was improvising up his own sphincter.

And what is jazz anyway? Is it Koop's *Waltz For Koop*, a Swedish approximation of lounge-core jazz, or is it Terry Callier's *Turn You To Love*, which is almost deep soul but is released on Elektra's 'classic jazz' label. The truth is, jazz is a bit of everything, something that isn't so surprising when you consider it was born out of marching bands, the blues, minstrel music and New Orleans creole. Jazz is Dixieland, swing, fusion, jazz-funk, jazz-rock, R&B, bossa nova, bebop, hard bop, hip-hop, cool jazz, hot jazz, West Coast jazz, modal jazz, acid jazz, soul jazz, free jazz, trad jazz, modern cheroot-smoking Sta-Prest button-down jazz, the lot. Some people now even call it the new chill-out (fools). Let's hope not. Chill-out has always seemed, to some jaundiced ears at least, a rather pejorative term, implying a type of music you listen to a) while slowly coming down from drugs, or b) the morning/afternoon after a heavy drug binge, when all your fragile temperament can cope with is some feint break beats, some aimless keyboards doodling, and rudimentary A-level acoustic guitar. For chill-out read drop-out.

But not everyone I asked was as enthusiastic as I was. There are some people who will never like it, as the *Daily Telegraph*'s Martin Gayford wrote recently: 'You can tell there must be something good about modern art just by considering the people who hate it – and the same is true of jazz.' Jazz is for people who don't like music, says my friend Bill; it must be fun to play, he says, because it sure ain't fun to listen to ('I remember this tune,' he'll say, warming to his theme, 'which is more than the guy playing it does'). It is, in the words of some forgotten 1980s comedian, six guys on stage playing different tunes. *GQ* ran a joke about it a while back: Q: 'Why do some people instantly hate jazz?' A: 'It saves time in the long run.' Even my six-year-old daughter hates it. After being subjected to hours of Charlie Parker in the car one weekend, she said, as though I hadn't realised it myself, 'I don't like this music. There are no songs for me to sing to.' (The only jazz tune she likes is 'Everybody Wants To Be A Cat', from Disney's *The Aristocats*, which, actually, is a great record – no honestly, it is.)[1] Unbeknownst to her, she was echoing John Lennon's little-known jibe: 'Jazz never does anything.'

Some people's innate hatred of jazz is simply the result of an unfortunate experience, but then anyone who's witnessed Art Blakey performing a three-and-a-half-hour drum solo is entitled to feel a little peeved (and I speak as someone who has seen one at close quarters, at Ronnie Scott's back in the mid-1980s, when, for about three months, jazz was unfeasibly trendy). On top of this some people just don't get it. Like the later work of James Joyce, the films of Tarkovsky or 'tax harmonisation', the fact that some things will always live just

---

[1] Musically I have tried to indoctrinate both my daughters, but with limited success, and while I've succeeded with the Beatles (Georgia likes 'the Octopus song') and the Strokes, many musical milestones have turned into millstones. Particular favourites remain the Monkees, Justin Timberlake, Kylie and the Scissor Sisters (see page 324).

beyond the common understanding is something jazz enthusiasts must learn to live with. Heigh ho.

Also, jazz has often been victim to the vagaries of fashion, destined to be revived at the most inappropriate moments. The last time jazz was really in the limelight was, as I said, back in the mid-1980s, when it became the soundtrack *du jour* in thousands of matt-black bachelor flats all over designer Britain, and when every style magazine and beer ad seemed to look like a Blue Note album cover. Jazz went from being a visceral, corporeal music to a lifestyle soundtrack. This was the age of the Style Council, of *Absolute Beginners* ... of Sting. Buying into jazz was meant to lend your life a patina of exotic sophistication, and was used to sell everything from Filofaxes and coffee machines to designer jeans and sports cars.

In his excellent book, *Jazz 101: a Complete Guide to Learning and Loving Jazz*, John F. Szwed wrote: 'The life and look of the black jazz musician offered a double attraction, that of the alienations of both artist and colour. Whatever jazz might have been as an actual occupation, the jazz musician offered one of the first truly nonmechanical metaphors of the twentieth century. Now, whether one has heard of Charlie Parker or not, we inherit a notion of cool, an idea of well-etched individuality, a certain angle of descent.' If jazz had started life as a subversive sexual extension of ragtime, blues, boogie-woogie and the New Orleans sound, by the end of the century it had become the soundtrack of accomplishment, a way of upstairs acknowledging downstairs in the manner of *nostalgie de la boue*.

But what about the music? In many ways, and for many people, jazz ended in the early 1960s, when Ornette Coleman, John Coltrane and Cecil Taylor suddenly became the avant-garde; in fact, almost everything that has happened to jazz in the last forty years could be called 'post-Coltrane' in much the same way that people use 'post-modern'. Obviously jazz didn't end then, but its public persona did; either jazz was 'free' and difficult (mad-looking Belgians with crazy hair, billowing luminescent smocks and angular clarinet-looking instruments), or else it was nostalgic (Harry Connick Jr, et al). Ironically, for a type of music so obsessed with the modern and the 'now', jazz has always been preoccupied with the past, so much so that during the 1980s and 1990s it became less and less able to reflect modern culture. Everyone wanted to sound like Miles or Dizzy; either that, or they went fusion mad, and ended up sounding and looking like Frank Zappa on steroids.

And so, after six long months I arrived at my final selection, the 100 best jazz CDs money can buy, the CDs that would produce the playlist on my iPod. The selections aren't necessarily all benchmarks, they're simply the best records to listen to, the ones that give me the most pleasure. For a while it seemed like my mission was simply to collect as many versions of 'A Night In Tunisia' as I could (and I did – my library now contains three killer versions, by Charlie Parker, Dexter Gordon and Dizzy Gillespie, as well as a vocal version by Eddie Jefferson that I'm still not sure about), although I eventually branched out into all areas of jazz, from New York stride piano to the Third Stream stuff (the classical/jazz crossover). There is very little trad, not much fusion, and rather a lot of stuff from the golden age of modern jazz, from 1955 to 1965. Oh, and nine albums by Miles Davis (eight of which have been uploaded in their entirety).[1]

Three years ago I could never have pictured myself wearing a metaphorical beret and nodding along to seemingly random trumpet sounds in the comfort of my own home. But here I am, imagining myself looking out over Los Angeles from Case Study house No. 22, with an AVO Classic Robusto in one hand and a large glass of amarone in the other. And all I can hear is Freddie Hubbard. Mmmm, jazz. *Nice.*

---

[1] The last appears on page 265.

17 iPod, uPod, We All Shop for 'Pod

In New York, the birth of a retail revolution

New York: the Sunday afternoon sun is dipping behind the extravagantly upholstered lofts and warehouses of SoHo. Along Prince Street, hordes of itinerant shoppers slope from vaulted window to vaulted window. They graze through the stores, their outsize cardboard carrier bags banging against their legs as they go. In New York, shopping in the Naughties is still devotional, and although they give the impression of being collectively absent-minded, the hundreds of baseball-capped, Gap-legged and Nike-topped New-New Yorkers strolling along Prince Street and Broadway this autumn afternoon have a purposeful glint in their eyes.

Nowhere is this glint more discernible than in Station A, on the corner of Prince and Green, just along from the gargantuan Prada store, and just round the corner from the hideously fashionable Mercer Hotel, where the media meets itself for latte and gossip. Here, a mass of excitable, yet slow-footed consumers look as though they have died and gone to shopping heaven. As computer technology has become the new religion, so Apple's Station A is its shrine.

Here is a world that offers so much in the shape of so much colour and speed, so many permutations of brushed metal and neoprene, and as many sorts of software as there are gigabytes on your average hard disc. There are currently 70 Apple Stores in the US, and though satellite operations are opening up all over the world – each one with the same manufactured feeling of austere indulgence, each one decorated with Apple's trademark Blueberry, Graphite and Lime – the New York store is the mothership, the lode star, the Starship Enterprise of Apple's brave new world. (Every location for every Apple store is hand-picked by a former Gap executive.) In a comprehensive and rather remarkable way, Apple has imbued consumerism with a new kind of dignity.

Since it opened at the turn of the century, Station A has become something of a Mecca, and has attracted the kind of adulatory talk usually reserved for monolithic clothing stores (Barney's, Comme Des Garçons, Prada). New York does gentrification well – especially in this part of town – but the Apple store has become something else again: it looks like some sort of post-modern church, a digital dreamland. With tills. It is the apple of the Big Apple's eye.

This is why Station A is so popular with the trend-weary deities of Downtown Manhattan. There is iCandy everywhere. Here, laptops and digital music players are presented as choice exhibits in a travelling exhibition, on podiums and in glass boxes, demanding attention; mouse mats and FireWire adaptors have a reverential air about them; neckband headphones and HotWire cables are displayed as though they are valuable works of art (which to Apple they sort of are; this is an expensive world with copper-bottom built-in margins: an iPod-friendly armband, which is made merely of rubber and a small amount of plastic can be yours for $30, while the company also offers iPod engraving, for $19.99).

Apple instils its products with a kind of holy superiority, implying entry to this virtuous and meritorious world can be sanctioned simply by investing in an iBook or a PowerPod Auto Adaptor (they even sanctify third-party products). When you slip in a pair of iPod earbuds connected to a brand, spanking-new Fourth-Generation memory box, and you spin the click-wheel onto a brand new download by Tom Baxter or an archive classic from Van Dyke Parks (I would suggest 'Another Dream' from *Clang Of The Yankee Reaper*), then you know that with just one single purchase you could become one of the chosen, one of the new-style great and the good, a member of Apple's seemingly inexhaustible army of consumer volunteers.

They come in wearing their chinos and backpacks, faceless investors in a digital future. And, boy, are they investing with gusto: they buy iMacs, PowerBooks, iPods ('I still think it looks like a bar of soap, Martha'), iTrips, miniature Altec Lansing speakers so they can listen to their iPod in their kitchens and their hotel rooms, Bluetooth wireless headphones, Tivoli radios, Lilipod waterproof iPod cases (or 'skins' as they're known), Xtreme iPod car chargers, every third-party accessory you can imagine. The iPod is now an industry, one that will soon be bigger than the music industry itself.

But how many iPods can Apple really sell? There are only so many pairs of ears in the world, only so many people prepared to succumb to the latest marketing wizardry of a company like this.

Many of the people in Station A are the same people I saw at the Franz Ferdinand concert at Roseland last night, a random army of chino and backpack-clad endomorphs, keen-eyed yet disorientated, as though they've just walked mistakenly into a recently-finished space-age theme park ... looking for ways to either enter the future or reacquaint themselves with their past (wondering if they can squeeze their own fantasy singles collection into the same sonic universe, or simply pondering the possibility of trying to like Maroon 5 – it can be done) ... all wandering around, lost in their own little iWorlds. Many of the semi-shaven East Village-type boys wear wraparound reflective sunglasses and three-quarter legged trousers while their girls wear short denim skirts, crop-tops and white Birkenstocks. Apple haven't just made it easy for their customers to take their products out of the study and into the living room, they can take them anywhere they like, to the banks of the Ganges or the streets of Downtown Manhattan.

A lot of the pilgrims here today are regulars, and you can tell they know the store as well as they know their own apartments (and seeing that New York apartments are so small, they might know it a bit better). I bump into two Labelholics from London, one of whom has his iPod tucked tightly inside his black patent leather Helmut Lang iPod case, bought at great cost from Colette, the insufferably trendy shop near Place Vendome in Paris. He couldn't be more pleased when I notice it.

It's a fact that Apple has produced a generation of Mac users who spend half their time gushing effusively about all things Apple (iMacs, iPods, iPhoto, iMovie, iTunes, etc.), and half their time bitching about their performance (they also bitch about the company's seemingly dismissive attitude towards its customers ... its secretive, paranoid attitude towards the press ... its obsession with discontinuing product lines ... its general intransigence). Every Apple product has a forum, a user group and several dozen websites (sometimes several hundred websites) devoted to it, where fans and fanatics can obsess to their hearts' content. Every new ergonomic slab of silicon and polycarbonate is dissected with boffin-like precision, and Apple's True Believers are fiercely protective of their toys: if they feel the company has let them down, they tell them (in no uncertain terms). Again and again and again.

Take thirty-four-year-old David Glickman, a management consultant from San Francisco. Since buying his iPod in 2003, he has invested in the following PodAccessories: a pair of noise-cancelling headphones, some Sony mini-speakers, an FM radio transmitter, various adaptors for charging his iPod in his car, a state-of-the-art cable to connect his toy to his stereo, and an adaptor so he and a family member can listen to his tunes simultaneously.

But their shopping habits caused Apple's commercial rebirth. Big time. In October 2004 Apple announced its fiscal fourth quarter earnings had more than doubled. It was the company's highest fourth-quarter revenue in nine years, with a net profit of $106m, or 26 cents per share, for the quarter ending 25 September. That compared with a profit of $44m, or 12 cents per share, in the same period in 2003. Sales were $2.35b, up 37 per cent from $1.72b the previous year. 'We shipped over two million iPods, our retail store revenues grew ninety-five per cent year-over-year, and the new iMac G5 has received phenomenal reviews and is off to a great start,' said Steve Jobs, rather too matter-of-factly. These two million sales represented a 500 per cent increase from the same period the year before, while in the previous quarter Apple had sold 860,000 iPods. Sales of Macintosh computers reached 836,000, a 6 per cent increase from 2003's final quarter. As soon as Jobs made the announcement, shares surged by 6 per cent, levelling off at $42.15, more than double the level from the year before. In the space of two years Apple had gone from being a $6 billion-a-year company to a $12 billion-a-year company, while the iPod itself had become a $2 billion-a-year business. The third-party businesses were booming too, with both Altec Lansing and Griffin Technology seeing huge, huge rises in profits.

Jobs believes that we are still in the foothills of the digital music revolution. iTunes, the store, has now sold more than 150m songs worldwide, but although they own 70 per cent of the global market (their closest rival, Napster, has 11 per cent), this is still a tiny fraction of total music sales. Pascal Cagni, Apple's European boss, says 'The iTunes music store is the key driver to establish the iPod as the Walkman of the twenty-first century.'[1]

It's a comparison that preys on Jobs' mind. Since it was introduced in 1979, Sony has sold over three hundred million

---

[1] The 150 millionth song downloaded from iTunes was, rather unexceptionally, 'Ex-Factor' by Lauryn Hill and was bought by a young downloader from Colorado called Beth Santisteven.

Walkmans; so far, Apple has sold a mere six million iPods, more than half of them in the last twelve months. Not only do they have to build on this success, they have to hold on to their dominance in the market, and make sure they ring-fence their success. Critics – including Microsoft's Bill Gates – have repeatedly suggested that Apple is in danger of repeating its mistake with the Macintosh in the Eighties, by pinning its faith exclusively on its own technology – this time on the AAC music file format as opposed to the MP3 format that everyone else uses (and that includes Microsoft). But Jobs is nothing if not bullish: Hewlett-Packard now sell its own PC-friendly version of the iPod (nicknamed the hPod), considerably increasing Apple's distribution power, while Jobs' deal with Motorola (enabling users to transfer music from iTunes directly to hand-held technology) means Apple will be able to tap into the 500 million+ handset market with a proven technology and brand, in the hopes of having attach rates in the tens of millions, as opposed to the few million iPods it has currently shipped, and thus dramatically expand the iTunes user base (the future doesn't just mean iTunes direct to your mobile, it means digital entertainment direct to your TV monitor, your hob, your sunglasses, anything you damn well like; LG Electronics have already produced one such gimmick, the Internet Fridge, a £6000 beast that has already found a home with those paragons of conspicuous consumption, the Beckhams).

The Hewlett-Packard deal was a big one, and analysts predict that HP's iPod will eventually outsell Apple's own product, given their enormous distribution channels. Jobs' decision to open up iTunes and iPod to Windows users was widely praised. One analyst, Charles Wolf, from Needham & Co., welcomed the decision, saying, 'In our opinion, Apple's decision to port iTunes to the Windows platform was the most strategically significant one the company made since Steve Jobs' return in 1997. It signalled that Apple would no longer confine its award-winning software to the Mac, but instead leverage it to address a market where ninety-five per cent of consumers use Windows PCs.'

The HP product bought into the Apple cult by launching durable, water-resistant Printable Tattoos, special iSkins that could be wrapped around their iPods. They allowed customers to personalise the look of their memory boxes with album cover art, as well as creating their own designs and photos printed on Tattoo media via HP colour printers. And who wouldn't want to buy into that?

When Apple and Hewlett-Packard announced the deal, HP CEO Cary Fiorina said, 'We explored a range of alternatives to deliver a great digital-music experience and concluded Apple's iPod music player and iTunes music service were the best by far. We have the opportunity to add value by integrating the world's best digital-music offering into HP's larger digital-entertainment system strategy.'

Apple recognises that the iPod is a better-known product than the Macintosh, which until recently was its hero product. When it started advertising the Mac G5 in the summer of 2004, the advertising strap line proclaimed the product was 'From the creators of iPod', which was tantamount to saying the iPod was Apple's Trojan horse. The new-look Mac showed how serious Apple was about selling computers, and, by associating the G5 with the music carrier, basically said that if you bought an iPod then what you really needed was a cool new Mac to go with it.

This had been happening ever since Apple launched the iPod, back in the autumn of 2001, and while their share of the personal computer market was small – it has hovered around the 3 per cent for years – people began swapping their PCs for Macs because of iPod compatibility (no matter that they could actually use their iPods with their PC if they had the right adaptor).

What defines a decade is obviously not a technology's invention, but rather a shift in price and performance that triggers a rush from lab to marketplace. Along with Microsoft, Apple has largely been responsible for orchestrating that shift. For a while we weren't sure why any of us out here in the real world needed computers – they did stuff, really quite clever stuff – but why would a person need such a thing? Why would we want a glorified abacus? Using a computer back then was a consumer decision, not any sort of necessity. In 1943, when the founder of IBM, Thomas Watson, was asked how he viewed the future of technology – his response, it is said, was that there would one day be a worldwide market 'for maybe five computers'. Soon we won't be able to live our lives without them, whether we like it or not.

The year wasn't all good though. In July Steve Jobs underwent life-saving cancer surgery, and on his return the company was once again embroiled in the Apple Computer versus Apple Corps lawsuit that for months had been talked about as potentially the largest non-class-action settlement in history. Following the scare, Jobs sent a memo to his staff, telling them his cancer was a far more curable form than typical pancreatic cancer. Ever the company man, he finished the missive by writing: 'I'm sending this from my hospital bed using my seventeen-inch PowerBook and an Airport Express.'

Then there was the furore over the amount Apple were charging UK iTunes customers for downloads – 79p, which at the time was approximately 1.15 Euros. Apple's French and German customers at the time were being charged just 0.99 Euros – about 67.8p. This was contravening European law, which explicitly states that UK consumers are supposed to enjoy the same benefits of the single market as other citizens of member states.

However, the future is bright – the future is Apple green. Given that the company's global market share is only about 3 per cent, industry analysts believe that it will increase substantially since its 'mind share' of the PC market seems much higher, now that the iPod has revitalized the brand and its product line is refreshed.

As I climb the stairs to Station A's mezzanine, on my way to the book department, I inadvertently walk into the middle of a seminar on iTunes. Some good-meaning soul – who I soon discover knows more about selling soap than he does about the internal workings of the iPod – is addressing about fifty wide-eyed innocents, steering them haphazardly through the labyrinthine wonders of all things Mac. He is rushing as he is running out of time, yet is still encouraging his slack-jawed audience to ask him questions. And so I do. But having failed to answer three questions successfully (I'm especially interested in changing encoders and the optimum bit rate of AAC conversion), he spends the rest of the session ignoring my raised hand.

I feel kind of vindicated, in a silly, childish sort of way. Meet Dylan Jones, I think to myself: iExpert, iBore.

18 Ask Not What You Can Do For Your iPod, Ask What Your iPod Can Do For You

'I want my MP3'

It's August 2004 and I am having breakfast in 7, a café in Playa d'en Bossa, where the Manumission podium dancers traditionally come after finishing their eight-hour stint, and before they traipse off to the after-party at Space, a few hundred yards away (not for recreation either; there they'll be dancing some more). They come for beers, *café con leche*, *ensamadas* (Spanish croissants, basically, with the consistency of compressed doughnuts), and to soak their feet in plastic washing-up bowls full of warm soapy water.

There are five of them, and seven of us; they've been up for twenty-four hours while we've only been up for two. They're still dripping with sweat; we're just covered in recently applied Auto-Bronzant, the sort that gives you an automatic tan while you're waiting for a real one. Nevertheless, we're all enjoying the same soundtrack, the same filtered noise oozing quietly from the café's overhead speakers. It's about 9.30 a.m. and the Tuesday morning sun is already high above the crenellated adobes on this side of the island. There are people everywhere – some dressed in the regulation day-glo logo-intensive sportswear worn by the serious clubber, some simply in tie-dye three-quarter-length shorts and loose-fitting surfer singlets. Unlike other resorts, unlike other beaches, in fact unlike anywhere else in the world, you can't tell whether these people have been up for hours, or days. Take a closer peek and some of them look like they've been up for years.

We sit there in all our finery, faces tilted to the sun, nodding along to the music, the girls all in flowing shimmery things, and the boys dressed in the modern Balearic summer wardrobe: Birkenstocks, loud shorts, even louder shirts, and expensive reflective and very girly sunglasses. This is the Ibiza look: young, glitzy, a little too flash. Men on holiday tend to dress at least five years younger than they normally do, which allows us to indulge ourselves with stuff we wouldn't dream of entertaining at home.

7's in-house music is as eclectic as music is everywhere on this island, as eclectic as it's been for thirty years, as it was thirty years ago, back in the days when Ibiza first started making a name for itself as the alternative egalitarian party capital of the world. Thirty years ago, if you had been sitting here – right here where I am now, watching a bunch of podium dancers wash their feet in the hot morning sun – or hereabouts, you would have heard anything from James Brown ('Give It Up Or Turn It A Loose') and George McCrae ('Rock Your Baby') to Pink Floyd ('Money') and Roy Harper ('One Of Those Days In England'). Today is no different, in essence, only more so. The only difference is it's not just in Ibiza this is happening, it's happening everywhere, all over the world, in nightclubs, in cafés and bedrooms from New Cross to New Delhi.

As we sit and sip our 2004 coffee, the stereo – such an old-fashioned word these days – pumps out a selection of tunes which encapsulates the way we all consume pop nowadays: the Rolling Stones' '19th Nervous Breakdown' is followed by the handbag house remix of Lou Reed's 'Satellite Of Love' which in turn is followed by John Barry's loungecore classic 'The Theme From The Persuaders', the 2002 bootleg remix of the Velvet Underground's 'I'm Waiting For My Man', and at least three club records of unfamiliar provenance (at least to me). It wasn't so long ago that having eclectic musical taste was anathema to the average punter. Ever since the dawn of pop – fifty years ago, when Elvis proved that white men really could sing the blues – youth culture has been defined by musical attrition, not musical détente. You liked rockabilly or you liked Motown; you liked Captain Beefheart or you liked the Skatalites; you liked Genesis or the Clash; Womack & Womack or the Jesus & Mary Chain. You never liked both, and if you did you weren't really taken seriously.

It is in Ibiza where I have my iPod crisis of confidence. We are on holiday in this huge, mad house, the sort of place the Addams Family might have stayed had they been part of the Ecstasy Generation. It is a gothic monument to kitsch, complete with 48-track recording studio, DVD porn den, snooker room, lap pools, a walk-in wardrobe full of what I assume are lap-dancers' wigs, a wigwam (obviously), two miniature ponds and a fantastically naff sculpture garden. When we describe the place to potential visitors, we say it is heartening to know that it is still possible to spend a million pounds in Woolworths. (When I get back to London I discover it is owned by a lottery-winning DJ from Birmingham, which seems to make perfect sense.)

Having spent four months converting my CDs to MP3s (or, rather, the Apple equivalent, AAC files, which are fundamentally MP4s), by the middle of May I had begun ripping my vinyl too. One night I'd been judging some student fashion awards in a tent in Battersea Park, and one of the organisers told me about a piece of kit called an iMic which allows you to record directly from vinyl into iTunes. This felt like the most serendipitous thing ever, and the next day I made my way to the hi-fi department in John Lewis in Oxford Street (which is where I had been told, in no uncertain terms, to go), and spent £39 on my Griffin iMic.

And boy, did it make me happy. The first recordings I remember making were when I was about ten, in the front room of our house in Deal, the listless coastal town in Kent, with me using an external cassette microphone to record various Tiny

Tots versions of Disney songs like 'Old Yeller' and 'Whistle While You Work'; this was going to be just as much fun, with hopefully better results.

I started with the singles, daunted somewhat by the thought of manually recording every song on some of my favourite LPs (especially Wire's *Pink Flag*, which, the last time I looked, had about sixty-three tracks on it). By recording singles, I could make quantum dents in my record collection, a sort of cathartic housekeeping and rather pathetic self-management technique which would subconsciously encourage me to keep going (this was going to take a long, long time). I installed the software, connected all the leads, and adjusted the volume control, just like I'd been doing for years when recording onto cassette or mini-disc, making sure my Devo and Aztec Camera singles weren't going to bounce up into the red and get all distorted. Then I'd lower the needle onto the vinyl, and quickly click on the record button on the iMic display, real-time recording every obscure and esoteric piece of my life that (for probably very sound reasons) hadn't found its way onto CD. You'd think that in this age of extravagantly produced boxed sets, where every raggedy cast-off is collated and framed with perfect digital efficiency, that it would be possible to find this stuff loitering about in record shops (where I always imagine the likes of long-deleted Roberta Flack and Donny Hathaway LPs metaphorically kicking a ball against a garage door, waiting for someone like me to come along and buy them). Either that, or they would be available on the Internet.

But no, the only place where this stuff existed was in my cupboards, and so I had to keep going. If I was seriously going to pour my whole life into my box, I had to squash it all in, and not just the bits that had been deemed acceptable for the CD generation. And so I began trawling through my record collection, uploading rare singles like Alternative TV's 'Love Lies Limp', the seminal (ha, ha) flexi-disc given away by *Sniffin' Glue* in 1977; the Red Crayola's 'Hurricane Fighter Plane' flexi-disc we were given at a Pere Ubu concert in Chiselhirst Caves in 1978; Tony Osborne's 'Shepherd's Song', a 1972 recording of a Dubonnet commercial; Iggy Pop's Siamese Records version of 'I Got A Right' (again from 1977, and the only version of this song worth having), and many, many more. Of course, the greatest thing about the iMic was its ability to import all my 12" singles, records which had defined my life after dark through much of my youth, which had almost become part of my DNA but which I very rarely listened to anymore. (One such example is Nuance's 'Loveride' on Island's original Fourth & Broadway label, a 12" I bought on my first trip to New York in 1984, when I was twenty-three, and which I rather crassly said was so powerful it was actually 'killing' people on the dancefloor, when I reviewed it for the *NME* on my return.)

So, come August, at least two-thirds of my life is in my 'Pod. There is still a fair bit of husbandry to take care of, but by and large I'm on the home straight. Or at least I think I am.

One afternoon in Ibiza, as we're all lazing by the pool, some of us working off hangovers, at least three of us working our way through Bob Woodward's *Plan of Attack*, and a couple of us attempting to do both, we start playing the iPod through the pool-side speaker system, pumping out one of many chill-out playlists I've compiled specifically for moments like this (in a fit of hubris, I have taken it upon myself to be the iPod DJ for a house full of gold-standard, first-generation iPodaholics). But to my dismay, the quality is not quite what I expected it to be. The songs sound a bit ... woody, a little dull, as though we are listening to them on an FM radio that isn't quite tuned in.

Bizarrely, the only songs that don't sound muddy are the ones recorded directly from vinyl; and not because music was better in those days, but because – *stupid man, why hadn't I realised?* – they've all been recorded on the default AIFF format. This meant that whereas all the songs recorded from CD had been via the MP3 (or rather AAC) format – i.e., compressed files – the vinyl recordings weren't compressed at all, as they were AIFF. The AIFF, or Audio Interchange File Format, is one that has been used in the Macintosh operating system for ages. In a way, you could say that they are the Macintosh equivalent of wave files (meaning uncompressed audio data). The quality is far superior to MP3s but the file size is huge, and a full song title in the AIFF format can take up to 30MB or more of disk space. AAC – Advanced Audio Coding – was designed to replace MP3 technology, which is now nearly twenty-five years old. But while the sound compression system is far more efficient and delivers better sound quality, nearly rivalling that of uncompressed CDs, the AIFF system actually *is* CD quality. Which is where I was obviously going wrong (by not using it, that is).

And then, with a cold sweat building up around my neck, like some sort of death-mask halo, I thought back to a couple of conversations I'd had six months previously. Robin, who had introduced me to the Altec Lansing speakers, and who seemed to be something of an expert in these matters long before I thought it was desirable to be so, had told me I ought to explore other importing preferences ('You see, I'm a sucker for quality,' he'd said, as though he knew I was an amateur, but was trying to soften the blow). While Richard, another good friend and the one person who had followed my burgeoning obsession with the iPod since its inception, had casually told me months ago that compressed files were not the way to go (he was installing a solid state music centre in his house and was full of derision for any sort of compression). Shit. How could they both be right? Not only would I have to do something about my importing process, I would have to do so without letting either of them know.

Should I dump all my AACs and bump up to AIFF? This would mean that while a song like, say, Miles Davis's 'So What' (which lasts for 9 minutes and 24 seconds) was only taking up 8.8 MB with AAC, if I was to convert it or import it as an AIFF, which is a non-compressed file, it would be taking up 95.1 MB, using over ten times as much space (you can fit around ninety-two four-minute AIFF files on an iPod mini). So although I could fill up my 40 GB iPod with approximately 10,000 songs using AAC (which is 666.6 hours, or nearly enough music to play non-stop throughout the entire month of February without hearing the same song twice), the quality would eventually be found wanting.

This is where AIFF comes in. Basically, it's better. If you read any of the dozens of iPod manuals which have been published in the last couple of years, you'll be told that AIFF files are only for fidelity fanatics, but that's not the case at all: to experience CD-quality sound you need AIFF files.

So I had a dilemma. Should I carry on regardless, recording everything on AAC, and to hell with the consequences? Or should I start again using AIFF, safe in the knowledge that my collection was as good as it possibly could be? It would be no good converting my AAC files to AIFF files (which can be done with two swift movements inside the iTunes gateway), as all I'd be doing was expanding an already compressed file, like magnifying an abridged book (it's still abridged, just bigger).

After several days of internal dialogue (I was too embarrassed to discuss it with anyone else), I decided to go for it. That night, as I was in the kitchen of our rented Balearic palace, I casually mentioned to Richard that I might – just might, you understand – start filling my iPod all over again, and go back through my CD collection importing everything on AIFF instead of AAC. He was painstakingly making a Caesar salad at the time, and, perhaps with a mixture of bewilderment and benevolent resignation, took a long hard pull on his beer, and gave me a seriously old-fashioned look that said, implicitly, 'You are a dear, dear friend, and whatever you decide to do will be OK with me, but I feel I have to point out to you right now that you should have thought of this *ages* ago, before you began all this nonsense, and that I want it to be logged that I think you are a sad, sad loser.'

Which I thought was fair enough, really.

Prior to this, I'd had other minor iPod disappointments, but none that was insurmountable. When I started listening to my iPod through headphones (something I've never been a huge fan of, preferring to listen to the iPod through speakers), I started to worry that I was going prematurely deaf, as the machine wasn't loud enough, although I soon realised this was because the European models are much quieter than their American counterparts. Some European countries – and principally I mean the French – are so concerned about the dangerous mix of excessive volume and unprotected eardrums that they've barred personal listening devices such as the iPod from being louder than 100 decibels. The American iPod can play up to a theoretical limit of 104 DB, which is 2.5 times louder than 100 DB. (There are various ways to accelerate the onslaught of tinnitus, although one of the easiest is Hans-Peter Dusel's iPod VolumeBooster utility, which can be found at www.bnv-gz.de/~hdusel/tools/iPodVolumeBooster. You could also invest in a pair of Etymotic's ER 6 Isolator headphones, which will cut out most extraneous outside noise. Failing that, you could start listening to Queens of the Stone Age. All of the time.)

My second problem involved my PowerBook's capacity, which after a few months I discovered wasn't as big as I'd thought it was – only 37 GB, making it impossible for me to fill my 40 GB iPod. I felt slightly conned when I found this out, as though the IT guys who'd sold me the laptop knew I was about to painstakingly import ten thousand songs onto iTunes and be unable to do anything else because my hard disk wasn't big enough. But I simply increased the memory (to 55 GB) and got on with it. After all, if I was intent on building a compact version of the Virgin Megastore, it was hardly surprising if I had to build the odd extension or two.

But having discovered my importing gaff, I vowed to go back in again, resigned myself to uploading everything I had already uploaded, but in a different, better format. Sure, at least a fifth of my iTunes collection had been transferred by AIFF from vinyl, but that still left over four thousand songs to be recorded – or rerecorded – again. Four thousand songs, roughly four hundred LP-length CDs, at roughly five minutes a pop (the time it takes to upload), meant another thirty-three hours in front of my PowerBook. Not only bearable, I reasoned, but potentially quite fun. Gore Vidal once said that the only danger in watching pornography is that it might make you want to watch *more* pornography, and I must admit the addictive nature of uploading meant that the thought of spending a day and half (non-stop, you realise), doing something I had already done before – doing lots of things I had already done before – was actually rather exciting. Sexy, even.

Consequently, I started making more lists – more considered this time – of the stuff I needed to upload ... started itemising my Steely Dan and Stevie Wonder CDs, and working out exactly how quickly I could work my way through the piles of CDs that I knew only contained one or two songs I wanted. And so I decided to go back in, back into the swatches of Sinatra, the acres of Moloko, the forests of Free Design. Far from dreading the task, it excited me – editing, deleting songs not deemed essential, reducing my musical sauce even more.

But just as I was About To Go Back In – like the tag-line from yet another *Alien* or *Jaws* sequel – I stumbled across another format altogether: Apple Lossless. I had worked out that to convert my entire iTunes library to AIFF, I would have to whittle down my collection, and slice off even more songs from my past. Did I really need all those Van Morrison songs? Could I live without all that Bob Dylan stuff I'd ripped basically because I thought I ought to (I only really like *Blonde On Blonde* and *Blood On The Tracks*, so why don't I leave it at that?)? And did I really need the first Blondie album? It would take me back to 1977 whenever I played it, obviously, but honestly, did I really like it? Would I appreciate any of its songs cropping up unannounced in the middle of a dinner party? And what the hell was I doing with the Keane album? It had three good songs on it, for Chrissakes, so why did I need it all?

And as I was mentally working my way through all of this stuff, a colleague suggested I investigate Apple Lossless, which is another way of importing your music at high quality, but without using so much space.

Jesus, I thought to myself, what now? Would I still be rerecording this stuff when I was in my fifties? But this turned out to be the best iTip yet. In the past, if you were an audiophile and weren't concerned about the amount of space your music files consumed, you would have chosen either the WAV or, more likely, the AIFF encoder, because of the resulting files' purity. But Lossless, which is a relatively new codec, offers almost exactly the same quality as AIFF at roughly half the size. Meaning that Miles Davis's 'So What', which in the AIFF format eats up a massive 95.1 MB, with Lossless comes in at a much more reasonable 55.5 MB – almost half. (Regardless of the format you choose, changing encoders and bit rates requires a trip to iTunes' Importing 'preference' panel – select Preferences from the iTunes menu in Mac OS X. Within this window you'll find iTunes' five encoding options in the Import Using pop-up menu, and when you select an encoder, its default setting will appear there. Choose AAC, for example, and you'll find that iTunes will encode a file at 128 Kbps, while MP3 files are encoded at 160 Kbps by default, even though the quality is less good.)

Armed with this knowledge, I started again; slightly irritated by the thought of repetition, but also quite fired up by it too – excited by the thought of once more hitting the air snare at the start of 'Like A Rolling Stone', excited by the thought of ripping the best bits of Blur's *The Great Escape* without having to play the whole thing again, excited by the thought of importing those 112 Van Morrison songs in their entirety.

A few weeks after my conversion to Lossless, I see an ad on the Internet. 'IBIZA HOUSE FOR RENT: Gingerbread style, 12 bedrooms, gym, Jacuzzi, petting zoo, indoor ice rink, popular with adult film makers.' I decide to book it for next year.

19 Journey to the Centre of the iPod

At last I am replete, at one with my machine

The PowerBook is sitting on the desk in my den, where it's been, by and large, for the last ten months. It sits, Zen-like, right in the middle, surrounded by my detritus, my . . . stuff. The KEF speakers still sit proudly behind it, as do the Sony twin-deck, the Audio-Technica turntable and the mammoth Kenwood tuner. Underneath the plasma on the far wall sit my almost-installed Japanese Eclipse iPod speakers, their wires still hanging over the edge of the cabinet like ivy. There are piles of CDs, piles of magazines, piles of newspaper clippings, piles of . . . piles.

My left index finger presses the Apple key on the PowerBook as the right one presses 's', for save. And as I do, the laptop goes 'ping!' in perfect C major, the happiest chord in the world, the I-1ove-everybody chord. Apple put this here for a reason, to make us all feel good about using their products, and it works. This 'ping!' isn't a D minor seventh, not the I'm-so-sad-I-can't-even-find-a-hooker blues chord, but the 'ping!' of eternal sunshine. Sure, it also sounds like it should herald the arrival of a filtered disco record, but is that such a bad thing?

'Ping!'

And so, finally, I have finished. I have collected every single piece of good music I own in one place. Every song I have ever liked has been uploaded onto my iTunes library and transferred to my iPod. My box of memories is full, fit to bursting. Every day, every week, every month of my life is represented here in one way or another – whether it's the night I lost my virginity, or the day I fell in love with my wife. Everything has its soundtrack, and that soundtrack is on my iPod. Can this be it? Is that all there is?

The term 'Elvis Year' is used to describe the year of something's peak popularity (2003, for instance, was the Atkins diet's Elvis Year – although which year was Elvis's Elvis Year is still a matter of debate). For the iPod, so far every year since 2001 has been its Elvis Year. The iPod has been such a cultural phenomenon, it has made a lot more people interested in Apple than Apple made people interested in the iPod. Millions of people own them, millions more talk about them in hushed tones, and the fusillade of third-party gadgets has contributed to an extraordinarily lush and prosperous eco-system. There is a veritable iPodNation out there, and it is now such an intrinsic part of the pop-cultural lexicon that 'i' references crop up everywhere. Take these examples from the *Future Dictionary of America:* iGod *n.* a portable device (typically of 500-yottabyte capacity) that simulates the wisdom and/or awe-inspiring terror of an omnipotent deity. e.g., 'I downloaded Buddhism on to my iGod last week and I've already reached a state of nirvana.' ... or ... iJob *n.* optical liposuction for people with unfashionable fat eyes, popular in the 2010s. The extracted material made an excellent teething gel for babies.

The iPod became so ubiquitous that Duke University in North Carolina started offering downloadable courses ... asking people what was on their iPod became an acceptable question in job interviews ... and in a move-on from Seventies 'key' parties, people in my neighbourhood began throwing iPod parties, where they placed their machines in a big bowl on the coffee table and then chose one at random to take home (imagine the horror of taking your little digital box of joy out to the car in the hope of pushing the sonic envelope, only to discover it contained the complete works of Courtney Love or the Manic Street Preachers!).

And what ructions it has caused! The music industry is in

such a state of flux that it seems unlikely to find a workable business model that resembles any they've employed during the last fifty years. The success of the iPod and digital downloading has affected the industry in so many different ways.

Since the beginning of the decade, magazines and newspapers have made a habit of cover-mounting CDs in the hope of generating sales. In November 2004 *Wired* magazine gave away a CD with a difference. All the songs came with a license that gave anyone the permission to do more than just listen to them. You could swap them, sample them, whatever. And most of the artists involved – Danger Mouse, Gilberto Gil, the Thievery Corporation, David Byrne, Paul Westerberg, etc. – went a step further and released their songs under the more expansive Sampling Plus license, meaning their music could be used by other people for commercial gain. Figuring the music industry is waging an unwinnable war against technology, *Wired* decided to set a precedent and put all this stuff ... out there.

There is also a fast-growing band of so-called 'podcasters' – mostly amateur programme-makers whose music radio shows are designed to be heard on MP3 players. Since September 2004, when new software called iPodder allowed listeners to download their favourite shows automatically, hundreds of advertisement-free radio channels have emerged in cyberspace. You just download the software at iPodder.org and decide which audio feeds to subscribe to, which are then stored on your iPod next time you sync with your laptop.

I myself have become a third-party extension, and since loading my machine have become something of an iPod bitch, encouraging people to send me their brand new machines so I can put my own memories on them. A newspaper editor, a shoe designer, a singer, an architect, a literary agent, the European head of a major fashion company, a solicitor or two ... all of them are now walking around with my memories bouncing around inside their heads ... Am I helping them, or are they helping me? I wonder – am I simply saving them an awful lot of time and trouble, or am I indulging myself by foisting my taste upon them?

Ironically, especially as the iPod could turn out to be Apple's greatest success story, it was Jonathan Ive and Steve Jobs' passion for music that helped push the product through in the first place. Yes, Jobs knew the company needed an MP3 player, and yes, like all Apple creations it was driven by commerce (and the thirst for digital convergence), but the iPod's soul, its core, is a testament to its creators' belief that music is as capable of defining our culture as it so obviously was twenty, thirty, forty years ago. Pop's continued relevance, both to consumers and to the industry that feeds them, relies upon constant, perpetual reinvention: every eighteen months or so there needs to be a collective Damascene conversion in order to keep the whole thing fresh, the sort of groundswell that automatically makes whatever came immediately before it seem arcane and unfathomable. And in its way, the iPod is the first music carrier, and digital music technology the first delivery system, to affect the music industry in the same way as music itself.

As I reached what I thought was the end of my digital tunnel, an interested party posed two very salient questions:

a) Having compiled all this ... stuff, what are you missing? What do you realise you still need? Will you ever need any Sham 69?

b) How are you going to remember where all this stuff is?

Well, the answer to the first question is easy: everything ... potentially. As every song on the iPod has the ability to challenge the assumptions of the one before, who knows what weird juxtaposition might work? Who's to say that there aren't a few buried gems on the many albums produced by Prince in the Nineties? Who's to say that Motley Crue are beyond redemption? Just how many Grateful Dead albums are there out there? They can't all be bad, can they? *Can they?* (However, there might not be any room for Sham 69, admittedly ...)

And as for question two: with ease. The iPod's propulsion makes everything easy to access, while keeping that very same 'everything' buried inside a labyrinth of interweaving algorithms (listen long enough and you might hear something you've never heard before).

So how was I, after my journey? Had I really captured the soul of this new machine? Or were my expectations simply resentment under construction? William Burroughs once said that we cut up the past to find the future, which, in a way, is exactly what the iPod has done, scrambling our back pages in order to create a bright new tomorrow. I certainly felt that my past had been well and truly trawled over, while I was simultaneously looking forward with a heightened sense of anticipation.

More importantly, was my journey actually over? Had my express train finally reached Digitopia? Far from it. No, I thought, this is only the beginning. Everything I do for the rest of my life can now be accompanied by my little white memory box. When my collection was finally all in one place, I began to think of it as an arc that has followed my life, from left to right in a descending curve that eventually falls out of peripheral vision, in the bottom right-hand corner of my sightline, around the time I am 110 (by which time, no matter what Jonathan Ive designs, I shall surely be dead).[1] Starting at the age of eight or nine with my parents' Frank Sinatra and Beatles records, my graph-line then drops down to my teens and Bowie and Roxy and Alice Cooper, then runs along the straight with the arrival of punk, new romantics, antediluvian disco, clubland and shiny Eighties pop, towards a retrenchment leading to enlightenment (i.e., when I started listening to my old records again). As the curve starts racing towards my thirties, I think of Van Morrison and Bruce Springsteen, and a pre-midlife curiosity for things I had previously ignored or missed. And then, just as my arc had begun tailing off ... up pops the iPod icon, just like it does on my PowerBook.

---

[1] This contrasts starkly with the way I visualise the calendar year, which I see as a clock, with January, February and March taking up the first fifteen minutes, and October, November and December filling up the last.

There it is! The UberPod, standing proud and tall, a black hole full of everything from my past, everything from my present, and as much from my future as I've got time for.

Crucially, it began dawning on me that my journey had been a destination in itself. John Lennon liked to say that life is what happens when you're busy making other plans (he even said it in song once), and my iPod journey is testament to that.[1] I have learnt so much about music, about myself, during the time I've been 'at one' with my machine, that I've begun to think that my hobby is a vocation after all, and that what I always thought was a parallel universe is in fact my own private universe, of which there is only one.

What I know for a fact is that this is the first time I can remember technology influencing content, or the consumption of content, in such a profound way. The iPod has totally rejuvenated my interest in music, and over my nine-month induction period I became a man obsessed, buying dozens and dozens of new CDs, dozens and dozens of old CDs I thought I'd never get round to listening to, and borrowing, burning, and downloading like a crazy person. The iPod reminded me that music is compelling, all-consuming and continually diverting. And, right now, the more I hear the more I want. John Peel, who was perhaps the greatest, and most vocal supporter of 'new' music – or at the very least a man who spent more time listening to music than probably anyone else has ever done – had this to say about his continual quest for the new:

There's always the possibility that you're going to come across

---

[1] Spending thirty years collecting the various bits and pieces required to build a decent version of the Beach Boys' *Smile* seemed like an honourable task, and one that has occupied an inordinate amount of my time, but having got there, having achieved my goal, when Brian Wilson finally released his rerecorded interpretation in 2004, all I felt was a massive sense of deflation. It was all right, I thought to myself, but a) It's not quite as good as the original, b) Now everyone's got it, and c) What do I do now?

a record that transforms your life. And it happens weekly. It's like a leaf on the stream. There are little currents and eddies and sticks lying in the water that nudge you in a slightly different direction. And then you break loose and carry on down the current. There's nothing that actually stops you and lifts you out of the water and puts you on the bank but there are diversions and distractions and alarums and excursions, which is what makes life interesting really. Not in a Roman Emperor kind of way where you have an *excess* of stimulation – I forget which Emperor it was that used to have animal skins thrown over him and then scamper into an arena and claw testicles off naked slaves with his bare hands, not quite *that* level – but a little excitement here and there. And music provides that. It's fantastic.

Without the iPod it's unlikely I would have bought Rilo Kiley's astonishing CD *The Execution of All Things*, nor bothered to buy the early work of Stephen Stills, stuff that I always thought I might like but had never cared enough about to find out about. And the way I feel about music now is a bit like that: I don't want to miss anything, don't want to miss the next Strokes record, wouldn't want to miss the new Coldplay CD, couldn't bear to miss Steely Dan's 'future project', can't wait to hear the new U2 (and there's always a new U2). Patti Smith once said, in the way she once said things (about 1975 I reckon, at the time of *Horses*), that the only reason she hadn't committed suicide was because she'd miss the next Stones album, and while I am about as far from committing suicide as a person can be, and while I have almost no desire to hear the next Stones album (and I'm fairly sure I wasn't that bothered in 1975, actually) I sort of see what she means. Music now feels as important to me as it did at the age of twelve, sixteen or twenty (and they were very good years – Bowie, the Ramones, Chic) – perhaps it always was, but I somehow *feel* it more now.

One of the least expected endorsements of the iPod came from the White House in April 2005, when George Bush announced he was a partial adopter. In between his return from Pope John Paul II's funeral in Rome and a meeting with Israeli Prime Minister Ariel Sharon, President Bush spent ninety minutes on an eighteen-mile bike ride at his Texas ranch accompanied by his iPod loaded with 'country', 'rock' and 'pop'. This was what was on it: Van Morrison's 'Brown Eyed Girl', John Fogerty's 'Centrefold', '(You're So Square) Baby, I Don't Care' by Joni Mitchell and the deeply suspect 'My Sharona' by powerpop wannabes the Knack.

I was less surprised to learn that Burt Bacharach owns one. When I interviewed the 77-year-old composer in his palatial Pacific Palisades dreamhome in LA – the sort of house I might have envisaged him living in during the 1960s, with all the pre-requisites of future-retro suburbia, including a bachelor den, a music room, pool house, barbeque patio and open-plan kitchen – he eulogised the little white box. It was uploaded for him by his twelve-year-old son Oliver, who filled it with his father's favourites, notably James Ingrams and old Motown. Bacharach never listens to his own records, at least his old ones ('Why should I? I know it all'), and if he listens to anything at all, it's stuff he's working on at the moment. When we met he was working on an orchestral 'concept' album with Dr Dre and Rufus Wainwright, and it sounded great, a lush and convoluted symphony that evoked all those common epiphanies of yesteryear.

And as for Steve Jobs and Apple? As the competition fails to come up with a credible 'iPodKiller', it appears their hegemony will continue until the idea of a machine that stores 15,000, 25,000, 50,000 songs seems – God forbid – old-fashioned or unnecessary. In October 2004 Steve Jobs announced the launch of the iPod Photo, a 60 GB iPod, capable of storing up to 15,000 songs as well as 25,000 wallet-sized full-colour digital images. At the San José launch, Jobs described how he could now create slide shows to accompany his music selections, as well as album covers, and started repeating the mantra, 'all of your songs and photos in your pocket'. Amazingly, the new iPod could do all this and was just one millimetre thicker than the G4. This was a remarkable feat of engineering, and immediately made me stop worrying about whether or not I'd be able to fit everything I own onto my 40 GB (all I had to do was upgrade).

This wasn't the only thing Apple had been planning in 2004. Steve Jobs' keynote address at the Macworld jamboree in San Francisco in January 2005 was one of his most surprising as well as being one of his most devotional. It was screened, as has become the norm, via satellite to Paris, this year to La Maison de la Radio, where Jobs was to address five hundred exuberant and expectant tech-heads from France, Germany, Italy, Spain, Britain, and everywhere else where tech-heads blossom in Western Europe. These 'keynotes' have become major events in Apple World; religious gatherings where the converted can come and pay homage to The One. They are a sort of Woodstock or Glastonbury of the gadget age.

After a brief introduction by a jacketless Pascal Cagni, the VP of Europe, Africa and the Middle East, Jobs made his entrance, to the thunderous applause of the five hundred in Paris and the many thousands in California. Suddenly there was an almost tangible aura of confidence in the room, one shared by everyone present. The audience in both time zones was identical – jeans, trainers, backpacks, denim shirts, denim jackets, denim everywhere! Everyone looked like a relative of Jobs, even the women. Sitting next to me was a fiftysomething Jobs clone with a black mock-turtleneck top – just like Steve! – with the sleeves rolled up to his elbows. Everyone looked like Jobs, regardless of age or sex. Three rows from the front, former Vice President Al Gore beamed away at the stage with the sort of benevolent glow rarely seen outside a revivalist meeting.

At an event like this it's difficult to decide whether you're at a religious gathering or a rock concert – and instead of watching Coldplay, Elbow, Athlete or the Dave Matthews Band, you get Jobs, live, via satellite, just like Elvis! He even looks like a preacher, and all his black crew-neck top needs to complete the transition is a gleaming white dog collar. At Macworld 2005 Jobs was magnificent, and as he strolled around the stage, explaining the new product launches, the crowd lapped it up, applauding every move, every little *bon mot*.

I feel as though I am witnessing a presentation by the Tyrell Corporation, the creators of the Replicants in *Blade Runner*. This was omnipotent branding like I'd never seen, every image, every surface covered with Apple's Hoefler & Frere-Jones-inspired typeface, every soundbite a logocentric clarion call. This wasn't just a computer rally, this was the living embodiment of an iPod economy ('four hundred third-party accessories and rising!')

Me, I am swept away, and experience the sort of thrill I might get watching Paul McCartney perform the unreleased Beatles song 'Carnival of Light' or seeing U2 perform in my living room. It produced an epiphany, and I sat, dumbfounded by the whole parade of twenty-first century hucksterism – I felt as giddy as I had done two decades previously, as Hall & Oates' 'Out of Touch' poured out of my Virgin Atlantic headphones as we glided over an ever-expanding eiderdown of brilliantly lit cloud, en route to New York for the first time. As a consumer package, Apple is nigh irresistible, and I am filled with the will to consume, like everyone else here, and feel a surge of excitement, a glimpse of how simply wonderful it is to be alive. Silly, I know, but that's what Jobs did to me.

His performance is simply awesome, and any cynicism I may have smuggled into the auditorium is kept discreetly in my pocket, unwanted and not needed. The crowd clap everything – not just the products, but every mistake, every failed cue, every evangelical display conjured up on Jobs' laptop. This wasn't a teenager playing an electric guitar, but a guy in his fifties mucking about on his computer! A man selling laptops instead of religion.

But what mucking about, and what products. In 2004 Apple launched over forty products, and the offering for '05 was just as impressive, including an abundance of new software, as well as a new computer, the MacMini (the 'headless Mac'), designed to entice all those iPod users to switch from their PCs, and the iPod Shuffle, Apple's move into the cheaper flash MP3 market – nearly as small and lighter than a pack of gum or a Swiss Army Knife, and meant to dangle from your neck on a lanyard.

'We wanted to make something that's even easier to use than the iPod,' said Jobs, as though he were selling microwaves out of the back of a van. 'Something happened in the iPod market – people discovered a new way to listen to their music that became the most popular way to listen to your music: shuffle. We think the iPod Shuffle is going to bring tons of people into this new era of digital music. We *love* this!'

They hadn't been doing too badly already, and in the run-up to Christmas had sold a staggering 4.5 million iPods, taking the total sold to over 10 million. Their profits for the final quarter of the year were $295 million, up from $63 million in the same period in 2003, and the biggest in their history. And the goals for the future had suddenly been ramped up: everyone from Mercedes and Ferrari to Volvo and Nissan (top end and bottom!) was putting iPod ports in their cars, and the powers-that-be thought there was no reason why profits wouldn't improve by 75 per cent over the next eighteen months. Who knew? Maybe everyone in the world would own an iPod. Maybe there would soon be an iPod big enough to take everything!

The launch of the 60 GB MotherPod was also indicative of the iPod's future – it's exponential, and will soon no doubt be able to suck everything into its shiny white casing. This begs me to ask myself whether or not I want a machine that acts as a mobile-phone-cum-video-streaming-type-personal-organiser-type thing, that allows me to send and receive e-mails while I watch *Taxi Driver*, write a column for *GQ* and look at my holiday snaps at the same time. But soon I may have no choice. By then Apple will have no doubt effectively turned into a record company, signing bands and releasing their stuff exclusively via iTunes. Who knows? In a short while it's quite conceivable that as we enter the age of the end of ownership, we'll be able to instantly download any song we like (i.e., every song that's ever been recorded anywhere by anyone) onto our mobile phone, while the whole notion of actually bothering to curate music ourselves will seem quaint and ridiculously time-consuming. Maybe the iPod could become totally cognitive, and anticipate mood through a mixture of logic and intuition?

The future looks limitless: nowadays it doesn't seem so fanciful to suppose that if, say, in a few years we want to imagine what it would sound like for Babyshambles (if Pete Doherty isn't dead by then) to record the Rolling Stones' *Aftermath* in its entirety, because of the sophisticated wizardry of digital manipulation, this would be entirely possible (just imagine, with your new Microsoft iPod Expo-Remix all you need do is press the 'Create' button, then 'Babyshambles', then 'Aftermath', then 'All', then 'Imagine' and in less time than it took you to come up with the idea in the first place, there it would be, playing in your home, in your car, in the homes and cars of everyone you know, or, maybe, simply playing in your head, where you'll indulge it for a few minutes before asking your machine to get Pink Floyd to cover the complete works of Orbital. Just imagine ...)

More prosaically, it will soon be possible for any domestic music player to take remix culture as far as anyone could possibly want it to: if you want to remix 'Blue Monday' so it lasts three hours, then why not? If your perverted sense of the zeitgeist determines that you fancy listening to a calypso remix of 'Smells Like Teen Spirit', then who's to deny you? No one.

But you might just enjoy the thought of playing the first track of every Beatles album as you drive to work tomorrow morning – and with digital potential, you'll be able to configure this on your music carrier in the time it takes you to find your car keys (and in my case, probably less time). Your machine will soon be able to download directly from any on-line music store, as well as being able to tune in to every radio programme that has been broadcast in living memory ...

Or, you just might want to wallow in a day's worth of Joni Mitchell – scramble the stuff up, tell your machine to try and anticipate your Saturday morning mood (with specially designated pauses for eating, peeing and reading the newspapers), and then just play away.

Which is just what I'm doing now, playing away, letting my machine whisk me away and sweep me through the farthermost reaches of my mind, taking me through my past, my present, and, by dint of random juxtaposition, my future too. Right now I am exerting complete control, keeping a tight hand on the tiller. For a while the world of abundance is as appealing as any Shangri-La, I know that for me personally, individuality will be the key to any successful navigation.

In the course of the next half an hour I will listen to a song I first enjoyed at the age of eight (the Rushmorean 'Hey Jude'); a song I've only heard once before in my life ('Willow Weep For Me' from Dexter Gordon's *Our Man In Paris*); two Johnny Cash tracks; and a song that means as much to me now as it did when I first heard it, a song that means so much to me it has the capacity to occasionally make me well up. That song is 'Being Boring' by the Pet Shop Boys (6.50, from *Behaviour*, Parlophone, October 1990, the melancholic classic written by Neil Tennant and Chris Lowe), and the salient lyrics are these: 'And now I sit with different faces in rented rooms in far off places, All the people I was kissing, Some are here and some are missing in my nineteen nineties, I never dreamt that I would get to be the creature that I always meant to be, But I thought in spite of dreams you'd be sitting somewhere here ...'

Well, while some people might not be with me now, the records we were listening to are all here in my little white memory box, all lovingly compiled and curated, just waiting for that time when I might need them again.

And I think that time is just about now ...

Appendices

There are those who would say that the iTunes facility is little but a glorified, animated list – a fully functional, battery-powered litany – which, I suppose, is why I like it so much. I no longer have to scour my CD shelves for the Eminem album with 'Stan' on it, I don't have to fanny around looking for a Sex Pistols single I'm not even sure I have any more (how can you lose a picture sleeve copy of 'Pretty Vacant'?), and there's no need for me to get down on my hands and knees and inspect the curling spines of my LPs searching for the Smiths' *Hatful Of Hollow* (which, I must admit, I haven't done since I was about twenty-three), or one of my rare Japanese limited edition David Bowie albums. With my PowerBook it's just a scroll in the park.

The list has become one of the defining characteristics of our time, whether it's one of those *100 Best ...* programmes on Channel 4 (*100 Best Wednesday Afternoon Game Shows, 100 Worst Channel 5 Programmes Starring An Ex-Member Of A Partially-Successful Boy Band ...*), or the first thirty pages of any blue collar men's magazine, or page three of any national broadsheet ('... in a massive, nationwide poll undertaken by the *Daily Telegraph* we've discovered that the country's favourite Lenny Kravitz song is 'It Ain't Over 'Til It's Over', principally because that was the only one most of you could remember ...'). Today's culture is a list culture, but then that's hardly surprising. The Internet, Satellite TV, DVDs, the constant repackaging and reorganising of old pop music (we live, in case you hadn't realised, in a compilation culture that threatens to disappear up its own fundament), the revisionist and often reductive nature of music magazines, the fact that fifty years of pop culture is now available as soon as you press the return button on your keyboard ... it's all conspired to turn the past into the present, and the future into the past.

Everything is there if we want it, which, it has to be said, we do. I do, anyway. iTunes has condoned my obsessive, nerd-like tendencies, outed me as a collector, a hoarder, an adolescent (though not so adolescent anymore) list-maker. And boy, have I leapt at the opportunity: B-sides that are better than their A-sides, ten solo Beatles songs about being in the Beatles, ten genitally-obsessed Red Hot Chili Peppers songs, Frank Sinatra songs he recorded wearing a hat, songs one of my best friends thought were by the Doors but were actually by R. Dean Taylor (one: 'There's A Ghost In My House'), the 350 greatest rap diss songs ... ever! (How about 'Takeover' by Jay-Z, which gives Mobb Deep the finger in the following fashion: 'You little fuck, I've got money stacks bigger than you/When I was pushin' weight, back in '88, you was a ballerina/I got your pictures I seen ya.'). Songs that send shivers up your spine when the singer sings the words 'Steve McQueen' (two: 'Absent Friends' by the Divine Comedy and 'Electrolite' by REM). Songs with either Blue in the title: 'Blue Eyes' (Elton John), 'Blue Hotel' (Chris Isaak), 'Blue Money' (Van Morrison), or Big: 'Big Log' (Robert Plant), 'Big Louise' (Scott Walker), 'Big Time' (Neil Young). The capacity for iTunes lists is exponential.

If songs really are little houses in which our hearts once lived, then surely it's our duty to build gargantuan pleasure palaces where they all can live. After all, the iPod is nothing if not a memory box.

Creating playlists on iTunes doesn't use up any more space, it just reconfigures the files in a different order, so you can make as many as you like (they're all joined by invisible umbilical c(h)ords). TV theme tunes? Download/upload them all! (For the record, the stars of Boss Cat, so-called in the UK because of a well-known cat food, were Top Cat, Spook, Fancy, Brain, Choo Choo and Benny. Oh, and Officer Dibble.) Britpop casualties? The playlist can be as long as you like!

After I'd collated around a dozen playlists (artist-specific: Beatles. Beach Boys. Springsteen. Steely Dan. Marvin Gaye. U2.

Afrika Bambaataa. REM. Coldplay. Libertines), I started to get inventive. Could I create a playlist featuring only records that had great hi-hat sounds (the best hi-hat sound ever recorded is on the O'Jays' 'I Love Music')?[1] Could I create a playlist which consisted of records that sounded like they were recorded by the Rolling Stones but obviously weren't? A playlist featuring Radiohead's best songs (actually quite a few: I had an irrational and rather childish dislike of them – spotty Oxford students, I thought, yuk – until my brother exasperatedly sat me down one night and talked, and played me through them; so three at least: 'High and Dry', 'Fake Plastic Trees' and 'The Bends', all from *The Bends*)? A playlist featuring piano-led songs all played in the key of E? How about an imaginary colloquial British rap concept album featuring alternating tracks by Mike Skinner and John Cooper Clarke?

After a while I realised I could do all this, and more. A lot, lot more ...

Appendix I: 'Hello, is that Peggy?' – 50 David Bowie Records

It was a dark, miserable winter weekday afternoon at the *Sunday Times*, some time around 1994: phones ringing, faxes whirring, subs screaming for copy, couriers coming and going, and the East London hail lashing down outside, hitting the windows like furious fingers on a keyboard.

My phone rings, I pick it up, and a familiar voice on the other end asks, 'Hello, is that Peggy?', although in the retelling I always imagine

---

[1] As for the best pre-digital, analogue drum sound – in case you were wondering, and I think you probably were – check out Elton John's 'Someone Saved My Life Tonight' on *Captain Fantastic and the Brown Dirt Cowboy* (DJM, 1975). The drums were played by Nigel Olsson, and produced by Gus Dudgeon. I met Dudgeon once, and when I told him I thought he had recorded the best drum sound in the history of twentieth century music, he looked at me quizzically, and said, without a hint of arrogance: 'That's weird. That's the second time I've been told that this month.'

it more as 'Hellooooo, is that Pigga-aaay?', in the sort of Mockney drawl that has been used by everyone from Anthony Newley to Damon Albarn via Mick Jagger and Keith Richards.

'Er, no, this is Dylan Jones. Is that David Bowie?'

It seems Bowie's mother had just moved, and as I'd just interviewed Bowie for the *Sunday Times*, my phone number was on the same page as hers (her name was Jones, after all). Bowie seemed as thrilled as I was flattered by this bizarre accident of serendipity, and stayed on the phone for twenty minutes, as I frantically made explanatory hand signals and mouthed 'IT'S DAVID BOWIE!' to anyone passing through the office.

Peggy's son was about to enter another of his purple patches – more golden years – and over the next decade would produce many records as good as those he made in his prime. (And as for the tin-pot Tin Machine, they had been sent back to the Land of Bad Ideas whence they came, and quickly locked up with the Glass Spider, the Laughing Gnome, *Labyrinth*-bloke and that weird guy from the 'Blue Jean' video.)

'I've got to stop mucking about and start making records for myself rather than other people,' he told me on the phone. 'Anyway, I better call my mum before I get round to that ...'

In the thirty-odd years that Bowie has been a star, he has recorded some of the most important music of the post-Beatles era, and although he is still largely known for the raft of ground-breaking albums he released in the Seventies, his work since then has been equally fascinating, and almost as prescient.

Today he is a lifetime away from the androgynous android of the Seventies, when Bowie could be found lolling about in the back of large American limousines, a crumpled heap of black kamikaze silk drinking Tequila Gold from a brown paper bag. This was when his ambition and ego were most blind. 'I get so much fan mail it has to be handled by a computer,' he said in 1975. Computers? What were they? 'I'm an instant star. Just add water and stir.' Any one of Bowie's Seventies personae might have been apocryphal, yet they were all excessive. These days he is no less compelling – he's just not so maniacal.

And the 50 best Bowie records (including quite a few from the last ten years) are ... I Dig Everything, Space Oddity, An Occasional Dream, Over The Wall We Go (as Oscar), The Width Of A Circle, Life On Mars, Queen Bitch, All The Young Dudes, Starman, Five Years, John I'm Only Dancing, Drive-In Saturday, Lady Grinning Soul, Sorrow, Rebel

Rebel (original mix), Sweet Thing, Can You Hear Me?, John I'm Only Dancing ('75), Stay, 'Heroes', Sons Of The Silent Age, 'Helden', DJ, Up The Hill Backwards, Under Pressure (with Queen), Let's Dance, Loving The Alien, Dancing In The Street (with Mick Jagger), Absolute Beginners (long version), Shades (from Iggy Pop's Blah Blah Blah), Amazing, Real Cool World, Sound And Vision Vs. 808 State, Looking For Lester, Buddha Of Suburbia, Pretty Pink Rose (a song he gave to guitarist Adrian Belew in 1990), Strangers When We Meet (single version), Hallo Spaceboy (Pet Shop Boys remix), I'm Afraid Of Americans, Seven, Thursday's Child, This Is Not America (Live at the BBC), I Would Be Your Slave, 5.15 The Angels Have Gone, Slow Burn, Everyone Says 'Hi', New Killer Star, Fall Dog Bombs The Moon, Changes (from *Shrek 2*), Rebel Never Gets Old (yet another Rebel Rebel remix, and a great record from gun to tape).

Appendix II: Found! *Everest* – The Great Lost Beatles Album

In 1970, with their friendship stretched to breaking point, John, Paul, George and Ringo came together at London's Abbey Road Studios to record one last album. The result was the towering *Everest*.

Side One
My Sweet Lord (4.30)
Harrison's original demo had a long, devotional 'Hey Jude'-style coda, though George Martin trimmed this down, turning the song into one of the Beatles' most poignant epics, not a million miles from 'All You Need Is Love'. Eric Clapton plays guitar on this, as does Bob Dylan, while Billy Preston (who is also rumoured to have supplied some of the lyrics) provides some searing organ work. As soon as *Everest* was released, it was this song that dominated the airwaves ('Every time I put on the radio it's "Oh My Lord",' said Lennon after the album's release, 'I'm beginning to think there must be a God.'), giving Harrison the confidence to branch out on his own, which, at the end of the year, he would do with enormous success.

Maybe I'm Amazed (3.50)
An anthem that could only have been written by McCartney, this achingly powerful love song would be the finest thing he'd write all

year. Surprisingly – especially considering that Lennon had always complained that McCartney got more than his fair share of A-sides – the rest of the band said it should be a single; McCartney, even more surprisingly, dragged his heels, preferring the more elegiac 'Let It Be'. (In the end only 'My Sweet Lord' was released as a single, a month after *Everest* itself – the Beatles couldn't agree on a follow-up.)

Cold Turkey (4.59)

The Beatles had alluded to drug-taking for years, usually with their collective tongue in their collective cheek, but Lennon's heroin confessional was a bitter pill for them to swallow. Considered for inclusion on *Abbey Road*, the song was rejected due to its harrowing nature (it is hard to imagine it sitting comfortably next to 'Maxwell's Silver Hammer'), and then shelved. Lennon thought about recording it himself with the Plastic Ono Band ('I thought, "Bugger you, I'll put it out myself,"' he moaned) but then Paul, George and Ringo grudgingly relented and allowed it on *Everest*. Clapton plays lead guitar.

Come And Get It (2.27)

'If you want it, here it is ...' originally intended for new Apple signings Badfinger, McCartney decided to use this instead for *Everest*, thinking the album needed more songs with its honest, simplistic approach. A trite treatise on greed – the song had been commissioned for the Terry Southern-penned movie *The Magic Christian* – it may also have been a dig at Allen Klein. Of all the songs on *Everest*, this is perhaps the one which most sounds like the Beatles of old. Ironic, really.

It Don't Come Easy (2.58)

Ringo had been hanging on to this song for a while and, as he was reluctant to sing another Lennon & McCartney composition (they offered him 'Teddy Boy' and a bizarre gospel arrangement of 'One After 909'), he insisted they record this, encouraging Harrison to get more involved in the production (George was responsible for the all-girl choir and the over-dubbed horns). Sick of being cast as the band's stooge, this was Ringo's stab at independence, although the rest of the band balked when he suggested the Who's Keith Moon accompany him on drums.

The Long And Winding Road (3.35)

Recorded initially during the 'Get Back' sessions in January 1969, the song was then offered to both Cilla Black and Tom Jones before McCartney recorded his own version. One of his most beautiful compositions – with a lyric that combines longing and loss, wonder and woe – McCartney recorded most of the instruments himself, fearful of sabotage by Lennon, who thought it 'soft'. Consequently, the final recording was closer to McCartney's demo than almost anything the band had ever done, its arrangement being sparse and almost jazzy. The long and winding road itself is the B842, which runs down the east coast of Kintyre into Campbeltown, near McCartney's farm in Scotland.

Side Two
Instant Karma (3.18)
Written in a single morning in January 1970 and recorded over the next two days, Lennon's urgent, psychological powerplay set the tone for much of his later solo work, with drums reverberating like someone slapping a wet fish on a marble slab. During the recording he asked George Martin to create a Phil Spector-like Wall Of Sound. 'It was fantastic!' said Lennon afterwards. 'It sounded like there were fifty people playing!' Considering Lennon's increasing cynicism, lyrically this is a curiously uplifting song. 'All we're trying to say to the world is, "You're gonna be great,"' said the author at the time.

Love (3.17)
'It's a beautiful melody and I'm not even known for my melody,' said Lennon after this was recorded. This delicate, uncomplicated ballad sounds as if it should have been on *Abbey Road*. Just before his death in 1980, Lennon recalled the song with great affection, not only because of its melody – he thought this and 'Imagine', which he would record a year later, were two of his best – but also because it depicted one of the more harmonious periods in his relationship with Yoko. McCartney adored it, and repeatedly told Lennon so.

What is Life? (4.09)
As Harrison had been getting increasingly frustrated with his inability to get more of his songs on Beatles LPs, and having built up rather a large backlog of material, he lobbied hard to get more tunes on *Everest*. Lennon and McCartney, as well as feeling slightly guilty about their behaviour in the past ('We've never even offered George B-sides,' admitted Lennon rather sheepishly at one point during the sessions),

knew that this also made commercial sense, seeing as Harrison had written two of *Abbey Road*'s most popular songs, 'Something' and 'Here Comes The Sun' (even though this contained an instrumental section that was borrowed from 'Badge', the song he wrote with Eric Clapton for Cream).

Teddy Boy (2.22)

Originally recorded as a demo by McCartney in January 1969 at Apple Studios (below the Beatles' offices in Savile Row), this rather slight tune was in the style of the whimsical 'Rocky Racoon'. One version included barn-dance calls from Lennon, though George Martin – a saviour to the very last – edited these out, favouring the simple approach heard here. Lennon hated the song ('He doesn't sound like a fucking teddy boy to me,' he is heard to mutter on one bootleg), but for the time being, bit his lip.

Let It Be (3.40)

Though first recorded in January 1969 for the 'Get Back' sessions, this has nevertheless become known as the Beatles' swan song. Written in the style of a modern hymn, McCartney chronicles the group's on-going dissolution and his own feelings of despair. 'I really was passing through my "hour of darkness" and writing the song was my way of exorcising the ghosts,' he said. Lennon was never fond of the song's Catholic sanctimony, but by this time all the Beatles had their own religious bent, although luckily Ringo's never made it onto a record.

Working Class Hero (3.44)

As cynical a song as Lennon had ever written, this sarcastic self-portrait was released almost in demo form, with only an acoustic guitar and Billy Preston's sombre organ for company. Its meaning was never as prosaic as people thought, a confusion helped by the fact that Lennon performed it as an anthem, Bob Dylan-style. Like 'Give Peace A Chance', this was another attempt by Lennon to top 'We Shall Overcome'. 'I think its concept is revolutionary,' said Lennon. 'I hope it's for workers and not for tarts and fags. It's just a warning to people ... it's a song for the revolution.'

EP Side One
Wah-Wah (5.26)
One of *Everest*'s highlights, this was another song which Harrison wrote specifically for the album. Although he had an enormous number of unrecorded tunes, he wrote eight songs especially for *Everest* (the rejects, which turned up on subsequent solo albums, included 'I'd Have You Anytime' – co-written with Bob Dylan – and 'Apple Scruffs', a tribute to the fans who congregated outside the Beatles' offices). 'I don't particularly seek acclaim,' George told John and Paul. 'It's just to get out whatever is there to make way for whatever else is there. Also, I might as well make a bit of money, seeing as I'm spending as much as the rest of you.'

Across The Universe (3.28)
Initially recorded in February 1968, Lennon's wistful incantation was obviously inspired by his LSD experiences, and while it was briefly considered as a single, his inability to finish it (or to write a suitable middle eight), meant it was replaced by McCartney's 'Lady Madonna'. 'It drove me out of bed,' said Lennon. 'I didn't want to write it, I was just slightly irritable and I couldn't go to sleep.' Lennon dusted this off and re-recorded it, as he figured it might be the last time he could use it. Edited onto the end of the track was a throwaway line by Lennon recorded during the famous rooftop session in Savile Row where the band taped 'Get Back': 'I'd like to say thank you on behalf of the group and ourselves, and I hope we passed the audition.'

EP Side Two
All Things Must Pass (3.03)
Harrison's plaintive, wistful song was first recorded on the occasion of his twenty-sixth birthday on 25 February 1969. Intended for the *Get Back* album – like a lot of stuff here – it's acoustic foundation fitted in nicely with the down-home rock'n'roll throwaways being bashed out then by John and Paul, though neither of them liked the song very much. As they were desperately trying to appease Harrison, they encouraged him to record another, fuller version of it for *Everest*. David Crosby, Stephen Stills and Graham Nash accompany the band on acoustic guitars and – slightly dodgy – harmonies.

Singalong Junk (2.34)
Written by McCartney in India in the spring of 1968, it was demoed

at George Harrison's house in Esher in May that year. It lay dormant until the *Everest* sessions in early 1970, although it epitomised the type of 'ballads and babies' material which McCartney would pursue once the band finally split later in the year. As if to echo Lennon's snippet on side one McCartney included two further cinema *vérité* moments from the rooftop performance, this time from a taxi driver captured in the street below, ('Is it their new record? Oh, great, I'm all in favour of it!') and a bowler-hatted vicar, ('Nice to have something for free in this country at the moment, isn't it?') And that was that.

Appendix III: They Did It Their Way – The 50 Best Cover Versions

Does anyone really want to hear William Shatner cover Pulp's 'Common People'? Maybe Shatner's agent and Jarvis Cocker's publishers, but anyone else? The cover version has become much abused recently, and the cute, arch, or contrary 'interpretation' is not as easy to master as it once was. And so . . . 1. 'Hallelujah' by Rufus Wainwright. 2. 'I'm Only Sleeping' by the Vines. 3. 'Windmills Of Your Mind' by Dusty Springfield. 4. ''Ol 55' by the Eagles. 5. 'Jersey Girl' by Bruce Springsteen. 6. 'Got To Get You Into My Life' by Earth Wind And Fire. 7. 'Ride Like The Wind' by East Side Beat. 8. 'Tomorrow's Just Another Day' by Elvis Costello. 9. 'Do Ya' by Utopia. 10. 'Dancing In The Moonlight' by Toploader. 11. 'Nothing Compares To You' by Sinead O'Connor. 12. 'Little Wing' by Derek and the Dominoes. 13. 'Macarthur Park' by Donna Summer. 14. 'Songbird' by Eva Cassidy. 15. 'The Only Living Boy In New York' by Everything But The Girl. 16. 'Someone To Watch Over Me' by Frank Sinatra. 17. 'Killing Me Softly' by the Fugees. 18. 'I'm Not In Love' by the Fun Lovin' Criminals. 19. 'Whisky In The Jar' by Thin Lizzy. 20. 'Largo' by the Swingle Singers. 21. 'Walk On By' by the Stranglers. 22. 'Goin' Back' by Nils Lofgren. 23. '(I Can't Get No) Satisfaction' by Devo. 24. 'Let 'Em In' by Starbelly. 25. 'Manha De Carnaval' by Stan Getz. 26. 'As' by George Michael. 27. 'La Vie En Rose' by Grace Jones. 28. 'We've Only Just Begun' by Grant Lee Buffalo. 29. 'Knockin' On Heaven's Door' by Guns N' Roses. 30. 'Louie Louie' by Iggy Pop. 31. 'The Look Of Love' by Isaac Hayes. 32. 'Up On The Roof' by James Taylor. 33. 'Wind Cries Mary' by Jamie Cullum. 34. 'So What?' by Ronny Jordan. 35. 'Reason To Believe' by Rod Stewart. 36. 'California Sun' by the Ramones. 37. 'They Shoot Horses

Don't They' by Beck. 38. 'A Whiter Shade Of Pale' by Annie Lennox. 39. 'Stop Your Sobbing' by the Pretenders. 40. 'Dancing In The Dark' by Pete Yorn. 41. 'Where The Streets Have No Name' by the Pet Shop Boys. 42. 'My Favourite Things' by Outkast. 43. 'A Forest' by Nouvelle Vague. 44. 'Only With You' by Norman Blake. 45. 'Baltimore' by Nina Simone. 46. 'Handbags and Gladrags' by the Stereophonics. 47. 'I Want To Know What Love Is' by the New Jersey Mass Choir. 48. 'Dear Friend' by the Minus 5. 49. 'Summertime' by Miles Davis. 50. 'My Little Red Book' by Love.

Appendix IV: The 100 Best Songs from the 100 Best Jazz Albums (in a very particular order)

100. The Don Ellis Orchestra
Electric Bath
(Columbia) 1967
Trumpeter Ellis introduced mathematics to jazz, experimenting with so many time signatures it sometimes seemed as though they were trying to construct the world's most convoluted equation. Imagine a song in 5/4, 7/4 and 19/4, and you can imagine a Don Ellis recording (and that's only the first four bars). He mixed 'third stream' jazz with rock and a proper orchestra, always having his tongue dangerously near his cheek. Released at the height of flower power, *Electric Bath* still sounds as energised and as arcane as it almost certainly did then.
   Upload: 'Turkish Bath'.

99. Herbie Hancock
Takin' Off
(Blue Note) 1962
The best jazz debut ever. Includes the massive hit single 'Watermelon Man'.
   Upload: 'Watermelon Man' (no shit, Sherlock).

98. Art Pepper
Winter Moon
(Galaxy) 1981
Alto sax genius, serial drug abuser (he unthinkingly recorded an album called *Smack Up*), this lush, dense, orchestral album came in the twilight of his career, and was unequivocally his best. Profoundly

sexy, his solo on 'Our Song' could make most women shed their clothes before closing the front door.

Upload: 'Here's That Rainy Day'.

97. Jamie Cullum
Twentysomething
(Universal) 2003

The Reading University graduate who prompted a record-label bidding war after building up a cult following on the smoky jazz-bar circuit. His debut album – a mix of original material and inspired covers – is the biggest-selling British jazz album ever, and deservedly so. One of the few modern jazz CDs you can rip in its entirety.

Upload: 'Singing In The Rain'.

96. Duke Ellington
Anatomy Of A Murder
(Columbia) 1959

Ellington's first soundtrack (to Otto Preminger's classic courtroom drama) is one of the best examples of 'crime jazz', the sort of melo-dramatic cloak and dagger, big band stuff heard in movies like *The Wild One*, *Sweet Smell Of Success*, and *The Man With The Golden Arm*.

Underappreciated at the time, this is now afforded classic status. The Ellington band never sounded do good, and they are especially gifted in the way they manage to articulate sex. 'Flirtbird', written about the female lead, Lee Remick, appears to have been inspired by her derriere.

Upload: 'Flirtbird'.

95. Julie London
The Liberty Years
(Liberty) 1989

With a face, a body and a demeanour straight out of Central Casting, Julie London was a chanteuse with a difference. 'Cry Me A River' is one of the greatest torch songs ever written, and London's version is definitive.

Upload: 'Cry Me A River'.

94. Miles Davis
Tutu
(Warner Bros) 1986

A comeback of sorts, not least commercially, as previous to this collaboration with Marcus Miller, Miles' most recent success had been with Stan Getz and Lee Konitz on *Conception* in 1975. A haunting record, its only downside is the (now) very obvious 1980s production (close your eyes and you could be in *Miami Vice*). Nevertheless, if only for its blatant commerciality, this is an indispensable Miles CD.

Upload: 'Tutu'.

93. Norah Jones
Coma Away With Me
(Blue Note) 2002

She appeared seemingly out of nowhere, although on closer inspection you can tell she has been exceptionally well-groomed. This debut album was such a success with critics and public alike that she won an astonishing five awards at the Grammys, including Album Of The Year, Song Of The Year ('Don't Know Why'), and Best New Artist. The biggest crossover star to emerge for years – this album stayed in the American Top Ten for 37 weeks – she already has the look of a hardy perennial. Her album is also a fantastic seduction tool (remember the laydeez love her).

Upload: 'Don't Know Why'.

92. Miles Davis
Porgy And Bess
(Columbia) 1958

George Gershwin said that jazz was folk music, and there's no greater example than this, the best-ever version of Gershwin's best-ever score. To capture the work's profoundity, Davis uses a flugelhorn – to awesome effect.

Upload: 'Bess, You Is My Woman Now'.

91. Bobbi Humphrey
The Best Of Bobbi Humphrey
(Blue Note) 1992

A female flautist of all things, who couldn't have existed without the records of Donald Byrd (see also: number 38). This CD is worth it just for the magnificent 'Harlem River Drive', which, in terms of songs which epitomise New York City, is as quintessential as Ella Fitzgerald's 'Take The A Train', the Ramones' '53rd & 3rd' or War's 'All Day Music'.

Upload: 'Harlem River Drive.'

90. 4Hero
Creating Patterns
(Talkin' Loud) 2001
Perfect room temperature chill-out and one of the best jazz albums of the twenty-first century.

Upload: 'Les Fleur'

89. Billie Holiday
The Voice Of Jazz: The Complete Recordings 1933–40
(Affinity) 1999
For many, Lady Day was the finest singer who ever lived, yet she died in typically ignominious circumstances. Having been a drunk and a junkie for most of her life, she was still begging for heroin on her deathbed, in a guarded ward at the run-down Harlem Metropolitan Hospital, in 1959, at the age of forty-four. A lifelong fan, Frank Sinatra came to visit her on the night she died. Holiday pleaded with him to get her a 'bag'. Hours later the dope arrived but the dealer couldn't get past the guards. Billie died minutes later of liver failure.

Upload: 'Strange Fruit'.

88. Various Artists
Get Easy! Volume 2
(Motor) 1995
The new generation of cool: Pizzicato Five, James Taylor Quartet, Corduroy, Workshop, Swing Out Sister, UFO.

Upload: 'Something In My Eye'.

87. Nina Simone
Jazz As Played In An Exclusive Side Street Club
(Bethlehem) 1958
Her first classic. Includes 'Love Me Or Leave Me' and 'I Loves You Porgy'.

Upload: 'My Baby Just Cares For Me'.

86. Hank Mobley
Soul Station
(Blue Note) 1960
A lightweight among the hard men of hard bop, Mobley was a tenor sax man with a 'round sound' rather than a direct punch.

Upload: 'Remember'.

85. Various Artists
Jazz On A Summer's Day
(Charly) 1959
Possibly the greatest jazz film ever (other notables include '*Round Midnight* and Clint Eastwood's *Bird*), this fairly prosaic documentary is a balmy depiction of the 1958 Newport Rhode Island Festival. At the time, Bert Stern's film was revolutionary, and still has enormous charm. Highlights include Anita O'Day's 'Sweet Georgia Brown', Gerry Mulligan's 'Catch Me If You Can', Dinah Washington's 'All Of Me' and Thelonious Monk's 'Blue Monk'. What Chuck Berry was doing at the gig is anyone's guess, and you might want to skip that track.

Upload: 'Sweet Georgia Brown'.

84. Diana Krall
Love Scenes
(Impulse) 1997
The first three tracks are worth the price of entry alone.

Upload: 'Peel Me A Grape'.

83. Art Blakey Quintet
A Night At Birdland Volume 1
(Blue Note) 1954
The classic live recording, from 1678 Broadway, New York's premier bebop club, starts with the voice of Pee Wee Marquette, Birdland's diminutive MC: 'Ladies and gentlemen, as you know we have something special down here at Birdland this evening ... a recording for Blue Note records.' His words were famously sampled on Us3's jazz-hop hit 'Canteloop'.

Upload: 'Split Kick'.

82. Count Basie
The Complete Atomic Basie
(Roulette/Blue Note) 1994

With songs and arrangements by Neal Hefti (who would whole-heartedly embrace fame when he wrote and performed the theme from the *Batman* TV series in the mid-1960s), this was one of Basie's greatest records, and one of his last. Recorded in 1957, it showed the band leader at the height of his powers – focused, totally syncopated, and aiming, as always, for the roof. Some say that Basie made better records – and some that were certainly more popular – but this is the one to own. (The CD extras are pretty cool too.)

Upload: 'Whirly Bird'.

81. Miles Davis
Ascenseur Pour L'echafaud
(Fontana) 1958

C'est bon. Ça c'est superb! C'est pas Courtney Pine!

Upload: 'Generique'.

80. Della Reese
Della
(RCA) 1960

Della's accelerated version of Irving Berlin's 'Blue Skies' (all 1.45 of it) is one of the most exhilarating two minutes in all jazz. She has tended to be forgotten, and her name is absent from three of the so-called classic texts (*The Penguin Guide To Jazz On CD, LP and Cassette* by Richard Cook and Brian Morton; *Jazz: the Rough Guide* by Ian Carr, Digby Fairweather and Brian Priestley; and *The Virgin Encyclopedia of Jazz* edited by Colin Larkin), yet her talent is beyond question.

Upload: 'Blue Skies'.

79. Mark Murphy
Rah
(Riverside) 1961

The Jazz singer's jazz singer. Cool, bossly-dressed, never seen without his shades.

Upload: 'Milestones'.

78. Working Week
Working Nights
(Virgin) 1985
The brainchild of British jazz guitarist Simon Booth, Working Week were at the centre of London's 1984 jazz revivalist scene, one hinging on a few esoteric nightclubs, a gaggle of jazz dancers and the patronage of a few style journalists. In spite of this, they produced one of the finest British albums of the decade. Includes the monumental 'Venceremos' with guest vocals by Everything But The Girl's Tracey Thorn.
   Upload: 'Sweet Nothing'.

77. Cannonball Adderley
The Best Of Cannonball Adderley
(Capital) 1969
The man who invented soul jazz.
   Upload: 'Mercy, Mercy, Mercy'.

76. Weather Report
Heavy Weather
(Columbia) 1976
The greatest fusion album of all time, one of the best-selling jazz albums, and an alternative soundtrack to 1977. Weather Report were a jazz supergroup – Wayne Shorter, Jaco Pastorious, et al – who turned elaborately arranged songs into FM-friendly hits, 'Birdland' included. The album spawned a new genre of radio broadcasting, 'smooth jazz', just as Sade would a decade later with 'quiet storm'.
   Upload: 'Birdland'.

75. New York Philharmonic
Manhattan
(CBS) 1979
Gershwin's 'Rhapsody In Blue', Woody Allen in his prime, a New York skyline: this is jazz writ large.
   Upload: 'Rhapsody In Blue', all of it, from penthouse to pavement.

74. Louis Armstrong
The Complete Hot Five And Seven Recordings
(Columbia) 2000 [Boxed Set]
Armstrong was one of the most important musicians the States has

ever produced, and his career not only spanned most of the twentieth century, it incorporated every different type of music, from gospel and blues to hillbilly and pop. Armstrong's unmistakable voice, full of cracks and fissures, is a cornerstone of early jazz, and his trumpet work is nothing short of pioneering. This collection of his best work, from 1925–9, includes some of the earliest recorded jazz and 'West End Blues', once called 'the most perfect three minutes of music' ever created.

Upload: 'Stardust'.

73. Mel Torme
Mel Torme Swings Shubert Alley
(Verve) 1960
Was he Mark Murphy for hipsters, or Robbie Williams for the old 'nowtro' generation? Either way, he had a weightless way with himself and his voice.

Upload: 'Too Close For Comfort'.

72. Ramsey Lewis
Finest Hour
(Verve) 2000
Clap hands, come here Ramsey! Lewis' best records always have a jaunty, uplifting feel to them – his piano to the fore, hand claps in the background. This is crossover jazz, offering 'the uninitiated an enticing gateway into the jazz idiom', in the words of writer Bill Dahl. Standouts include lackadaisical versions of 'Wade In The Water' and Dobie Gray's 'In The Crowd'.

Upload: 'Wade In The Water'.

71. Herbie Hancock
Maiden Voyage
(Blue Note) 1964
One of the best of Hancock's early Blue Note albums, this is basically the Miles Davis band of the time, with the trumpeter replaced by the young Freddie Hubbard. Hancock's career has mirrored Quincy Jones's, as he's had success as a pianist, arranger, composer, bandleader, producer and solo artist (remember 'Rockit'?).

Upload: 'Dolphin Dance'.

70. Mark Isham
The Moderns
(Virgin) 1988
Go on, be a devil: buy a beret. Jazz 'style' is so cinematic that it is often used to pep up soundtracks. This is one where it undeniably works.
Upload: The title theme.

69. Wynton Marsalis
Blood On The Fields
(Columbia) 1997
Just in case you didn't know, this won the 1998 Pulitzer Prize for music, which is more than *Kid A* did.
Upload: All of it.

68. Bernard Herrmann
Taxi Driver
(Arista) 1976
The saxophones come out at night.
Upload: 'All The Animals Come Out At Night'.

67. Lou Donaldson
The Righteous Reed!
(Blue Note) 1994
From fashion shows to cocktail reception and dinner party and back again, Lou Donaldson's sax shuffles, glides and leaps.
Upload: 'The Long Goodbye'.

66. Mose Allison
I Don't Worry About A Thing
(Atlantic Jazz) 1962
When asked to describe himself, the piano-playing blues singer simply said, 'middle-class white boy'. Who could sing like a dream.
Upload: 'I Don't Worry About A Thing'.

65. Art Tatum
20th Century Piano Genius
(Verve) 1992
A child prodigy who became famous for his locomotive fingers in the

Thirties. Whenever Tatum played on the radio, listeners often thought three people were playing.

Upload: 'Someone To Watch Over Me'.

64. Jimmy Smith
Back At The Chicken Shack
(Blue Note) 1961
Smith is the man who revolutionised jazz by playing the Hammond B-3 organ, an instrument he kept in his shed for two years while learning to play it. By the time he had recorded this he had already completed 19 albums for Blue Note, although this is the one that made his name. According to Frank Wolff, one of the brains behind Blue Note, 'He was a stunning sight. A man in convulsions, face contorted, crouched over in apparent agony, his fingers flying, his foot dancing over the pedals.'

Upload: 'On The Sunny Side Of The Street'.

63. The Michael Franks Anthology
The Art Of Love
(Warners) 2003
Californian jazz-pop that's so laid-back it makes Nick Drake sound like the Buzzcocks. The man is a guilty pleasure, albeit one enjoyed by many others on this list (and not just the dead ones).

Upload: 'Eggplant'.

62. Steely Dan
Aja
(MCA) 1977
Donald Fagan and Walter Becker had already become the American Beatles by the time they released *Aja*, and albums such as *Can't Buy A Thrill*, *Countdown To Ecstasy* and *Pretzel Logic* had confirmed them as the most important band of the early 1970s. With the release of *Aja*, and its hipster cool, slick arrangements and sarcastic guitar solos, they could no longer hide their secret: they were buttoned-down jazzers at heart, and this was a jazz record in everything but name.

Upload: 'Black Cow'.

61. Rahsaan Roland Kirk
The Inflated Tear
(Atlantic) 1967
Welcome to the hydra-headed sax player. Imagine Swamp Thing, blind, in dark glasses, with three horns strung round his neck, all of which he could play at once. That was Kirk, the only man ever to have mastered the art of circular breathing, which allowed him to blow solos that lasted for hours on end, sometimes for days.

Upload: 'A Laugh For Rory'.

60. Miles Davis
In A Silent Way
(Columbia) 1969
The first jazz-rock album. 'There are no wrong notes in jazz,' Davis once said, and with this album he proved it. The trumpeter had first flirted with rock the year before, on *Filles de Kilimanjaro* (his collaborator Gil Evans shaping the title tune from the chords of Hendrix's 'The Wind Cries Mary'); this, though, was something quite different, a full-length 'album' album, an electronic masterpiece that feels like the jazz buff's answer to Van Morrison's *Astral Weeks* or *Veedon Fleece*. A few years later with *On The Corner*, Miles would combine James Brown with Stockhausen and the world would hate him for it. With good reason. But this rocks (albeit quietly).

Upload: 'Shhh/Peaceful'.

59. Ella Fitzgerald
Day Dream: Best Of The Duke Ellington Songbook
(Verve) 1995
Ella's 'Take The A Train' did for jazz what 'Down In The Tube Station At Midnight' did for punk (as well as being a better record).

Upload: 'Take The A Train'.

58. Us3
Hand On The Torch
(Blue Note) 1993
Jazz came back in a big way in the early 1990s, particularly with the *Rebirth Of Cool* albums. Most of these featured braggadocios beating their chests about their heritage over an endless stream of jazz samples (evoking John Coltrane's name doesn't turn you into John Coltrane), although they inspired others to do better. Based around the piano

lick from Herbie Hancock's 'Cantaloupe Island', Us3's 'Cantaloop' (geddit?) was produced by Geoff Wilkinson and Mel Simpson. Worried that Blue Note would sue, they were shocked when the company gave them access to its entire back catalogue.

Upload: 'Cantaloop'.

57. Cassandra Wilson
Blue Light 'Til Dawn
(Blue Note) 1993
Having spent a decade using a well-stirred mixture of blues, standards and original material, this was her first album for Blue Note, an exceptionally well-reviewed collection that includes a killer version of Ann Peebles' 'I Can't Stand The Rain', a song thought to be uncoverable. The best time to play it is straight after the Norah Jones album, to hear your guests ask if this is a follow-up.

Upload: 'I Can't Stand The Rain'.

56. Herbie Hancock
Gershwin's World
(Verve) 1988
One twentieth-century genius reinvented by another.

Upload: 'Overture (Fascinating Rhythm)'.

55. Tubby Hayes
Down In The Village
(Verve Redial) 1962
Vibes and sax, sexy vibes, all recorded at Ronnie Scott's.

Upload: All of it.

54. Django Reinhardt
Swing De Paris
(Proper) 1934
The first acknowledged European jazz genius, Django, was a Belgian gypsy whose Hot Club of France recordings in the 1930s turned him into a global celebrity (unheard of at the time). Often called the best guitar picker to ever draw breath, his style stemmed from the fact he only had two operational fingers on his left hand (it was damaged in a caravan fire in 1928).

Upload: This is a five-CD boxed set gathering titles by the Quintette du Hot Club de France, as well as Reinhardt's recordings from the period. So close your eyes and take your pick ...

53. Wes Montgomery
Incredible Jazz Guitar
(Riverside/OJC) 1960
An axe hero before we knew they existed, this is the album that elevated Wes to the jazz elite, and while jazz is considered to be one long line of musical miscegenation, this still sounds brand spanking new. No damaged majesty here.
Upload: 'Mister Walker'.

52. Dave Holland Quintet
Not For Nothin'
(ECM) 2001
The most recent album the purists all like. And guess what? It's great.
Upload: 'For All You Are'.

51. Herbie Hancock
Empyrean Isles
(Blue Note) 1964
Includes the poptastic 'Cantaloupe Island', soon to become a jazz standard.
Upload: 'One Finger Snap'.

50. Sarah Vaughan With Clifford Brown
(Polygram) 1990
'Lullaby Of Birdland' has the catchiest and most haunting intro of any jazz record.
Upload: Call me contrary, but it has to be 'Lullaby Of Birdland'.

49. Charles Mingus
Mingus Ah Um
(CBS) 1959
The man who played the double bass like no other, a first-rate jazz composer, and a colossus of cool who wrote one of the most fascinating jazz autobiographies of them all (the semi-fictional *Beneath the*

Underdog), Mingus is an endearing cultural icon. This record is a tribute to his own heroes: 'Goodbye Pork Pie Hat' is a salute to saxophonist Lester Young; 'Open Letter To Duke' is a homage to Ellington; while 'Bird Calls' cites Charlie Parker.

Upload: 'Pussy Cat Dues'.

48. Airto
Touching You . . . Touching Me
(Warners) 1979
Drummers shouldn't make albums? Really? Well, just listen to this.

Upload: 'Toque De Cuica'.

47. Miles Davis
Miles Ahead
(Columbia) 1957
It's strange to think that Miles was recording this masterpiece at exactly the same time Elvis was recording 'All Shook Up', but then it's also bizarre to think that the Bee Gees were recording 'Staying Alive' at the same time as the Clash were completing their first album. At this point in his career, Miles seemed to bang out another classic album every six months, and this is one of his best.

Upload: 'The Duke'.

46. Koop
Waltz For Koop
(Jazzanova Compost) 2001
Strictly speaking a lounge-core classic, this is so full of jazz it almost feels genuine. Koop are another example of PoMoMoR (PostModernMiddleoftheRoad), a musical genre you'll have heard in the last branch of the Body Shop you inadvertently wandered into. Often confused with chill-out pop, since the big Easy Listening revival of 1994 the likes of Koop, Zero 7, Röyksopp, Groove Armada and Lemon Jelly seem content to lay muted trumpets over hip-hop beats until the cows come home. The usually redoubtable Nick Hornby has called this 'a cliché, lazy shorthand for a sort of Vacuous, monied-up hip'. Not so: it's great.

Upload: 'Tonight'.

45. Sonny Clark

Cool Struttin'
(Blue Note) 1958
Clark's death, at thirty-one, was down to alcohol abuse and heroin dependency. How very jazz.

   Upload: 'Blue Minor'.

44. Various Artists

Brazilica!
(Talkin' Loud) 1994
You may not be able to buy Jorge Ben's 1972 masterpiece *Ben* (Philips) on CD right now, but there are plenty of other places to look for cracking Brazilian music. This is one genre that has benefited immensely from the CD format, and reissues and compilations come thick and fast. Talkin' Loud's Talkin Jazz compilations have been real curate's eggs (*More Themes From The Black Forest*, for instance, contains the Dieter Reith Trio's wondrous version of Burt Bacharach's 'Wives And Lovers', but also a lot of iffier material), although this one is completely successful, containing a varied selection of some of the more esoteric examples of Brazilian jazz.

   Upload: 'Roda'.

43. Coleman Hawkins

Body & Soul
(Sony) 2000
Adolphe Sax may have invented the saxophone, but this man defined it.

   Upload: 'My Ideal'.

42. Keith Jarrett

The Melody At Night, With You
(ECM) 1999
An album of lush, laid-back cover versions, this feels like having sex in church.

   Upload: 'I Loves You, Porgy'.

41. Joao Gilberto

The Legendary . . .
(World Pacific) 1990
The eternal wunderkind of Latin beat.

   Upload: 'Bim Bom'.

40. Thelonious Monk
Genius Of Modern Music Vol. 1
(Blue Note) 1951

Part bebopper, part free-jazz thinker, Monk was enigmatic in the extreme. Years before Elton John, he persisted with the funny glasses, wore ecclesiastical robes and played some of the strangest piano you'll ever be lucky enough to hear. His tunes were, in the words of one critic, 'rigorous investigations of musical ideas'; i.e., using the damping pedal to eliminate certain notes, using keys as a drummer might, and sometimes just wandering off stage in search of God knows what when he was supposed to be playing a solo. Includes 'Round Midnight', the most recorded jazz song of all time.

Upload: 'Humph'.

39. Nina Simone
Baltimore
(CTI) 1978

The second Simone masterpiece. This collection of straightforward covers is undoubtedly her best work, the defining record in her career: a selection of haunting covers that spotlights her remarkable gift for interpretation. Highlights include 'Everything Must Change', the heartbreaking 'That's All I Want From You', and Randy Newman's maudlin-to-the-max title track, a song she makes her own.

Upload: 'Baltimore.'

38. Donald Byrd
Black Byrd
(Blue Note) 1973

Gil Scott Heron without the attitude, this was at one time the best-selling jazz LP in Blue Note's history – a fusion album before fusion began, jazz-rock with electric trumpets and flugelhorns-a-go-go. It still kicks, thirty years after it was meant to.

Upload: 'Flight Time'.

37. John Coltrane
Blue Train
(Blue Note) 1957

Cool bop. This is one of Coltrane's easiest records, 'the most convenient and tolerable example of the first period of a difficult musician,' according to Richard Cook, author of *Blue Note Records: the Biography.*

Recorded with a classic line-up – pianist Kenny Drew, bassist Paul Chambers, trumpeter Lee Morgan, trombonist Curtis Fuller and drummer Philly Joe Jones – the album consists of four very distinct pieces, each one representing a stage of spiritual development. Its popularity was helped enormously by the cover: Coltrane in close-up, his eyes looking down, deep in thought, his right hand raised to his lips. It is perfectly enigmatic, while the album's title suggests cool, mellow, dinner party pop.

Upload: 'Locomotion'.

36. Wayne Shorter
Speak No Evil
(Blue Note) 1965
A mix of hard bop and free jazz, this is Shorter's best work, calm and ingenious at the same time. It's also got one of the very best Blue Note album covers, and considering there have been books devoted to the subject, that's praise.

Upload: 'Witch Hunt'.

35. Duke Ellington
Far East Suite
(RCA Bluebird) 1967
In his fifty-year career, Ellington composed over two thousand pieces of 'negro music' (he preferred the term to 'jazz'), including sprawling orchestral suites, pop, dance tunes and everything in between. He also kept an orchestra on the road his whole professional life, and in that respect resembled Bob Dylan (and his 'never-ending tour'), a wandering journeyman. Being on the road enabled Ellington to indulge in his other great passion, sex (he was a self-confessed 'sexual inter-course freak'). It was this lust for travel that caused him to visit the Middle East and Japan in 1963 and 1964, a tour that resulted in this, a record ranking among his greatest achievements.

Upload: 'Tourist Point Of View'.

34. Sonny Rollins
Volume Two
(Blue Note) 1957
After *Meet The Beatles*, this is the most imitated album cover ever. Contains the tenor saxophonist's best tune, 'Why Don't I', although

anything on this album could be considered a solid-gold classic. It's tasty.

Upload: 'Reflections'.

33. Lee Morgan
The Sidewinder
(Blue Note) 1964

At the time, the title was Blue Note's biggest to date, making No. 25 on the *Billboard* chart. It was the jazz track of choice on jukeboxes everywhere in 1964, and with some modifications (added strings, basically), would later turn up on a Chrysler TV commercial. The song can still fill dancefloors today, and has an enduring R&B groove that never dates. Morgan tried following this up with songs such as 'The Rumproller', but none was as popular. The trumpeter was shot dead by his common-law wife in 1972 while onstage at the infamous black-and-tan New York jazz club, Slug's Saloon.

Upload: 'Hocus-Pocus'.

32. Francis Albert Sinatra & Antonio Carlos Jobim
(Reprise) 1967

Sinatra's best album. Deal with it.

Upload: 'Meditation'.

31. Dexter Gordon
Our Man In Paris
(Blue Note) 1963

A shining example of late-period bebop, and one of the most successful records of Blue Note's 'blue' period. The CD includes 'A Night In Tunisia' and various bonus tracks including 'Our Love Is Here To Stay' from *An American In Paris*. Gordon had all the jazz problems – heroin addiction, alcoholism, too many wives. His life was less learning curve than learning cliff. But he had a resurrection, including an Oscar nomination for his portrayal of an alcoholic sax man in Bertrand Tavernier's 1986 film *'Round Midnight*.

Upload: 'Scrapple From The Apple'.

29. The Oscar Peterson Trio
Night Train
(Verve) 1963
You'll hear 'Night Train' playing in any nightclub scene in any 1960s film.

Upload: 'Things Ain't What They Used To Be'.

28. Bix Beiderbecke
The Bix Beiderbecke Story
(Columbia) 1990
The white Louis Armstrong, whose horn style was like 'a bullet hitting a chime'.

Upload: 'In A Mist'.

27. John Coltrane
My Favourite Things
(Atlantic) 1961
On 'My Favourite Things' Coltrane played a soprano sax, a horn that produced a sound that was almost like some eastern-Indian instrument. The public loved it, and this soon became one of the best-selling jazz albums of the age. In 1962, Coltrane explained how he adapted the *Sound Of Music* waltz to a model jazz riff: 'this piece is built on two chords, but we prolonged the two chords for the whole piece.' An impressed, if rather irritated Miles Davis said, 'Only he could do that and make it work.' And he was right.

Upload: 'Summertime'.

26. St. Germain
Tourist
(Blue Note) 2000
In 2001 this was the sound on every hip catwalk show in London, Paris, Milan and New York. Ludovic Navarre's second album is the first jazz masterpiece of the twenty-first century.

Upload: 'Rose Rouge'.

25. Dizzy Gillespie
Groovin' High
(Savoy) 1999
One of the kings of bebop, 'Diz' always dressed the part: in an act of self-parody he would wear a large, flowing tie *à la Boheme*, with a

beret, goatee and extravagant horn-rimmed glasses (always with plain glass inside them), and speak in beat vocab. He turned himself into a fashion plate as well as an icon, and his style became so closely associated with jazz that whenever cartoonists try and represent a jazz motif, they simply copy Diz. And the music? Well, it rocked, obviously.

Upload: 'Dizzy Atmosphere'.

24. The Swingle Singers With The Modern Jazz Quartet
Place Vendome
(Musical Rendezvous) 1967
The world's greatest vocal group gets hip, while Bach never sounded so cool (sorry Walter Carlos).

Upload: 'Air For G String'.

23. Herbie Hancock
Headhunters
(CBS) 1973
The world's first proper fusion record, *Headhunters* was Hancock's reaction to funk, rock and everything else that was storming the charts in the early 1970s. It was funky and rocky and owed not a little to Sly Stone ('Thank You Falettinme Be Mice Elf Again' in particular), but essentially it was without boundaries, which made it all the more exciting. There was a huge African influence too. 'The roots of music came from there,' says Hancock.

Upload: 'Watermelon Man'.

22. The Gil Evans Orchestra
Out Of The Cool
(MCA) 2000
Rip it: it's one of the few albums all critics agree on (they like it).

Upload: 'Sister Sadie'.

21. Quincy Jones
Straight No Chaser: The Many Faces Of . . .
(Universal) 2000
Michael Jackson's producer has a legacy stretching back to Count Basie and Thelonious Monk. He blew brass, wore a dashiki and wrote 'Soul Bossa Nova', now for ever associated with Austin Powers.

Upload: 'Jive Samba'.

20. Bill Evans Trio
Sunday At The Village Vanguard
(Riverside/Original Jazz Classics) 1964

One of the most important recordings in all jazz, this is the best example of Evans' ability to encourage successful interplay between his band. Having left Miles Davis' group because he couldn't cope with the hostility at gigs (he was white and played in a more subtle way than his colleagues), Evans formed a trio and, having released two good albums, 1959's *Portrait In Jazz* and 1961's *Explorations*, spent one Sunday in June 1961 recording what would be the most fitting testament. According to his producer Orrin Keepnews (great name, Orrin), it was 'a relatively painless way to extract an album from the usually foot-dragging pianist'. On the follow-up, *Waltz For Debby*, recorded on the same day, hear 'Milestones' played on the piano.

Upload: 'Gloria's Step (Take 2)'.

19. Tania Maria
The Queen Of Brazilian Jazz
(Manteca) 2003

'I chose music and music chose me,' says the passionate and capricious Sao Luis-born singer, whose uncompromising records mix Afro-Latin and pop with jazz and funk. They brim with vim.

Upload: 'Triste'.

18. John Coltrane
A Love Supreme
(Impulse!) 1964

One of the most popular jazz records of all time, a collection of songs that highlight jazz at its very highest level of achievement. Coltrane was a genius, but he's also tagged with encouraging everyone who came in his wake to think a saxophone solo could last several weeks. When Coltrane died, aged forty, Philip Larkin wrote that the only compliment one could pay him was one of stature: 'If he was boring, he was enormously boring. If he was ugly, he was massively ugly.' Nevertheless, this is genius. (On no account buy Alice Coltrane's version of her husband's classic; it will disturb the neighbours, give you a piercing headache and quite possibly damage your laptop.)

Upload: 'Acknowledgement'.

17. Art Blakey & The Jazz Messengers
A Night in Tunisia
(Bluebird) 1957

This is the complete legacy of Art Blakey's first sextet, the one he formed after Horace Silver, Donald Byrd and Hank Mobley left to set up by themselves. The album features Dizzy Gillespie's exotic title track, a song that was made for Blakey by dint of his hypnotic patterns, and a song he would record nearly a dozen times over the next decade. This version is perhaps the most glorious: thirteen minutes of frantic hard bop, and one of those records you can play again and again and again.

Upload: 'Off The Wall'.

16. Chet Baker
The Best Of Chet Baker Sings
(Pacific Jazz) 1989

With trumpet sounds as light as a kite, and a voice that was always verging on the slightly 'off' – there are those who'll tell you that he should never have sung at all – Baker's records were the perfect balance of sunshine and shade. His most successful outings were classic love songs, and he became renowned as something of a romantic balladeer, although his own life was somewhat more tortured. He was the star of a great Bruce Weber film, *Let's Get Lost*, and is soon to be the subject of a major Hollywood biopic. (Leo DiCaprio has been obsessed with Baker for years, and is slated to play him in the movie.)

Upload: 'I Remember You'.

15. Miles Davis
Milestones
(Columbia) 1958

The tightly coiled title track is the best record Miles ever made. John Coltrane was part of his band then and, when the saxophonist got too big for himself, the trumpet player would say, 'Coltrane, you don't have to play everything.' But of course he did.

Upload: 'Two Bass Hit'.

14. Charles Mingus
The Black Saint And The Sinner Lady
(Impulse!) 1963

On its release, Mingus was adamant that people think of this as a folk record[1] (he was beginning to tour as the Charles Mingus New Folk Band), although as he had periodically spent time as a patient in New York's Bellevue mental institution, people were used to such bizarre outbursts (it's not a folk record). The album has the feel of an Elmer Bernstein film score – theatrical, controversial – and is considered by many critics to be the best jazz record ever made. It was also the first jazz record to use overdubs.

Upload: 'Duet Solo Dancers'.

13. Duke Ellington
Money Jungle
(Blue Note) 1962

Since he's regarded as America's greatest composer in any genre, it's difficult to pick individual albums to sum up Ellington. But this is one of his best 1960s album. Quirky, but cool.

Upload: 'Wig Wise'.

12. Dave Brubeck
Time Out
(Columbia) 1959

In the late 1950s, Brubeck was the biggest jazz star in America, a white pianist who conquered a middle America just coming to terms with the expansionist dreams of suburbia. He was the hipster it was OK to like, the jazzer who wouldn't frighten the Stepford Wives when they popped around for cocktails on Saturday night. Brubeck's critics thought he was all puff and bluster. '[His audience] enjoy being offered titles such as "Blue Rondo A La Turk",' wrote one, 'because the implication is there that they understand blues, rondos and even Turks.' The album contains 'Take Five', one of the most popular jazz

---

[1] In the early Sixties, Thelonious Monk used to play regularly at the Blue Note, on 3rd Street in New York. He used to rehearse in the afternoons, a half-eaten sandwich left on top of the piano. Bob Dylan once dropped in to see him play, and told him he played folk 'up the street'. 'We all play folk music,' replied Monk.

records of all time, and deservedly so. Not owning this CD is like not owning *Revolver* or *London Calling*.

Upload: 'Take Five'.

11. Dexter Gordon
One Flight Up
(Blue Note) 1964

The follow-up to *Our Man In Paris*, and Gordon's second European album. The Donald Byrd tune 'Tanya' runs to 18 minutes, a whole side of old-style vinyl, and is one of the most evocative pieces of music ever recorded.

Upload: 'Coppin' The Haven'.

10. Miles Davis
Birth Of The Cool
(Capitol) 1956

Tired of what he felt was the rigidity of bebop – Davis had trumpeted in the Charlie Parker Quintet – and unable to emulate Dizzy Gillespie's quick-fire playing, the man in the green shirt, as he was soon to be labelled, got together with Gil Evans. This led to jazz with bigger spaces and lighter textures – cool jazz.

Upload: 'Move'.

9. The Horace Silver Quintet
Song For My Father
(Blue Note) 1964

Another huge hit for Blue Note, and one of Silver's most memorable records. The title track is based on a Portuguese rhythm, a device Silver's father had been encouraging him to try for some time (hence the title). Silver was so pleased with the result that he asked for a photo of his dad to be used as the cover. (The piano refrain was famously appropriated for Steely Dan's 'Rikki Don't Lose That Number' ten years later.)

Upload: 'Song For My Father'.

8. Ella Fitzgerald
Sings The Cole Porter Songbook
(Verve) 1956

The record that turned a great American voice into a national treasure.

This collection was the brainchild of Norman Granz, the founder of Verve records, who had been trying to sign the First Lady of Song for six years. Thinking she had been recording substandard material, when he finally got her he put her in a studio for three days, and this is the result. It was so successful he followed it with collections based around Rodgers and Hart, Duke Ellington, George Gershwin, Irving Berlin and Kern and Mercer, although this was the most memorable. Her version of 'Ev'ry Time We Say Goodbye' knocks Mick Hucknall into a cocked flat cap.

Upload: 'Night And Day'.

7. Keith Jarrett
The Koln Concert
(ECM) 1975
The subdued nature of this live album is due to the fact that before the concert Jarrett hadn't slept for twenty-four hours. Not only that, but because the piano was in such disrepair, Jarrett had to avoid using the tinny high notes. 'When I finally had to play it was a relief because there was nothing more of this story to tell,' says Jarrett. 'It was, "I am now going out there with this piano, and the hell with everything else."' This improvised set not only turned Jarrett into a jazz superstar, it turned the tiny ECM label into a major force, selling three million copies in the process.

Upload: 'Part 1'.

6. Clifford Brown
Clifford Brown With Strings
(Verve) 1955
Imagine the opening of a French movie, as the camera pans across Parisian rooftops at dusk, and then drops several storeys below before entering a small basement window. There we see curls of cigarette smoke climb towards a vaulted ceiling, and saxophones glinting like polished weapons. Well, that pretty much sums up what Clifford Brown sounds like. He was a sentimental horn player, some say the best of his generation, but he was killed in a car crash a year after this was recorded, so never fulfilled his potential. This is his legacy.

Upload: 'Laura'.

5. Charlie Parker
Yardbird Suite
(Castle Pie) 2000

Parker was the king of bop, the fastest saxophonist in the west, and at the time – the mid 1940s – one of the coolest men in America. This collection has many of his classics – 'Ornithology', 'Ko-Ko', 'Groovin' High', etc. – as well as his greatest ever recording, the incomparable 'A Night In Tunisia', which must rank as not only just one of the greatest jazz records of all time, but one of the greatest records, period. Parker had a terrible impulse towards self-destruction, and before his untimely death in 1955 (from a heroin overdose: he was thirty-four, although the coroner thought he was sixty) became quite adept at burning candelabra at all ends. As well as being responsible for recording some of the finest music of the twentieth century, he also came up with the ultimate jazz truism: 'If you play something that seems to be wrong, play it again, then play the same thing a third time. Then they'll think you meant it.'

Upload: 'A Night In Tunisia'.

4. Miles Davis
Sketches Of Spain
(CBS) 1960

The soundtrack to a movie that's yet to be made, Miles's foray into the Spanish interior includes stunning versions of classical composers Rodrigo's 'Concierto De Aranjuez' and Gil Evans' 'Solea'; the former is arguably the most successful jazz treatment of any European classical work, while the latter is simply one of the most beautiful things Miles ever recorded. As the original liner notes suggest, the music is so natural, so innate, it is as if Miles had been born of Andalusian gypsies. Initially recorded by critics as a lesser Miles work, it has gradually grown in stature over the years.

Upload: 'The Pan Piper'.

3. Stan Getz/Joao Gilberto
Getz/Gilberto
(Verve) 1964

For over forty years, Astrud Gilberto has been singing the gentle lyrical samba ballads of Brazil, a career kick-started by a happy accident in a New York recording studio in 1963. Earlier that year, Stan Getz called up the Brazilian pianist Antonio Carlos Jobim, asking him to bring along some of his new material. Getz was looking to record the follow up to *Jazz Samba* and *Jazz Samba Encore* – his two breakthrough LPs, which had resulted in the hits 'Desafinado' and 'One Note Samba'. The sensual sun-kissed samba Jobim brought to the studio that day was 'The Girl From Ipanema'; he also brought along a friend, the guitarist Joao Gilberto. The song vividly showcased Getz's pure-toned tenor sax and the intimate, burry voice of Gilberto, though as recording progressed it became evident that Gilberto could only sing in Portuguese. And so Getz asked Gilberto's 24-year-old Bahia-born wife Astrud to sing for him. Her contribution was initially considered so slight that she was not even credited on the album, though stardom beckoned when an edited version of the song went to number five in the US chart.

Upload: 'The Girl From Ipanema'.

2. John Coltrane
Giant Steps
(Atlantic) 1960
This was a breakthrough album for Coltrane, in particular its title track, and in the words of one critic, 'was thick with constant chord changes (moving the rate of a new chord every other beat) and with a melody whose endlessly unfolding odd intervals – giant steps – appeared to be designed to make life difficult for its soloist.' Coltrane also experimented with modal jazz on this album, which isn't too surprising: at the time he was working with Miles Davis on *Kind Of Blue*.

Upload: 'Spiral'.

1. Miles Davis
Kind Of Blue
(CBS) 1959
Miles' soft muted trumpet sound (dry as a martini) has become synonymous with 'cool' jazz, and there is no better example of the genre, or of his art, than this album. *Kind Of Blue* is the best-selling recording in his catalogue and the best-selling classic jazz album ever. It regularly tops All Time Favourite lists, and has become a template for what a jazz record is meant to be. It is perhaps also the most influential jazz record ever released. Musically, it's where modal jazz really hit paydirt, and where linear improvisation came to the fore (Davis playing Beckett to John Coltrane's Joyce), and its tunes have

been covered by everyone from Larry Carlton to Ronny Jordan. Its influence is far-reaching: 'Breathe' from Pink Floyd's *Dark Side Of The Moon* was based on a chord sequence from this album. From its vapory piano-and-bass introduction to the full-flight sophistication of 'Flamenco Sketches', *Kind Of Blue* is the very personification of modern cool. And, according to Steely Dan's Donald Fagen, it is also something else far more important: 'Sexual Wallpaper'.

Upload: 'So What'.

Appendix V: Hip-Hop iPod – the 25 Essential Hip-Hop Albums

Post-rationalisation is common in pop, especially among record company executives. Think of the number of people who nearly signed the Beatles/Sex Pistols/Culture Club/Run DMC/Primal Scream/ Coldplay who have had to create a plausible reason for why they didn't. And while there are still those out there who have never embraced hiphop because they think it largely consists of someone complaining or being shouty over a sample of someone else's record, there are just as many who pretend to like it ... and some who really do.

1. Kayne West: *The College Dropout* (Roc-A-Fella) 2004. 2. Run DMC: *Raising Hell* (Profile) 1986. 3. Eminem: *The Slim Shady LP* (Interscope) 1999. 4. Public Enemy: *It Takes A Nation Of Millions* (Def Jam) 1988. 5. Afrika Bambaataa: *Looking For The Perfect Beat* (Tommy Boy) 2001. 6. Wu-Tang Clan: *Enter The Wu-Tang* (Loud) 1993. 7. EPMD: *Strictly Business* (Priority) 1988. 8. Eric B. & Rakim: *Paid In Full* (4th and Broadway) 1987. 9. Dr Dre: *The Chronic* (Death Row) 1992. 10. OutKast: *Aquemini* (La Face) 1998. 11. Grandmaster Flash & The Furious Five: *The Message* (Sugarhill) 1983. 12. De La Soul: *3 Feet High And Rising* (Tommy Boy) 1989. 13. Snoop Doggy Dogg: *Doggystyle* (Death Row) 1993. 14. Notorious B.I.G.: *Ready To Die* (Bad Boy) 1994. 15. Beastie Boys: *Paul's Boutique* (Capitol) 1989. 16. The Roots: *Phrenology* (MCA) 2002. 17. Nas: *Illmatic* (Columbia) 1994. 18. N.W.A.: *Straight Outta Compton* (Ruthless) 1998. 19. A Tribe Called Quest: *The Low End Theory* (Jive) 1991. 20. Lauryn Hill: *The Mis-education Of Lauryn Hill* (Sony) 1998. 21. *The Neptunes Present ... Clones* (Star Trak), 2003. 22. The Fugees: *The Score* (Ruffhouse) 1996. 23. The Streets: *A Grand Don't Come For Free* (Locked On), 2004. 24.

Various Artists: *The Best Of Enjoy Records* (Hot) 1989. 25. Ice Cube: *Death Certificate* (Street Knowledge) 1991.

Appendix VI: Honey Still for Tea? – English Country Garden Rock

'How many foxgloves, tum-ti-tum-ti-tum ...?' Ah, how poignantly does that hymn to horticultural loveliness resound in Albion's soul. Why, even the nation's rockers couldn't resist the allure of the lawn-mower's snoozy drone and the distant peal of church bells. Here is 90 minutes of the rosiest English Country Garden records.

Think back to a time before tower blocks and bondage trousers, before geometric haircuts and multi-pleated skirts, before logo-intensive training shoes and baseball caps worn back to front. Think back to a time – roughly from the mid-1960s to the mid-1970s – of tea cakes, cricket and big country houses, when all was well in the English country garden, when rich young men with acoustic guitars, flutes and ever-so whimsical keyboards made pastoral music that more than complemented their surroundings.

This was the period when rock stars began moving to the stockbroker belt, hanging out in country houses, assuming aristocratic airs and graces, buying vintage sports cars and often sporting garish candy-stripe blazers. Escaping the suburbs of South-east London and Liverpool, and then the penthouses of Mayfair, John Lennon famously moved to Weybridge, Charlie Watts bought Lord Shawcross's 13th century moated farmhouse in Lewes, and Bill Wyman became lord of the manor after buying Gedding Hall. Soon every self-respecting rock god was moving to the country, dressing like Kevin Ayers (whose *Joy Of A Toy* from 1969 is English Country Garden Rock at its most freshly mown and herbaceously bordered) and penning lullabies to dewy-eyed debutantes.

Of course, a lot of this stuff was rubbish (Clifford T. Ward come on down!), and only a few artists ever managed to capture it without drowning in self-parody. Herewith not only those records which best represent the genre ('Pinball', 'Song For Insane Times', 'River Man'), but also records which discuss the genre ('House In The Country', 'Sunny Afternoon', 'Time Of The Season' 'Country House'). It was a style which didn't really survive punk, and though people such as Dream Academy, Everything But The Girl and Paul Weller have made various records which might warrant inclusion, the very thought would probably be anathema to them. And as for the Americans, well, they obviously don't get a look in (so there's no room for either Neil Young's magnificent 'Country Home' or CSNY's 'Our House').

So be it. To get in the mood, wrap your iPod in a brocade skin and ponder these liner notes from Traffic's 1991 retrospective, *Smiling Phases*: 'There is a land where crickets chirrup in sunlit meadows and bright red poppies wave a greeting across the hedgerows. And in that land, across the valley, nestling on the side of a hill is a white painted cottage, with roses round the door. The deep silence of the English countryside is gently interrupted by the rhythmic sound of breathing from four young musicians, slumbering inside ...'

The Zombies
'Time Of The Season' (3.26)
Single (Decca) *1968*

'What's your name ... who's your daddy, is he rich like me?' Such an admission, and from one so young! This remarkably atmospheric record was the Zombies' last hit before they split up; before embarking on a solo career, singer Colin Blunstone went to work in an insurance office, blowing his cover for ever. But he could always cast his mind back to a time of eternal sunsets when he drove up gravel drives in fancy rented Rollers.

The Kinks
'House In The Country' (2.55)
Album: Face To Face (Pye) *1966*

The first British rock star to acknowledge the fact that his peers were no longer living like students, Ray Davies' study of the 'rockbroker belt' is a classic of its kind ('... a house in the country, where he likes to spend his weekends ...'). *Face To Face* was something of a concept album, as it also includes 'Sunny Afternoon' and 'Most Exclusive Residence For Sale' (every rock star gets sick of the country eventually).

Kevin Ayers
'Song For Insane Times' (3.57)
Album: Joy Of A Toy (Harvest) *1969*

Scenario: a group of trustafarians sit around an open fire in a large country house in the middle of Surrey, passing around bottles of Rioja and the old Jazz Woodbines. Poetry is read, long players are played at length, bodily juices exchanged. (On this track Ayers was backed by the Soft Machine.)

Roy Harper
'One Of Those Days In England' *(3.18)*
Single (Harvest) *1977*
An unusually jaunty (if slightly world-weary) ballad from the sombre singer-songwriter, a snapshot of Blighty seen through (cracked) rainbow-coloured glasses. Harper once had a spell in Lancaster Moor Mental Institution and spent a year in prison in Liverpool.

Donovan
'I Like You' *(5.10)*
Album: Cosmic Wheels (Epic) *1973*
The original Pre-Raphaelite elf, Donovan Leitch is probably better known for his twee 1960s jingles ('Mellow Yellow', 'Sunshine Super-men', the *Gift From A Flower To A Garden* album), although this is one of the better things he recorded. 'Sad city sister, on avenue of palm ...' etc, etc.

Brian Protheroe
'Pinball' *(3.03)*
Album: Pinball (Chrysalis) *1974*
A much-neglected classic from the mid-1970s which at the time of its release received heavy airplay from Capital Radio's Nicky Horne. 'Got a call from a good friend, come on down for the weekend, didn't know if I could spare the time ...' Quite literally mellow madness. (The song has recently been resurrected by its inclusion of Sean Rowley's *Guilty Pleasures* CD, although I ought to add that this is most definitely not a guilty pleasure.)

Gary Shearston
'I Get A Kick Out Of You' *(3.19)*
Album: Dingo (Antilles) *1974*
Bryan Ferry's exquisite versions of 'You Go To My Head' and 'These Foolish Things' are perhaps better known, but this interpretation of a cocktail party standard is a lost masterpiece. Drinks on the lawn, anyone? (And a quick download when no one's looking?)

Nick Drake
'The River Man' (4.28)
Album: Five Leaves Left (Island) *1969*
Drake's wistful style was as influential in Britain as Gram Parsons' was in America. This melancholy paean is one of his most beautiful, both musically and lyrically: 'Going to see the river man, going to tell him all I can, about the ban on feeling fine ...'

Greenslade
'Bedside Manners Are Extra' (6.13)
Album: Bedside Manners Are Extra (Warner Brothers) *1973*
Keyboard-heavy 'progressive' rock group whose record sleeves were designed by graphic Yes-man Roger Dean, Greenslade sounded worryingly at times like Supertramp. This, however, is consummate English Country Garden Pomp Rock.

Brian Eno
'By This River. . .' (3.02)
Album: Before And After Science (Polydor) *1977*
When originally released this album came complete with four watercolour prints by Eno collaborator Peter Schmidt; pictures which portrayed a very particular kind of domestic bliss.

Pink Floyd
'A Pillow Of Winds' (5.08)
Album: Meddle (Harvest) *1971*
When led by Syd Barrett, Floyd managed to combine English psychedelic fairytale rock with electric free-form amorphous rock. It was only after he left that they developed their huge, architectural noise – a wall of sound which was occasionally offset by the odd space age folk song. Like this one.

Blur
'Country House' (3.57)
Album: The Great Escape (Parlophone) *1995*
On paper this is simply a mid-1960s Kinks record given a mammoth late twentieth century production and some amped-up irony. Played through the PowerBook's mini-speakers as I type this, it sounds like it too, although that isn't necessarily a bad thing.

The Kinks
'Sunny Afternoon' (3.31)
Album: Face To Face (Pye) *1966*
Written in response to that year's Labour electoral victory, this was a tongue-in-cheek examination of Ray Davies' new life as a member of the pop aristocracy: 'The taxman's taken all my dough, and left me in my stately home.' Davies himself called the song 'Magic ... you just know when you've made a great record.' Released in June 1966 this immediately went to Number 1.

Kevin Ayers
'Girl On A Swing' (2.48)
Album: Joy Of A Toy (Harvest) *1969*
The former Soft Machine member's first solo album was full of innocence and whimsy, a drug-addled masterpiece of childish eccentricity. Ayers was helped on the album by Robert Wyatt, who played drums, and pianist/arranger David Bedford.

Colin Blunstone
'Say You Don't Mind' (3.20)
Album: I Don't Believe In Miracles (CBS) *1982 reissue*
Recorded in 1971, this plaintive Denny Laine tune reached the British charts in February 1972. Blunstone's other solo hits include 'Wonderful', 'How Could We Dare To Be Wrong', and the album's title track, written by Russ Ballard.

Jethro Tull
'Living In The Past' (3.20)
Single (Island) *1969*
Though Ian Anderson increasingly looks like a character from a Monty Python film (especially when he stands on one leg to play his flute), and though much of his group's material has inclined to the fatuous, this – one of their better moments – is a fine example of medieval rock. Dig that woodwind.

Traffic
'No Face, No Name, No Number' (3.30)
Album: Mr Fantasy (Island) *1968*
Traffic were the first British band to seriously 'get it together in the country', and this song certainly proves it. 'No Face ...' was recorded

in a cottage in Berkshire where the group lived for over three years, playing host to various visiting luminaries, including Eric Clapton and Pete Townshend. Hello skies, hello trees.

The Beatles
'Fool On The Hill' (3.00)
EP: Magical Mystery Tour (Parlophone) *1967*
'Day after day ...' Recorded during the Sgt Pepper sessions, McCartney's airy creation is, according to the late Ian MacDonald, author of the marvellous *Revolution In The Head: The Beatles' Records & The Sixties*, 'poised peacefully above the world in a place where time and haste are suspended'.

Kevin Ayers
'Lady Rachel' (5.16)
Album: Joy Of A Toy (Harvest) *1969*
'She climbs up the stairs, by the light of a candle ...' Yet more fairy-tale nonsense from the lord of louche. Pass the spiked iced tea.

Paul Weller
'Sunflower' (4.06)
Album: Wild Wood (Go! Discs) *1993*
The early Style Council videos showed Weller's ironic regard for England in the summertime, and many of his songs have been blatantly in this vein, including 'Long Hot Summer', 'Have You Ever Had It Blue?' and most of his solo work.

XTC
'Chalkhills And Children' (4.45)
Album: Oranges And Lemons (Virgin) *1989*
During the 1980s, as bandleader Andy Partridge locked himself in the studio, XTC turned from new wave punsters into psychedelic post-modernists trapped for ever in Pepperland. Determined to appear as mild eccentrics, they are nevertheless capable of penning great pop songs such as this Beach Boys In The Cotswolds slice of verdant reverie.

Stackridge
'Anyone For Tennis?' (2.30)
Album: Friendliness (MCA) *1972*
Lashings of ginger beer! This Bonzo-esque jaunt from these West
Country rockers is quirky, boater-tossing nonsense. They also spe-
cialised in fey instrumentals with titles like 'Lummy Days' and 'God
Speed The Plough'. There's wind in them thar willows.

John Martyn
'Small Hours' (8.40)
Album: One World (Island) *1977*
Martyn's most atmospheric record, and one of his most commercial.
The title says it all, a tune to sequence just before dawn, when the
stimulants are perhaps proving a little too much, and your iPod needs
recharging.

Appendix VII: The Greatest 'Punk' Playlist in the World Ever!

If any iTunes entries work as AAC files (i.e., condensed and lo-fi),
then it's these: rough, visceral, and probably first heard over a dodgy
PA system in a dodgier club with condensation dripping down the
walls, beer dripping down the stairs, and God-knows-what over-
flowing in the loos.

1. '(White Man) In Hammersmith Palais' by the Clash. Single, 1977.
Epic (as opposed to CBS, or Sony, come to that). 2. 'All Around The
World' by the Jam. Single, 1977. Urgent. 3. 'Alone Together' by the
Strokes. *Is This It*, 2000. Frantic. 4. 'Are You Receiving Me?' by XTC.
Single, 1979. Electric. 5. 'Armagideon Time' by the Clash. Single B-
Side, 1979. Loping. 6. 'Autonomy' by the Buzzcocks. *Another Music
In A Different Kitchen*, 1978. Elliptical. 7. 'Blank Generation' by
Richard Hell & The Voidoids. Single, 1977. Vacant. 8. 'Butterfly Col-
lector' by the Jam. Single B-Side, 1978. Bitter. 9. 'Can't Stand Me
Now' by the Libertines. Single, 2004. Contemporary. 10. 'Complete
Control' by the Clash. Single, 1977. Awesome. 11. 'Damaged Goods'
by the Gang Of Four. Single, 1978. Post-modern. 12. 'Dancing With
Myself' by Generation X. Single, 1980. Manic. 13. 'Dead Leaves And
The Dirty Ground' by the White Stripes. *White Blood Cells*, 2001. Blue.
14. 'Don't Worry About The Government' by the Talking Heads.

Album: '77, 1977. Academic. 15. 'Emergency' by 999. Single, 1978. Afterthought. 16. 'Feel A Whole Lot Better' by the Flamin' Groovies. Single, 1976. Proto. 17. 'Femme Fatale' by the Velvet Underground. *The Velvet Underground and Nico*, 1967. Whipped. 18. 'Garageland' by the Clash. *The Clash*, 1977. Retort. 19. 'Gloria' by Patti Smith. *Horses*, 1975. Cover. 20. 'God Save The Queen' by the Sex Pistols. Single, 1977. Incendiary. 21. 'Hate To Say I Told You So' by the Hives. *Your New Favourite Band*, 2003. Fat. 22. 'High School' by the MC5. *Back In The USA*, 1970. Juvenile. 23. 'Hong Kong Garden' by Siouxsie & The Banshees. Single, 1978. Gothic. 24. 'I Got A Right' by Iggy Pop. Single, 1977. Sonic. 25. 'I Remember You' by the Ramones. *The Ramones Leave Home*, 1977. Haunting. 26. 'International' by Thomas Leer. Single, 1978. Cosmopolitan. 27. 'Keys To Your Heart' by the 101'ers. Single, 1976. Pubby. 28. 'Kill City' by Iggy Pop. *Kill City*, 1977. Affected. 29. 'London Calling' by the Clash. *London Calling*, 1979. Rallying. 30. 'Love Lies Limp' by Alternative TV. Flexi-disc, 1977. Floppy. 31. 'Marquee' Moon' by Television. *Marquee Moon*, 1977. Electric. 32. 'New Rose' by the Damned. Single, 1976. First (of sorts). 33. 'No More Heroes' by the Stranglers. Single, 1977. Doors. 34. 'Outdoor Miner' by Wire. Single, 1978. Poppy. 35. 'Police Car' by Larry Wallis. Single, 1978. Hairy. 36. 'Public Image' by Public Image Ltd. Single, 1978. Reinvented. 37. 'Pump It Up' by Elvis Costello and The Attractions. Single, 1978. Four-eyed. 38. 'Rip Her To Shreds' by Blondie. *Blondie*, 1977. Dyed. 39. 'Roadrunner' by Jonathan Richman. Single, 1977. Rockin'. 40. 'Safety-Pin Stuck In My Heart' by Patrik Fitzgerald. Single, 1978. Acoustic. 41. 'Sex & Drugs & Rock 'n' Roll' by Ian Dury and The Blockheads. Single, 1977. Generic. 42. 'She's Lost Control' by Joy Division. *Unknown Pleasures*, 1979. Black. 43. 'Sketch For Summer' by the Durutti Column. The Sandpaper album, 1978. Sandpapery. 44. 'So It Goes' by Nick Lowe. Single, 1976. First. 45. 'Suspect Device' by Stiff Little Fingers. Single, 1978. Irish. 46. 'Teenage Kicks' by the Undertones. Single, 1978. And again. 47. 'The Day The World Turned Day-Glo' by X-Ray Spex. Single, 1977. Illuminated (Neon!). 48. 'The First Time' by the Boys. Single, 1978. Shouty. 49. 'The Sound Of The Suburbs' by the Members. Single, 1978. Suburban. 50. 'Whole Wide World' by Wreckless Eric. Single, 1978. Solo.

Appendix VIII: From Burt Bacharach to Groove Armada: the Chill-out Lounge on Planet Relaxo

Ray Davies & The Button-Down Brass
Up Up And Away (2.10)
Album: Star Tracks (Phillips) *1971*
Not The Kinks' frontman, the almost as legendary 1960s trumpeter, here excelling himself on an almost punky cover of Jimmy Webb's soaring signature tune. Recorded in 1968, this track includes drumming which would shame the Buzzcocks' John Maher.

Burt Bacharach
Wives & Lovers (2.46)
Album: Hit Maker! (Kapp) *1965*
As lounge instrumentals go, they don't get much better than this, the definitive recording of the first commercially successful jazz waltz (should a person want such a thing). Sublime.

Groove Armada
At The River (3.13)
Album: Vertigo (Pepper) *1997*
Classic chill-out tune, using a repeated sample of country singer Patti Page in Zen-like fashion. There is a 45-minute version of this put together by some DJs soon after release, although it might be rather excessive to upload it (if you could find it, that is), and might eat up some valuable MBs. A tonic for anyone 'fond of sand dunes and salty air'.

Herb Alpert & The Tijuana Brass
Casino Royale (2.37)
Single (A&M) *1967*
The ex-army trumpeter's blistering version of David and Bacharach's theme from the bizarre Bond-spoof movie starring David Niven, Peter Sellers and Woody Allen. Alpert's quasi-American sound (dubbed 'Ameriachi') was never as pertinent as it is here, and the horns were never so piping. Sort of like a hot pie.

Sneaker Pimps
6 Underground (3.48)
Single (One Little Indian) *1996*
A quintessential chill-out tune, this suffered the misfortune of being included on the soundtrack of *The Saint*, the shocking remake of the 1960s TV series starring Roger Moore. Only this one starred Val Kilmer. It's still a remarkable record though ...

Sergio Mendes & Brasil '66
Mas Que Nada (2.39)
Single (A&M) *1966*
One of the group's first hits, this strange blend of bossa nova and jazz became a dancefloor staple in London during the early 1980s.

Garbage
Milk (4.46)
Album: Garbage (Mushroom) *1996*
The Bond-theme that never was, this glamorous nocturne was described at the time of release as the sort of music playing in the background when spies used to hang around casinos in the dark days of the Cold War.

Geoff Muldaur
Brazil (3.28)
Album: Brazil (Milan) *1992*
Included on the belated soundtrack LP of Terry Gilliam's 1985 extravaganza, Muldaur's manic version of Ary Barroso's famous song 'Aquarela Do Brasil' is post-modern in the extreme.

Martin Denny
Exotique Bossa Nova (2.20)
Album: The Versatile Martin Denny (Liberty) *1966*
Denny's surreal marriage of quiet jazz and exotic sound effects was labelled 'Exotica' in the 1960s, with the almost psychedelic Hawaiian jungle sounds incorporated into his records – finger cymbals, bamboo

sticks, congas, sea birds – creating a particular kind of music that has often been copied but never replicated.

Primal Scream
Inner Flight (5.02)
Album: Screamadelica (Creation) *1991*
Bobby Gillespie's almost quaint homage to *Smile*-era Beach Boys (how I wish everyone would stop that, especially REM). And drugs? Did anyone mention drugs?

Tony Hatch
Man Alive (2.00)
Album: Downtown With Tony Hatch (Pye) *1967*
No one has written more great television scores than the Hatchet (though admittedly no one has written more appalling ones, too). 'Man Alive' (1965) is one of his best – full of adrenalin, vibrancy and a sense of urgency.

Original Theme
The Odd Couple (1.16)
Album: Television's Greatest Hits Volume II (Tee Vee Toons Inc.) *1986*
Neal Hefti's magisterial theme tune was first heard in the original 1967 film, though the best version hails from the spin-off television series, which ran for five years from 1970. Hefti, of course, also wrote the theme tune to the *Batman* series and worked with Sinatra.

Sweetback
Love Is The Word (4.34)
Album: Stage (2) (Epic) *2004*
Three-quarters of Sade, Sweetback's second CD contains a diverse collection of chill-out beats, lo-fi samples and salty vocals. This uses bites from 'Grease' and the Isley Brothers' 'Between The Sheets'.

Bert Kaempfert & His Orchestra
A Swingin' Safari (3.07)
Album: A Swingin' Safari (Polydor) *1962*
Stabbing horns, penny whistles, silly strings and African rhythms – Kaempfert's music would seem perverse if it wasn't so seductive.

Helmut Zacharias
Tokyo Melody (3.06)
Single (Polydor) *1964*
A German orchestra, through a glass darkly. Still a very strange, deceptive record.

Moloko
Pure Pleasure Seeker (6.30)
Album: Things To Make And Do (Echo) *2000*
Sheffield art-dance types Roisin Murphy and Mark Brydon make unplugged nu-lounge for nu-people. This CD contains the Boris Dlugosch disco remix of their Iberian chill-out classic 'Sing It Back'.

Santo & Johnny
Sleepwalk (2.23)
Album: Mermaids Soundtrack (Epic) *1990*
A remarkably twangy guitar surf standard which manages to bring Hawaii into your front room in a little over two minutes. The Chantays had nothing on them.

The Art Of Noise
Robinson Crusoe (3.49)
Album: The Best Of The Art Of Noise (China) *1992*
A faithful recreation of the 1960s TV theme. Eerie.

John Barry
The Girl With The Sun In Her Hair (2.50)
Album: The Persuaders! (CBS) *1971*
This mellifluous tune, written for a shampoo commercial, is excessively swamped in strings, showing that even Barry's less austere work was head and shoulders (!) above the competition.

Massive Attack
Protection (7.51)
Album: Protection (Circa) *1994*
More council house corridor gloom, more vocals by Tracey Thorn, more smoke and mirrors than you can shake a very large spliff at, this is still a remarkable record, as atmospheric as they come.

The Beach Boys
Our Prayer (1.06)
Album: 20/20 (Capital) *1969*
Originally recorded in 1966 for *Smile*, this is a wordless rhapsody, what Brian Wilson called 'rock church music'. (As we all know now, in 2004 Wilson famously rerecorded the album, with an almost note-for-note reproduction of 'Our Prayer' as well as everything else on the album. With the right sort of software, it will soon be possible to replicate any noise, any sound, from any decade, and make it sound contemporary; or vice versa.)

Virna Lindt
Shiver (2.53)
Album: Shiver (Compact) *1984*
A sublime spy-movie pastiche, all the way from Stockholm, via the murky backwaters of North London. Imagine Thomas Leer working with John Barry and you have this marvellous exercise in musical subterfuge. An old grey trenchcoat will never let you down ...

Ray Coniff
Music To Watch Girls By (2.57)
Album: It Must Be Him (CBS) *1970*
A preposterous take on the battle of the sexes, this track (which is not strictly instrumental, though it has the dynamics of one) has been covered by the likes of James Last, Andy Williams and Floyd Cramer (and has been heard on a dozen TV commercials), but this is the definitive version.

Grandaddy
Underneath The Weeping Willow (2.23)
Album: The Sophtware Slump (V2) *2000*
Happy? Sad? Just what is chill-out meant to make you feel? Are you meant to wallow in nostalgia, feel upbeat about the future? Grandaddy are not exactly the Carpenters, but there is a silver lining around their dense, dark cloud.

Francis Lai
Un Homme Et Une Femme (2.34)
Album: Un Homme Et Une Femme (United Artists) *1966*
The grand prizewinner at the 1966 Cannes Film Festival, Claude

Lelouch's piece of escapist schmaltz has one of the most identifiable soundtracks of the decade. Since this came out, French country roads have never seemed the same.

Burt Bacharach
Pacific Coast Highway (3.20)
Album: On The Move (Chevrolet) *1970*
Conjures up images of swaying palms, the cool Californian breeze and open-top sports cars hurtling through Santa Monica. So successful was this tune that it was used to advertise the 1970 range of Chevrolets, including the Caprice, the Monte Carlo and the Chevelle SS 396.

Moby
Novio (2.35)
Album: I Like To Score (Mute) *1997*
A sequestered, churchy ambience; a medieval-like choir; a bit of piano – my word, is this a car ad I see before me?

Swing Out Sister
Coney Island Man (3.44)
Album: The Kaleidoscope World (Phonogram) *1989*
A modern companion piece to Bacharach's 'Pacific Coast Highway', by pop's finest exponents of Motown Lounge.

Nelson Riddle
Lolita Ya Ya (3.20)
Album: Lolita (MCA) *1961*
The jaunty and rather barmy refrain from the soundtrack to Kubrick's black comedy. So 1960s it hurts.

Rithma
The Return (3.25)
Album: Las Salinas Sessions (Jockey Club Salinas) *2004*
The music you hear as you sip your San Miguel – it's just before lunch, and you're on your second beer – as you gaze across the Med from the Jockey Club in Las Salinas (you're in Ibiza, by the way).

Duncan Lamont
Desafinado (2.16)
Album: The Best Of The Bossa Novas (MFP) *1970*
During the 1960s and 1970s the British Music For Pleasure label made a virtue out of so-so artists covering popular material. In the process, however, a lot of good, and sometimes great, records slipped through the net. This is one of the greats, a beautiful interpretation of Jobim's classic bossa nova. Deleted for over thirty years (well, as soon as the first batch had sold out, actually), this is one of the hardest records of any in the book to find, should you want to.

Alan Moorehouse
Fool On The Hill (2.53)
Album: Beatles, Bach & Bacharach Go Bossa (MFP) *1971*
Moorehouse calls the arrangement of this and other songs here ('Minuet In G', 'Musette in D', 'Do You Know The Way To San Jose', etc.) 'Happy Bossa', mixing flute, flugelhorn, tenor sax and electric harpsichord – a veritable soufflé of a record.

Zero 7
I Have Seen (5.04)
Album: Simple Things (Ultimate Dilemma) *2001*
Dark brown vocals and savvy studio pop, this whole album is a work of art. Unlike their follow-up, three years later, which was rubbish.

Liberace
Theme From A Summer Place (2.25)
Album: The Best Of Liberace (MCA) *1972*
Wladziu Valentino, Liberace's camp extravagance made him one of the most popular pianists of the 1950s, and his melodramatic vamping (lots of trills and double octaves) was more influential than most people realise. This track shows him in rather restrained form.

Murry Wilson
The Warmth Of The Sun (2.13)
Album: The Many Moods of Murry Wilson (Capitol) *1967*
Jealous of his son's success, the father of Brian, Dennis and Carl Wilson released this largely self-penned and produced LP. It includes this extravagant version of one of Brian's most endearing tunes.

The B-52's
Follow Your Bliss (4.10)
Album: Cosmic Thing (Reprise) *1989*
Recorded for their comeback LP by Nile Rodgers, this guitar-based instrumental is as good as any 1960s surf single – summertime incarnate.

The Beach Boys
The Nearest Faraway Place (2.36)
Album: 20/20 (Capitol) *1969*
Composed, performed and produced by Bruce Johnson, this shows the Brothers Beach at their most whimsical, recorded during a period when they were largely ignored. The strings here are arranged by Van McCoy. 'Bruce did a very beautiful thing with [this],' said Brian Wilson.

John Barry
Into Vienna (2.44)
Album: The Living Daylights (Warner Brothers) *1987*
The great forgotten Bond movie, the great forgotten soundtrack. This is a delicious Barry instrumental which is also included on the LP as is 'If There Was A Man' by the Pretenders. The other great forgotten Bond score is *Never Say Never Again*, and in particular Lani Hall's theme tune (which, incidentally, has only one chorus).

Air
La Femme D'Argent (7.08)
Album: Moon Safari (Source) *1998*
If an Air CD falls over in the forest and no one hears it, is it still ironic?

The Swingle Sisters
Largo (2.58)
Album: Going Baroque (Philips) *1965*
Bach has always been easily adapted by the MOR fraternity, while The Swingle Singers almost made a career out of it. Their first album, *Bach's Greatest Hits*, established Ward Swingle's singers as the most adventurous vocal group of their day, though this recording (from the Harpsichord Concerto in F Minor) on their follow-up LP is their best work.

Francis Lai
Theme De Catherine (2.50)
Album: Vivre Pour Vivre (United Artists) *1967*
This extraordinary epiphany is typical of Lai's lush 1960s French movie themes. He also wrote frothy concoctions for *Love Is A Funny Thing, Love Story* and, er, *Emmanuelle*.

Appendix IX: iBizaPod: Dance Records 1970–2004 (version 1.0 the First 50, Afrika Bambaataa – George McCrae)

One quarter of the ultimate dance playlist, featuring every decent floor-filler from the days before disco to the nights full of the Streets: 'Planet Rock' by Afrika Bambaataa, 'More More More' by Andrea True Connection, 'Ring My Bell' by Anita Ward, 'Dancing In Outer Space' by Atmosphere, 'Let The Music Play' by Barry White, 'Funky Nassau (Part One)' by The Beginning Of The End, 'Be With You' by Beyonce, 'Crazy In Love' by Beyonce, 'Where Is The Love' by the Black Eyed Peas, 'Love Town' by Booker Newberry III, 'Can't Take My Eyes Off You' by the Boys Town Gang, 'Stomp' by the Brothers Johnson, 'Young Hearts Run Free' by Candi Staton, 'Blinded By The Lights' by the Streets, 'Frontin'' by Pharrell, 'Sing It Back' by Moloko, 'Finally' by Ce Ce Peniston, 'I'm Every Woman' by Chaka Khan, 'I Feel For You' by Chaka Khan, 'Change Of Heart' by Change, 'Searching' by Change, 'The Glow Of Love' by Change, 'Would I Lie To You' by Charles and Eddie, 'I Want Your Love' by Chic, 'Le Freak' by Chic, 'Dance Dance Dance' by Chic, 'Good Times' by Chic, 'Casanova' by Coffee, 'Brick House' by the Commodores, 'You Gave Me Love' by Crown Heights Affair, 'Galaxy Of Love' by Crown Heights Affair, 'You're The One For Me' by D Train, 'One More Time' by Daft Punk, 'Instant Replay' by Dan Hartman, 'What A Fool Believes' by Aretha Franklin, 'Upside Down' by Diana Ross, 'I'm Coming Out' by Diana Ross, 'Get Dancin'' by Disco Tex and the Sex-O-Lettes, 'Love To Love You Baby' by Donna Summer, 'Could It Be Magic' by Donna Summer, 'I Feel Love' by Donna Summer, 'Saturday Nite' by Earth Wind and Fire, 'Lose Yourself' by Eminem, 'Best Of My Love' by the Emotions, 'What A Difference A Day Makes' by Esther Phillips, 'Love Come Down' by Evelyn 'Champagne' King, 'I Found Lovin'' by the Fatback Band, 'Praise You' by Fatboy Slim, 'Who Loves You' by the Four Seasons, 'Burn

Rubber On Me' by the Gap Band, 'Rock Your Baby' by George
McCrae . . .

Appendix X: The 20 Best Reggae Records

It's not cool to say that reggae had its finest hour in the 1970s, but it
pretty much did. It was new (relatively), it was embraced by a punk
fraternity who suddenly discovered they weren't allowed to like any
white music pre-'76 that wasn't the Stooges or the MC5, and it
legitimised jazz Woodbines. One curious byproduct of its popularity
was a generation of white trustafarians speaking in broad home
counties patois. And t'ing.

Culture
Two Sevens Clash
(Joe Gibbs) *1977*
During 1977's summer of hate, this was the reggae record on everyone's turntable, a record so full of propaganda it made the Clash's
album seem wishy-washy by comparison. It's become something of a
polemical classic, although we listen to it today mainly for its sweet
sounds.

Augustus Pablo
King Tubby Meets The Rockers Uptown
(Rockers/Jetstar) *1998*
Recorded between 1972 and 1975, this is the best dub album ever
made – moody, mellow, scary, and Oriental. Contains the benchmark
single 'Baby I Love You So', which largely defined dub for the non-
Jamaican audience. The melodica never sounded so eerie.

Third World
96 Degrees In The Shade
(Island) *1976*
Often dismissed as inauthentic by purists, Third World's biggest crossover hit was their 1978 Philly/reggae version of the O'Jays' 'Now That
We've Found Love'. Their best LP is this one, though, which includes
a cover of Bunny Wailer's 'Dreamland' and the astonishing title track
(whose lyric deals with Jamaican hero Paul Bogle and his role in the
1865 Morant Bay rebellion against the British).

Doctor Alimantado
Best Dressed Chicken in Town
(Greensleeves) *1978*
A DJ and toaster, Alimantado (born Winston Thompson, Kingston, Jamaica) was loved by punks and rastas alike, not least for his forthright and often ironic lyrics. This album is basically a collection of homegrown singles, the title track being one of the most eccentric reggae records ever made.

Bob Marley and the Wailers
Songs Of Freedom
(Island) *1992*
The biggest-selling CD box set in history (1.5m copies and rising), this is an all-encompassing, definitive overview of Marley's career. The John Lennon or Che Guevara of reggae, Marley was a poster-boy as well as a figurehead, although at least a dozen of his songs have become classics in their own right, including 'I Shot The Sheriff', 'Buffalo Soldier', 'Waiting In Vain', 'Could You Be Loved', the live 'No Woman No Cry', etc.

Shabba Ranks
Golden Touch
(Two Friends) *1990*
Ragga's one true international superstar, Ranks' 'rockstone' voice was perfectly equipped to deal with 'slack' (sexually explicit) themes, although the material on this album is actually quite varied (tracks range from 'Build Bridges Instead' to 'Wicked In Bed Part 2').

Lee Perry
Arkology
(Island Jamaica) *1997*
Perry's production techniques were surreal at the best of times, and his 'underwater' echoes and dense reverbs still make for arresting listening. This triple-CD, 52-track set has about as much Lee Perry as you need in your life. Contains five versions of Junior Murvin's quintessential cut 'Police And Thieves' (dub, toast, saxophone version, DJ cut, extended version), maybe the best reggae track of all time.

The Abyssinians
Satta Massagana
(Heartbeat) *1993*

The Abyssinians' vocal style was not only responsible for redefining Jamaican 'close-harmony' singing, it also developed its own sense of gravitas, one which has never been equalled. This CD collects their first album – *Forward On To Zion*, released in 1976 – together with some re-recorded songs and four extra tracks, 'Leggo Beast', 'Reason Time', 'There Is No End', and 'Peculiar Number' (which isn't peculiar at all, really).

Black Uhuru
Guess Who's Coming To Dinner
(Taxi) *1980*

Sly & Robbie's finest hour or so, a collection of their best work for the band, including 'Shine Eye Girl', 'Leaving To Zion' and 'Plastic Smile'. Massively popular in Jamaica at the time, this is music of dope and oppression, like a lot of good reggae (or, as my dad called it once in 1976, without a scintilla of irony, asking me if I liked it, 'Reggie').

Barrington Levy
Collection
(Greensleeves) *1990*

This houses many of his big dancehall hits, including the absolutely essential single 'Here I Come', a 12" masterpiece in which Levy claims – quite wrongly, in fact – to be 'broader than Broadway'. The other stuff here is fine, but no collection is complete without this song.

Big Youth
Screaming Target
(Trojan) *1973*

The big toasting disc of the early 1970s, for years this was the yardstick for roots style. Not only that, but Augustus Buchanan, as he was known as a child, was the first Jamaican singer to brandish his dreadlocks on stage in a defiant proclamation of his Rastafarian beliefs. Consequently this album became *the* cool accessory of 1973.

Peter Tosh
Legalize It
(Island) *1976*
Pass the bong, old boy. As much as the roots movement of the late 1960s and early 1970s called for a re-evaluation of Rastafarianism, it also espoused the 'religious' aspect of smoking an awful lot of ganja. And ex-Wailer Tosh was a big fan. Aha ...

The Congos
Heart Of The Congos
(Black Ark) *1977*
Another favourite of the punk era, this was regularly played down the Roxy in-between sets by the Pistols, the Buzzcocks and Subway Sect. Produced by legendary producer Lee 'Scratch' (née 'Bonkers') Perry, the standout track here is 'Fisherman'. (Note: the CD re-release contains an extra disc of dub and 12" versions.)

Bunny Wailer
Blackheart Man
(Island) *1976*
A founder member of the Wailers, this was produced during reggae's golden spell and remains one of the best releases of the period (and the best solo album by any of Bob's band). The title track's a killer, as is 'This Train' and 'Rasta Man'.

Steel Pulse
Handsworth Revolution
(Island) *1978*
Originating from Handsworth, Birmingham, during the punk era, the band were named, prosaically, after a race horse. Closely aligning themselves with Rock Against Racism, they signed to Chris Blackwell's Island and released this, which remains their defining moment. They may have played at Bill Clinton's inauguration in 1993, but they'll be remembered largely for 'Ku Klux Klan', included here.

The Slits
Cut
(Island) *1979*
Girls were never encouraged to make reggae, especially slumming white girls from Notting Hill. The Slits, who had survived traumatic

support slots on tours with the Clash and the Buzzcocks, were labelled punk-incompetents by the music press, who were belligerently sexist towards them. But their avant-garde reggae became a delight, and their debut album contains their finest five minutes, the single 'Typical Girls'.

Various Artists
Dread Meets Punk Rockers Uptown
(Heavenly) *2001*

A bunch of classic tracks selected by Don Letts, the DJ at the Roxy, the original London punk club in 1976. This is the stuff he used to spin: King Tubby, Big Youth, Horace Andy, the Congos, Junior Murvin, Culture, U-Roy and the like. It's a punky reggae party.

Various Artists
Tougher Than Tough: The Story Of Jamaican Music
(Mango) *1993*

Unashamedly populist, this vast four-CD collection is book-ended by the Folkes Brothers' original version of 'Oh Carolina' from the late 1950s, and Shaggy's raga update from 1993. In-between are the Upsetters, Burning Spear, Shabba Ranks, Barrington Levy, Dennis Brown, U-Roy, Prince Buster and more.

Various Artists
Hardcore Ragga: The Music Works Dancehall Hits
(Greensleeves) *1990*

Produced by Augustus 'Gussie' Clark, and including the work of Gregory Isaacs, J.C. Lodge, Shabba Ranks and Rebel Princess, this heralded the arrival of digital recording and reggae embracing new technology. The tunes weren't bad, either.

Various Artists
Lovers Rock: Serious Selection Volume I
(Rewind Selecta) *1995*

The genre got its name from a label that devoted itself to the soft, lilting sounds of 'reggae lite'. Early Lovers Rock tunes were criticised for being 'sung by girls who sounded as though they were still worrying about their school reports', although the best of the mid-1970s material rivals any Motown ballad.

Appendix XI: It's Still Sinatra's Playlist

(How Little It Matters) How..., (Love Is) The Tender Trap, A Foggy Day, All Of Me, All Or Nothing At All, All The Way, Autumn In New York, Autumn Leaves, Bang Bang (My Baby Shot M...), Baubles, Bangles And Beads, Bonita, Call Me, Change Partners, Cheek To Cheek, Chicago, Come Fly With Me, Day By Day, Desifinado, Dindi, Don't Sleep In The Subway, Drinking Again, Drinking Water (Aqua De Be...), Fairy Tale, Five Hundred Guys, Five Minutes More, Fools Rush In, French Foreign Legion, From Here To Eternity, From The Bottom To The Top, Gentle On My Mind, Have You Met Miss Jones? Hey! Jealous Lover, High Hopes, How Could You Do A Thing..., How Insensitive (Insensatez), I Concentrate On You, I Could Have Danced All Night, I Get A Kick Out Of You, I Love Paris, I Love You, I Thought About You, I Will Drink The Wine, I'll Be Seeing You, I'm Gonna Live Till I Die, I'm Walking Behind You, I've Got My Love To Keep M..., I've Got The World On A Stri..., I've Got You Under My Skin, I've Heard That Song Before, If It's The Last Thing I Do, If You Never Come To Me, Impatient Years, In The Wee Small Hours Of..., It Happened In Monterey, It Might As Well Be Spring, It Was A Very Good Year, It's Nice To Go Trav'ling, Just One Of Those Things, Lean Baby, Learnin' The Blues, Leaving On A Jet Plane, Let's Get Away From It All, Love And Marriage, Me And My Shadow, Meditation (Meditacao), Melody Of Love, Mind If I Make Love To You?, Moonlight In Vermont, Mr. Success, My Funny Valentine, My Kind Of Town, My Way, New York New York, Nice 'n' Easy, Night & Day, No One Ever Tells You, Not As A Stranger, Oh! Look At Me Now, On A Clear Day (You Can Se...), Once I Loved (O Amor En Paz), One For My Baby, One Note Samba (Samba De...), Pennies From Heaven, Put Your Dreams Away, Quiet Nights Of Quiet Stars..., Same Old Saturday Night, Saturday Night (Is The Lone...), Send In The Clowns, September Song, So Long My Love, Some Enchanted Evening, Someone To Watch Over Me, Somethin' Stupid, Something Wonderful Happ..., Song Of The Sabia, South Of The Border, Strangers In The Night, Style, Summer Wind (yes, probably the third best Sinatra song, and the one that all Pub Frank singers should aspire to), That Old Black Magic, That's Life, The Best Is Yet To Come, The Coffee Song, The Gal That Got Away, The Girl From Ipanema (Gar...), The Good Life, The Lady Is A Tramp, The Most Beautiful Girl In T..., The Second Time Around, The Sunny Side Of The Street, The World We Knew (Over A...), There Used To Be A

Ballpark, They Can't Take That Away, This Happy Madness (Estra...),
This Town, Three Coins In A Fountain, Time After Time, Too Marvellous
For Words, Triste, Two Hearts Two Kisses (Ma...), Wave, Well Did You
Evah, What Are You Doing The Re..., What Now My Love?, Who
Wants To Be A Milliona..., Witchcraft, You Make Me Feel So Young,
You'd Be So Nice To Come..., You'll Get Yours, You're Sensational,
Young At Heart, Zing Went The Strings Of M...

Appendix XII: Guilty Pleasures

The editing process involved in filling your iPod leads, quite naturally,
to lots of stuff being de-acquisitioned, and in the first few weeks of
loading my things up onto iTunes I realised that a lot of CDs no longer
warranted space in my home or my life, let alone my memory box:
why on earth had I entertained the idea of Aimee Mann, a singer-
songwriter who makes Leonard Cohen and Damien Rice seem like the
Cheeky Girls? Why did I own so much Lenny Kravitz? What had
possessed me to buy all those Oasis CDs? What were Oasis anyway,
but a warning as to what the Beatles may have sounded like if George
Harrison had been replaced by Status Quo's Francis Rossi?

The beauty of the iPod is its by-now transparent championing of
the frail and the unloved, the 'naff' and the unfairly maligned (basically
the aural equivalent of a Subaru Justy, a Nissan Serena or a Vauxhall
Belmont). Guilty pleasures were made for the iPod, a device that
encourages – nay, demands! – obtuse juxtaposition of content (willowy
hauteur, over-reaching camp, grown-up nursery rhymes, Will Young
records). Fancy book-ending the Climax Blues Band's 'Couldn't Get It
Right' with the Pentangle's 'Light Flight' and Peter Skellern's 'You're
A Lady'? No problem, sir – sold to the man in the lead trilby and the
ocelot tie!

My 35 guiltiest pleasures are – cymbal crash, drum roll – the
following: 10cc's 'The Dean And I', Abba's 'SOS', Al Stewart's 'Year
Of The Cat', Andrew Gold's 'Lonely Boy', Argent's 'God Gave Rock 'n'
Roll To You', Art Garfunkel's '99 Miles From LA', Bob Seger's 'Still
The Same', the Boys Town Gang's 'Can't Take My Eyes Off You',
Cher's 'Save Up All Your Tears', Chicago's 'Wishin' You Were Here',
Christopher Cross's 'Ride Like The Wind', Duran Duran's 'Ordinary
Day', ELO's 'Wild West Hero', Eric Clapton's 'Wonderful Tonight'
(almost unforgivable, this, I know, but I do like it, especially the live
version he released at the beginning of the Noughties), Extreme's

'More Than Words', Gay Dad's 'Oh Jim', Haddaway's 'What Is Love?', Hall & Oates' 'Kiss On My List', Huey Lewis & The News' 'Power Of Love', Jake Thackray's 'Lah-Di-Dah', John Paul Young's 'Love Is In The Air', Johnny Mathis's 'Gone Gone Gone' (the greatest disco single ever made; 'Fact,' as David Brent still likes to say), Meat Loaf's 'Two Out Of Three Ain't Bad', Natasha Bedingfield's 'These Words', Neil Sedaka's 'The Immigrant', Nick Heyward's 'Whistle Down The Wind', the Ozark Mountain Daredevils' 'Jackie Blue', Phyllis Nelson's 'Move Closer' (a record I remember smooching to for simply ages in the middle of the dancefloor at the Wag Club in Soho ... when everyone else had gone home), Rainbow's 'Since You've Been Gone', the Rods' 'Do Anything You Wanna Do', the Seekers' 'World Of Our Own', the Scorpions' 'Wind Of Change', Sheryl Crow's 'All I Wanna Do', Steve Forbett's 'Romeo's Tune' (genius!), Wishbone Ash's 'Blowin' Free' (how embarrassing!), Yes's 'Owner Of A Lonely Heart' and Jackie Trent's 'Where Are You Now?', which, if you catch me on the right day, I'll nominate as the greatest piece of recorded music ever made. Wow, I feel like a shower (but in a good way).

Appendix XIII: Those 112 Van Morrison Songs in Short

The Eternal Kansas City, Joyous Sound, Heavy Connection, Tore Down A La Rimbaud, Ancient Of Days, Evening Meditation, What Would I Do, A Sense Of Wonder, Astral Weeks, Beside You, Sweet Thing, Cyprus Avenue, The Way Young Lovers Do, Madame George, Ballerina, Slim Slow Slider, Orangefield, These Are The Days, Celtic Ray, Northern Muse (Solid Ground), She Gives Me Religion, Vanlose Stairway, Across The Bridge Where A..., Scandinavia, Bright Side Of The Road, Gloria (Them), Baby Please Don't Go (Them), Have I Told You Lately, Brown Eyed Girl (not the radio version, which edits the 'making love' line), Warm Love, Wonderful Remark, Jackie Wilson Said, Full Force Gale, Here Comes The Night (Them), Domino, Did Ye Get Healed?, Cleaning Windows, Whenever God Shines His Li..., Queen Of The Slipstream, Dweller On The Threshold, Real Real Gone, When Will I Ever Learn To Li..., Sometimes I Feel Like A Mot..., Coney Island, Enlightenment, Rave On John Donne/Rave..., It's All Over Now Baby Blue (Them), Mystery, Hymns To The Silence, Wild Honey, Give Me A Kiss, Call Me Up In Dreamland, Blue Money, Gypsy Queen, Higher Than The World, Inarticulate Speech Of The..., Irish Heartbeat, The Street Only Knew Your..., September Night, Stepping Out Queen, Troubadours, You

Make Me Feel So Free, And It Stoned Me, Moondance, Crazy Love, Caravan, Into The Mystic, Come Running, These Dreams Of You, Brand New Day, Everyone, Glad Tidings, Foreign Window, A Town Called Paradise, In The Garden, Here Comes The Night, One Irish Rover, Mystery, I Forgot That Love Existed, Someone Like You, Gypsy, Listen To The Lion, Saint Dominic's Preview, Redwood Tree, Not Supposed To Break Down, Flamingoes Fly, In The Forest, Till We Get The Healing Done, Close Enough For Jazz, Before The World Was Made, Wild Night, Like A Cannonball, Old Old Woodstock, Starting A New Life, Tupelo Honey, I Wanna Roo You, Moonshine Whiskey, Fair Play, Linden Arden, Who Was That Masked Man, Streets Of Arklow, You Don't Pull No Punches, Bulbs, Cul De Sac, Comfort You, Come Here My Love, Country Fair, Natalia, Hungry For Your Love, Evening In June.

Appendix XIV: Driiiiiive time! The Only Rock Records You'll Ever Need

1. 'Under My Wheels' by Alice Cooper. 2. 'Ramblin' Man' by the Allman Brothers. 3. 'Can't Get Enough' by Bad Company. 4. 'More Than A Feeling' by Boston. 5. 'Thunder Road' by Bruce Springsteen. 6. 'White Room' by Cream. 7. 'Layla' by Derek & The Dominoes. 8. 'Tunnel Of Love' by Dire Straits. 9. 'The Boys Of Summer' by Don Henley. 10. 'China Grove' by the Doobie Brothers. 11. 'Already Gone' by the Eagles. 12. 'Frankenstein' by the Edgar Winter Group. 13. 'Do Ya' by the Electric Light Orchestra. 14. 'Bad Love' by Eric Clapton. 15. 'Stay With Me' by the Faces. 16. 'Go Your Own Way' by Fleetwood Mac. 17. 'Hocus Pocus' by Focus. 18. 'All Right Now' by Free. 19. 'Radar Love' by Golden Earring. 20. 'Sweet Child O' Mine' by Guns N' Roses. 21. 'Funk No. 49' by the James Gang. 22. 'Crosstown Traffic' by Jimi Hendrix. 23. 'Rocky Mountain Way' by Joe Walsh. 24. 'Kashmir' by Led Zeppelin. 25. 'Free Bird' by Lynyrd Skynyrd. 26. 'Wide Open Space' by Mansun. 27. 'Trouble' by Coldplay. 28. 'Bat Out Of Hell' by Meat Loaf. 29. 'Like A Hurricane' by Neil Young. 30. 'She Sells Sanctuary' by the Cult. 31. 'The Spirit Of Radio' by Rush. 32. 'A Wish Away' by the Wonder Stuff. 33. 'Baba O'Riley' by the Who. 34. 'Why Can't This Be Love' by Van Halen. 35. 'With Or Without You' by U2. 36. 'Anything That's Rock 'n' Roll' by Tom Petty and the Heartbreakers. 37. 'The Boys Are Back In Town' by Thin Lizzy. 38.

'Seven Seas Of Rhye' by Queen. 39. 'Man On The Moon' by REM. 40. 'Since You've Been Gone' by Rainbow. 41. 'Cuddly Toy' by Roachford. 42. 'Big Log' by Robert Plant. 43. 'Happy' by the Rolling Stones. 44. 'Black Hole Sun' by Soundgarden. 45. 'Take The Money And Run' by the Steve Miller Band. 46. 'Animal Zoo' by Spirit. 47. 'Lay Down' by the Strawbs. 48. 'Made Of Stone' by the Stone Roses. 49. 'Money' by Pink Floyd. 50. 'Hungry Heart' by Bruce Springsteen. (Bizarrely, this was originally written for the Ramones, until Springstein's manager persuaded him to record it himself.)

Appendix XV: Sweet Soul Music

Walk into any Megastore or HMV, or connect to iTunes via your Mac, and you'll find hundreds and hundreds of 1960s soul compilations, compilations which have not only reconfigured the Motown/Stax era so much that you feel they only select from a finite number of songs, but which have also become played so often on the radio they feel like jingles (and not particularly good jingles at that). So how does one reclaim the 1960s soul record? Ridiculously, the only way to do this is to become more and more obscure, by celebrating only the most esoteric collections, by discovering the most marginal performers (play the Supremes or the Four Tops at your dinner party and people will naturally assume you've left the radio on ... and NEVER TALK TO YOU AGAIN). So right now I would suggest that there is no need to upload or download any soul to your iPod, no need at all ... (See Chapter for any recommendations.) As Alan Partridge so eloquently put it, I'd give it a few minutes if I were you ...

Appendix XVI: The 50 Best Soundtracks

1. Get Carter (recently voted the best British film of all time). 2. The Italian Job (which actually *is* the best British film of all time). 3. The Last Waltz (buy the CD boxed set). 4. The Harder They Come (Jimmy Cliff). 5. One From The Heart (Tom Waits). 6. Pulp Fiction (from the days when Tarantino's films were as good as their soundtracks). 7. American Graffiti (which sums up a period of American pop culture in around fifty songs). 8. The Umbrellas Of Cherbourg (cute kitsch). 9. Once Upon A Time In America (Ennio Morricone's best score). 10. Blade Runner (Vangelis). 11. Once Upon A Time In The West (Morricone's second best score). 12. 8 Mile (Eminem and friends). 13.

Hable con Ella (heart-breaking). 14. Dazed & Confused (retro and nowtro at the same time). 15. The Virgin Suicides (Air). 16. Good Will Hunting (Elliott Smith sounding like Simon & Garfunkel). 17. Blow-Up (Quincy Jones, et al). 18. Grease (for karaoke purposes mainly). 19. Koyaanisqatsi (Philip Glass). 20. Escape From New York (John Carpenter). 21. Midnight Cowboy (John Barry). 22. The Deadly Affair (Quincy Jones). 23. Angel Heart (especially the DeNiro dialogue). 24. Paris, Texas (Ry Cooder). 25. Across 110th Street (the only blaxploitation album you need). 26. Pat Garrett And Billy The Kid (Bob Dylan). 27. Alfie (the first one, dopey; Sonny Rollins). 28. The Thomas Crown Affair (while the Pierce Brosnan remake is indisputably a better film, the original soundtrack is breathtaking). 29. High Society (the best filmed musical ever?), 30. Live For Life (Francis Lai's best work). 31. Saturday Night Fever (disco nirvana). 32. Natural Born Killers (musical supervisor, Trent Reznor!). 33. Lolita (Lolita Ya Ya). 34. The Blues Brothers (to be listened to only when wearing sunglasses). 35. Kill Bill Vol. 1 (skip the movie). 36. Diva (La Wally and all the rest). 37. Stop Making Sense (even if you don't like Talking Heads). 38. A Hard Day's Night (every track). 39. The Royal Tenenbaums (Mark Mothersbaugh). 40. GoodFellas (or Taxi Driver, come to that). 41. Thief (aka Violent Streets, Michael Mann's best film), 42. Death In Venice (Mahler's Fifth). 43. New York New York (Scorsese's most underrated film). 44. The Wicker Man (Willow's Sons). 45. La Dolce Vita (Nino Rota). 46. O Brother, Where Art Thou? (and the many versions of I Am A Man Of Constant Sorrow). 47. The Fabulous Baker Boys (Dave Grusin). 48. The Moderns (Mark Isham). 49. The Graduate (often overlooked, still brilliant). 50. 2001: A Space Odyssey (It's a boy! Stanley Kubrick's deployment of classical pieces – including Richard Strauss's bombastic 'Also Sprach Zarathustra' – throughout this sci-fi masterpiece influenced a generation of film-makers, and during the next ten years Mahler, Chopin, Vivaldi, Barber and every other classical bigwig found their way into the movies. Imagine Apocalypse Now without Wagner, Gallipoli without Albinoni or A Clockwork Orange without Beethoven ... Up until then Hollywood had a love/hate relationship with the classics. In the early 1930s Sam Goldwyn was approached by a fledgling screenwriter who suggested to the legendary producer that they film a biopic of Tchaikovsky. 'Great,' said Goldwyn impatiently, 'but who can we get to do the music?') And A Night At The Roxbury? Well, it just didn't make it.

Appendix XVII: 21st Century Pop:
The 30 Best Records Released This Century

My problem, with new music anyway, tends to be the fact that I have opinions about things *immediately* (often irrationally, and occasionally misguidedly). So, sometimes, and I stress that it's only sometimes, *I hate it ... and then I love it* (absolutely). Sometimes literally in the space of a few hours. Happened with Radiohead, happened with the Streets, happened with Damien Rice, Franz Ferdinand (who I thought sounded like the bastard, malevolent offspring of Squeeze and OMD, a sort of gay Blur), the list goes on. So my judgement is cloudy on this topic. However ... 1. *Is This It* by the Strokes. 2. *The Libertines* by the Libertines. 3. *A Grand Don't Come For Free* by the Streets. 4. *Smile* by Brian Wilson. 5. *Speakerboxx/The Love Below* by OutKast. 6. *Parachutes* by Coldplay. 7. *Kid A* by Radiohead. 8. *Gold* by Ryan Adams. 9. *The Rising* by Bruce Springsteen. 10. *Twentysomething* by Jamie Cullum. 11. *O* by Damien Rice. 12. *Songs From The West Coast* by Elton John. 13. *Justified* by Justin Timberlake. 14. *Think Tank* by Blur. 15. *Simple Things* by Zero 7. 16. *American III: Solitary Man* by Johnny Cash. 17. *Things To Make And Do* by Moloko. 18. *Bowie At The Beeb* by David Bowie. 19. *How To Dismantle An Atomic Bomb* by U2. 20. *Discovery* by Daft Punk. 21. *Poses* by Rufus Wainwright. 22. *A Rush Of Blood To The Head* by Coldplay. 23. *The Eminem Show* by Eminem. 24. *Your New Favourite Band* by the Hives. 25. *Songs For The Deaf* by Queens Of The Stone Age. 26. *Musicforthemorningafter* by Pete Yorn. 27. *So Much For The City* by the Thrills. 28. *Elephant* by the White Stripes. 29. *No Cities Left* by the Dears. 30. *Waltz For Koop* by Koop.

Appendix XVIII: Jangly Guitar Pop

It sounds a little like the Beatles, like the Byrds, like many of those six-string bands who wanted to sound like they knew their way around a fretboard in the mid-1960s. Power Pop, Skinny Tie Pop, Beatlesesque ... four guys in Oxfam suits wearing metaphorical ill-fitting Ringo wigs ... the world is full of them. And still they come ... 'Mr. Davies' by Tahiti 80. 'Feel A Whole Lot Better' by the Byrds. 'Lyin' Eyes' by the Eagles. '(The Angels Wanna Wear My) Red Shoes' by Elvis Costello. 'Let It Grow' by Eric Clapton. 'I Get A Kick Out Of You' by Gary Shearston. 'Great Big No' by the Lemonheads. 'Monday

Monday' by the Mamas and the Papas. 'I See The Rain' by the Marmalade. 'Echo Beach' by Martha and the Muffins. 'Every Night' by Matthew Sweet. 'Rose Of Cimarron' by Poco. 'Never Do That' by the Pretenders. 'Near Wild Heaven' by REM. 'Waiting On A Friend' by the Rolling Stones. 'Serenade' by the Steve Miller Band. 'Santa Cruz' by the Thrills. 'Sunlight' by the Youngbloods. 'There She Goes Again' by the Velvet Underground. 'Time Of The Season' by the Zombies. 'Is That Love' by Squeeze. 'When You Walk In The Room' by the Searchers. 'Shake Some Action' by the Flamin' Groovies. 'Listen To Her Heart' by Tom Petty. 'There She Goes' by the La's. 'She Bangs The Drums' by the Stone Roses. '(Don't Fear) The Reaper' by the Blue Oyster Cult. 'Put The Message In The Box' by World Party. 'Into Tomorrow' by Paul Weller. 'Cruel To Be Kind' by Nick Lowe. 'Long May You Run' by Neil Young. 'What Am I Doing Hanging Round' by the Monkees. 'Forest Fire' by Lloyd Cole and the Commotions. 'This Charming Man' by the Smiths. 'Just A Camera' by the Keys.

Appendix XIX: The iPod's Greatest Hits:
100 Songs You Absolutely Must Have in Your Life
(Version 1.0)

1. 'Tiny Dancer' by Elton John. 2. 'Scar Tissue' by Red Hot Chili Peppers. 3. 'Pure Pleasure Seeker' by Moloko. 4. 'School Spirit' by Kayne West. 5. 'Cannonball' by Damien Rice. 6. 'I Want You' by Bob Dylan. 7. 'Ceremony' by New Order. 8. 'Butterfly Collector' by the Jam. 9. 'Babe I'm Gonna Leave You' by Led Zeppelin. 10. 'High' by James Blunt. 11. 'High and Dry' by Radiohead. 12. 'Save The Country' by The 5th Dimension. 13. 'Planet Rock' by Africa Bambaataa. 14. 'Std 0632' by Alan Hull. 15. 'I Can't Stand The Rain' by Ann Peebles. 16. 'Tighten Up' by Archie Bell and The Drells. 17. 'A Night In Tunisia' by Art Blakey. 18. 'Miss You' by the Rolling Stones. 19. 'Ready For Love' by Bad Company. 20. 'Rough Boy' by ZZ Top. 21. 'What A Waste' by Ian Dury and The Blockheads. 22. 'Theme From Shaft' by Isaac Hayes. 23. 'The Pretender' by Jackson Browne. 24. 'Magnolia' by J.J. Cale. 24. 'Silly Games' by Janet Kay. 25. 'Grace' by Jeff Buckley. 26. 'She's Gone' by Hall and Oates. 27. 'Behind The Mask' by the Yellow Magic Orchestra. 27. 'Chalkhills and Children' by XTC. 28. 'Blue Red and Grey' by the Who. 29. 'Dead Leaves and The Dirty Ground' by the White Stripes. 30. 'Such A Night' by Dr John. 31. 'Black Water' by the

Doobie Brothers. 32. 'A Girl Like You' by Edwyn Collins. 33. 'Indian' by Eg and Alice. 34. 'Miss Otis Regrets' by Ella Fitzgerald. 35. 'Big Tears' by Elvis Costello. 36. 'I Found A Reason' by the Velvet Underground. 37. 'Walk On' by U2. 38. 'Hey Fellas' by Trouble Funk. 39. 'Hidden Treasure' by Traffic. 40. 'New York's A Lonely Town' by the Tradewinds. 41. 'Plain Sailing' by Tracey Thorn. 42. 'Broken Bicycles' by Tom Waits. 43. 'I Need To Know' by Tom Petty and the Heartbreakers. 44. 'Just One Victory' by Todd Rundgren. 45. 'Encore' by DJ Danger Mouse. 46. 'New York Minute' by Don Henley. 47. 'On The Dunes' by Donald Fagen. 48. 'The True Wheel' by Eno. 49. 'Debris' by the Faces. 50. 'My Friend The Sun' by Family. 51. 'The Chain' by Fleetwood Mac. 52. 'Janis' by Focus. 53. 'The Night' by Frankie Valli. 54. 'Kites Are Fun' by the Free Design. 55. 'Think It Over' by the Thorns. 56. 'Private Plane' by Thomas Leer. 57. 'Humph' by Thelonious Monk. 58. 'Advice For The Young At Heart' by Tears For Fears. 59. 'Come With Me' by Tania Maria. 60. 'Don't Worry About The Government' by Talking Heads. 61. 'Mr Davies' by Tahiti 80. 62. 'From My Window' by Swing Out Sister. 63. 'Rudy' by Supertramp. 64. 'Hoover Dam' by Sugar. 65. 'The Gardener Of Eden' by the Style Council. 66. 'Somewhere Down The Line' by Rogue (one of my absolute favourite records of all time). 67. 'Different Drum' by the Stone Poneys. 68. 'Pastime Paradise' by Stevie Wonder. 69. 'Serenade' by the Steve Miller Band. 70. 'Feel So Real' by Steve Arrington. 71. 'Cybele's Reverie' by Stereolab. 72. 'Johnny's Garden' by Stephen Stills. 73. 'I Was Dancing In The Lesbian Bar' by Jonathan Richman. 74. 'Jump To The Beat' by Stacy Lattisaw. 75. 'Do Nothing' by the Specials. 76. 'Journey' by the Gentle People. 77. 'Give Me The Night' by George Benson. 78. 'Costa del Sol' by Gero. 79. 'Sister Sadie' by the Gil Evans Orchestra. 80. 'Beautiful' by Gordon Lightfoot. 81. 'Undun' by the Guess Who. 82. 'Wake Up Everybody' by Harold Melvin and the Blue Notes. 83. 'This Is Mine' by Heaven 17. 84. 'Little One' by Herbie Hancock. 85. 'The Girl With The Loneliest Eyes' by the House Of Love. 86. 'Tiny Girls' by Iggy Pop. 87. 'A Song For Europe' by Roxy Music. 88. 'The Seed (2.0)' by the Roots. 89. 'A Laugh For Rory' by Roland Kirk. 90. 'Gradually Learning' by the Rockingbirds. 91. 'The Fool' by Robert Gordon. 92. 'Me and My Monkey' by Robbie Williams. 93. 'Scattered' by Ray Davies. 94. 'Jive Samba' by Quincy Jones. 95. 'Babies' by Pulp. 96. 'Prototype' by OutKast. 97. 'Loveride' by Nuance. 98. 'Lotus' by REM. 99. 'Starfish and Coffee' by Prince. 100. 'Vanilla Sky' by Paul McCartney.

Appendix XX: Funeral music

You can't be proscriptive with funeral music, as it's probably the most personal record selection you'll ever make. Rather morbidly, I've been refining this list for a decade, since I hit thirty, although the principal characters have largely remained the same. Having experimented with the Beatles, Van Morrison and various other random selections (for a while the Pet Shop Boys' 'Being Boring' was making the cut) I decided to focus my energies in one particular area: the Beach Boys.

As a pub discussion this has always been a successful diversion, and usually encourages people to show off a bit. And the topic comes around with such regularity, you really ought to have put some thought into it (my friend Adrian certainly has: he maintains he wants to leave this mortal coil to the strains of Joy Division's 'Atmosphere', which, after a couple of minutes, segues into Russ Abbott's 'Atmosphere').

On page three of my will is a clause detailing my funeral arrangements – I want to be cremated and to have my ashes scattered in the churchyard at Alvediston, in Wiltshire, where I was married – followed by a list explaining exactly what music I want played at the ceremony – four songs by the Beach Boys:

1) 'In My Room', the classic single that most people in the church will know.
2) 'The Warmth Of The Sun', another rather maudlin song that Brian Wilson wrote after JFK's assassination.
3) The killer blow, so to speak, which starts as the casket is conveyed into the furnace: 'Till I Die', the original version from the 1971 *Surf's Up* LP. Hopefully everyone will be in floods by now. Cathartic, eh?
4) Now the coffin has gone, hankies have been returned to handbags and trouser pockets, and people begin filing out of the church, accompanied by 'All Summer Long', the amazingly exhilarating song you hear at the end of George Lucas's *American Graffiti*. This sends the mourners out on a happy note, hopefully into the sunshine.

Playlist XXI: Edie and Georgia's iPod playlist

My daughters were both indoctrinated at an early age (they are just about seven and five), Edie being rocked to sleep by hours and hours of Sinatra, and Georgia being forced to listen to the Beatles whenever we went anywhere together in the car. They have both been through this first moptop phase (Edie favouring 'Yellow Submarine' and Georgia 'Octopus's Garden') and have developed extremely strong ideas of what they do and don't like. Right now, as I'm writing this, their *Desert Island Discs* would include Kylie, Justin Timberlake, the Scissor Sisters, Fountains of Wayne (especially 'Stacy's Mom') and the *Shrek 2* soundtrack. They especially like the Butterfly Boucher version of Bowie's 'Changes', but Georgia got confused when she heard the rather creaky version on *David Live*, in particular when Bowie says 'shit on' instead of 'spit on'. Profanity is a huge problem with modern pop, especially rap, and there have been dozens of times when we've been listening to something and I've had to cough at appropriate moments (especially with Eminem records). And you can't make them like something they don't: I tried playing some old punk the other day – *Ramones Leave Home* – and they thought it was just terrible ... so I had to put on Justin Trousersnake again (although I didn't call him that, obviously ...). So, forget Disney, here comes ... 1. 'Lose Yourself' by Eminem. 2. 'The Blob' by The Five Blobs. 3. 'Flawless (Go To The City)' by George Michael. 4. 'Rockin' Robin' by The Jackson 5. 5. 'White Horses' by Jackie. 6. '(Theme from) The Monkees'. 7. 'Daydream Believer' by The Monkees. 8. 'Pleasant Valley Sunday' by The Monkees. 9. 'I'm Not Your Stepping Stone' by The Monkees ('The stepping stone one!'). 10. 'Last Train To Clarksville' by The Monkees. 11. 'I'm A Believer' by The Monkees (a song they principally love because of the version used over the end credits of *Shrek*). 12. 'A Little Bit Me A Little Bit You' by The Monkees. 13. 'These Boots Are Made For Walking' by Nancy Sinatra. 14. 'Hey Ya!' by OutKast. 15. '(There's Always Something There To Remind Me' by Sandie Shaw. 16. 'Georgy Girl' by The Seekers (the 'Georgie' song, in case there were any doubt). 17. 'We Are Family' by Sister Sledge (and Edie's favourite record). 18. 'Is This It' by The Strokes (which Edie liked at first because the noise at the beginning apparently sounds like a cat. Go figure ...). 19. 'Señorita' by Justin Timberlake. 20. 'Rock Your Body' by Justin Timberlake. 21. 'Mary' by The Scissor Sisters. 22. 'Stacy's Mom' by Fountains Of Wayne ('They say mom and not mum!'). 22. 'Can't Get You Out Of My Head' by Kylie Minogue. 23. 'Fragile' by Kylie Minogue. 24. 'Dat Dere' by Oscare Brown Jr. 25. 'Egyptian Reggae' by Jonathan Richman.

Index